THE LIFE WORTH LIVING IN ANCIENT GREEK AND ROMAN PHILOSOPHY

The account of the best life for humans – i.e. a happy or flourishing life – and what it might consist of was the central theme of ancient ethics. But what does it take to have a life that, if not happy, is at least worth living, compared with being dead or never having come into life? This question was also much discussed in antiquity, and David Machek's book reconstructs, for the first time, philosophical engagements with the question from Socrates to Plotinus. Machek's comprehensive book explores ancient views on a life worth living against a background of the pessimistic outlook on the human condition which was adopted by the Greek poets, and also shows the continuities and contrasts between the ancient perspective and modern philosophical debates about biomedical ethics and the ethics of procreation. His rich study of this relatively neglected theme offers a fresh and compelling narrative of ancient ethics.

DAVID MACHEK is a Research Fellow at the Department of Philosophy, Universität Bern. He has published articles in journals including *Apeiron, Archiv für die Geschichte der Philosophie, Journal of the History of Philosophy,* and *Philosophy East and West.*

THE LIFE WORTH LIVING
IN ANCIENT GREEK AND
ROMAN PHILOSOPHY

DAVID MACHEK

University of Bern

CAMBRIDGE
UNIVERSITY PRESS

Shaftesbury Road, Cambridge CB2 8EA, United Kingdom

One Liberty Plaza, 20th Floor, New York, NY 10006, USA

477 Williamstown Road, Port Melbourne, VIC 3207, Australia

314–321, 3rd Floor, Plot 3, Splendor Forum, Jasola District Centre, New Delhi – 110025, India

103 Penang Road, #05–06/07, Visioncrest Commercial, Singapore 238467

Cambridge University Press is part of Cambridge University Press & Assessment, a department of the University of Cambridge.

We share the University's mission to contribute to society through the pursuit of education, learning and research at the highest international levels of excellence.

www.cambridge.org
Information on this title: www.cambridge.org/9781009257862

DOI: 10.1017/9781009257916

First published 2023
First paperback edition 2024

A catalogue record for this publication is available from the British Library

Library of Congress Cataloging-in-Publication data
NAMES: Machek, David, author.
TITLE: The life worth living in ancient Greek and Roman philosophy / David Machek.
DESCRIPTION: Cambridge ; New York, NY : Cambridge University Press, 2022. | Includes bibliographical references and indexes.
IDENTIFIERS: LCCN 2022027084 | ISBN 9781009257879 (hardback) | ISBN 9781009257916 (ebook)
SUBJECTS: LCSH: Philosophy, Ancient. | Ethics, Ancient. | Conduct of life. | Wisdom.
CLASSIFICATION: LCC B111 .M24 2022 | DDC 180–dc23/eng/20221129
LC record available at https://lccn.loc.gov/2022027084

ISBN   978-1-009-25787-9   Hardback
ISBN   978-1-009-25786-2   Paperback

To my grandparents
mým prarodičům

Majka, Jára, Janko a Sáma

[Odysseus visiting the Kingdom of the Dead]

'But you, Achilles,
there's not a man in the world more blest than you –
there never has been, never will be one.
Time was, when you were alive, we Argives
honored you as a god, and now down here, I see,
you lord it over the dead in all your power.
So grieve no more at dying, great Achilles.'

I reassured the ghost, but he broke out, protesting,
'No winning words about death to me, shining Odysseus!
By god, I'd rather slave on earth for another man –
some dirt-poor tenant farmer who scrapes to keep alive –
than rule down here over all the breathless dead.'
(Homer, *Odyssey* xi.548–559, transl. Fagles)

Contents

Acknowledgements

The help with imagining, writing and publishing this book came from many quarters. I would like to thank Hilary Gaskin at Cambridge University Press for her faith in this project; the Swiss National Science Foundation for the generous *Ambizione* grant, which enabled me to embark on a larger project such as this;* the section of the History of Philosophy at the philosophy department in Bern, and Richard King in particular, for the supportive intellectual atmosphere; the students of my Bernese seminar on the value of human life in ancient and modern philosophy, which took place under the sombre auspices of the peaking COVID-19 pandemic. I am also grateful to Jan Vihan, Jiří Holba, Vladimír Mikeš and Filip Lexa for inspiring conversations over the theme of this book; and to Elena Cagnoli Fiecconi, Chris Gill, Doug Hutchinson, Jakub Jirsa, Filip Karfík, Karel Thein and Georgia Tsouni, who read parts of the manuscripts and contributed with most helpful suggestions and corrections. A special thank you goes to those who took on the burden of reading the entire typescript: to James Warren and Richard Kraut, who served as readers for the Press and provided meticulous and inspiring reports, as well as two of my friends and close intellectual collaborators – Jorge Torres, with his untiring intellectual vigour, and Máté Veres, with his passion for the rigours of serious academic work, helped to improve the manuscript immensely. The remaining blunders are all my own fault. In academic and intellectual terms, my greatest debt is to Brad Inwood. His extensive, encouraging comments on the first four chapters of the manuscript were indispensable for getting the project off the ground. More fundamentally, Brad played a decisive formative role during my PhD in Toronto by inspiring and helping me to take up the serious study of Greek language and philosophy, and thus to expand my expertise beyond

* The project 'Carving up moral motivation in ancient Chinese and early Greek thought', project number 179994.

Chinese philosophy, the proper subject of my PhD. Finally, a different kind of thanks goes to my family, and particularly to my wife, Markéta, my closest life companion. Markéta's unwavering loyalty and support has found a particularly powerful expression in her generous offer to take on the onerous task of preparing the indices.

Abbreviations

Alexander Aphrodisias

Eth. Quest.	*Ethical Questions*

Aristotle

DA	*De anima* (On the Soul)
EE	*Eudemian Ethics*
GA	*Generation of Animals*
GC	*Generation and Corruption*
HA	*History of Animals*
Met.	*Metaphysics*
Mete.	*Meteorology*
NE	*Nicomachean Ethics*
PA	*Parts of Animals*
Ph.	*Physics*
Pol.	*Politics*
Protr.	*Protrepticus*
Rh.	*Rhetoric*

Cicero

DND	*De natura deorum* (On the Nature of the Gods)
Fin.	*De finibus* (On Moral Ends)
Off.	*De officiis* (On Duties)
Tusc.	*Tusculan Disputations*

Diogenes Laertius

DL	*Lives of Eminent Philosophers*

Epictetus

Diss.	*Dissertationes*
Ench.	*Enchiridion*

Epicurus

Ep. Men.	*Letter to Menoeceus*
KD	*Key Doctrines*
VS	*Vatican Sayings*

Galen

PHP	*De placitis Hippocratis et Platonis* (On the Doctrines of Hippocrates and Plato)

Lucretius

DRN	*De rerum natura* (On the Nature of Things)

Marcus Aurelius

Med.	*Meditations*

Plato

Alc.	*Alcibiades*
Ap.	*Apology*
Charm.	*Charmides*
Clit.	*Clitophon*
Cr.	*Crito*
Euthyd.	*Euthydemus*
Grg.	*Gorgias*
Leg.	*Laws*
Men.	*Meno*
Phd.	*Phaedo*
Phlb.	*Philebus*
Resp.	*Republic*

Plotinus

Enn.   *Enneads*

Plutarch

De com. not.   *De communibus notitiis contra Stoicos*
                    (On Common Conceptions)
De st. rep.   *De Stoicorum repugnantiis* (On the Stoic
                    Self-Contradictions)
De virt. mor.   *De virtute morali* (On Moral Virtue)

Seneca

Ep.   *Epistulae morales ad Lucilium* (Moral Letters)

Sextus Empiricus

AP   *Against the Professors*

Stobaeus

Ecl.   *Eclogae*

Introduction

Not to be born is the first choice, the prize beyond any other. But once he has seen the light, the next best is to go back to that dark place from which he came as soon as possible. In thoughtless youth all seems well at first – then suffering begins and every blow strikes home: envy, factions, war, and murder. Troubles abound. And afterwards comes hateful, feeble old age, crabbed and friendless – the evils compound.

(*Oedipus at Colonus* 1225–38; trans. Fainlight and Littman)

But the wise man neither rejects life nor fears death. For living does not offend him, nor does he believe not living to be something bad. And just as he does not unconditionally choose the largest amount of food but the most pleasant food, so he savours not the longest time but the most pleasant. He who advises the young man to live well and the old man to die well is simple-minded, not just because of the pleasing aspects of life but because the same kind of practice produces a good life and a good death. Much worse is he who says that it is good not to be born, 'but when born to pass through the gates of Hades as quickly as possible.' For if he really believes what he says, why doesn't he leave life? For it is easy for him to do, if he has firmly decided on it. But if he is joking, he is wasting his time among men who don't welcome it.

(Epicurus, *Ep. Men.* 125–127; trans. Inwood and Gerson)

I.1 Questions and Objectives

The central and familiar concern of ancient ethics is to give an account of a good or happy human life (*eudaimonia*).[1] A happy life is the best possible life for humans. This project addresses a different and less familiar ancient concern about the value of human life: what does it take for humans to

---

[1] Scholarly treatments of ancient theories of happiness abound. Some of the most representative examples include Kraut (1989); Annas (1993); Richardson Lear (2004); Cooper (2012); Rabbås (2015).

have a life worth living (*biôtos*)? Are only happy lives worth living, or can also unhappy lives be worth living for those who live them, perhaps even regardless of their prospects of achieving happiness during their lifetime? If so, under what conditions? Let me start with unpacking these questions by introducing central terms and distinctions that inform this interpretative project. At this stage, I intend these to be uncontroversial and intelligible from both the ancient and modern perspective.

The notion of a life worth living can be understood in a twofold sense. We can ask whether it is *worth being born* at all; or whether it is *worth staying alive*, once we have been born. Answers to these questions can come apart: it may be better for you not to have been born in the first place, but the continuation of your life could still be worthwhile with a view to any existing goods or commitments in your life; alternatively, you may come to the conclusion at some point that your life has been worth it, but that staying alive any longer is not worthwhile. In both cases, to ask what it takes to live a life worth living means to ask about the *threshold* – the minimal value that a human life must reach if it is to be at least barely worth living, or worthwhile. 'Life worth living', or 'worthwhile life' means *a life that is just barely good enough to be worth living or a life that is better than that*. It covers a whole range of lives that clear the threshold of a life worth living, from lives that are not good but just barely worth living up to the lives that are most worth living.

Two default assumptions can be made about this threshold. First, the threshold is just barely above zero: when the good things in one's life are greater than the bad things, then life is worth living; if the bad things prevail, then it is not. The things in one's life are life's *contents*. Typical bad contents are pain, poverty or vice; typical good contents are pleasure, virtue or friendship. A compelling account of a life worth living is able to specify which of these good and bad contents are relevant for reaching the threshold or falling short of it, and why, and how much each of them matters for so doing. Second, the relationship between a happy life and a life worth living can be understood in terms of a threshold–target distinction. A happy life is the life most worth living; Aristotle expresses this intuition when he says that it is 'most worthwhile to live' (*malista zên axion*) for the person who lives well, or happily (NE iii.9, 1117b11–12). But unless one holds that *only* happy lives are lives worth living, there is a scope for lives that are not happy but still good enough to be worthwhile.

The notion of a life worth living is different from the notion of a meaningful life. When we ask whether a life is worth living, we ask whether this life is worth living for the person who is living it. This internal evaluative perspective underlies the ancient accounts of the happy or good life: the good life is a life that is good for the person who is living it. But we can also ask whether a life has a value from a standpoint that is external to the individual whose life is being evaluated, such as from the standpoint of other human beings, society or the universe. When an individual life makes a positive contribution to such a larger structure, or matters for other humans, it can be called *meaningful*, in contrast to useless, futile or even harmful. There is a chance that whatever makes your life meaningful makes it also worth living, and vice versa. For instance, by being a good parent, you make your life matter in positive ways for your family and perhaps even for the world at large, but your role as a good parent is also likely to make your life more rewarding for you – for example, by being a source of fulfilment and satisfaction. We should not assume, however, that worthwhileness and meaningfulness fully overlap; perhaps there are lives that are worth living but not meaningful or, conversely, lives that are meaningful but not worth living. Consider a typically ancient, and controversial, case: the lives of slaves. Many of them are certainly making a positive contribution to the welfare of the city, and so their lives are meaningful, but does that necessarily also make them worthwhile?

Staying within the internal evaluative perspective, the question of what makes a life worth living needs to be further distinguished from a question whether the mere fact of being alive (*zēn monon*) has some value *independently* of life's contents. Many philosophers agree that mere living has instrumental value, because it is the necessary condition for living well. But could it also have a non-instrumental value, regardless of whether one lives well or badly? Some ancient philosophers make remarks to that effect. For instance, the Stoics include mere living on the list of the so-called preferred indifferents, that is, objects of selection that are non-instrumentally valuable, such as health or wealth. What are we to make of such claims? Would the fact of being alive, while living a bad life, still be non-instrumentally valuable? Could the non-instrumental goodness of mere living, if any, possibly outweigh, in part or fully, the badness of lives with some very bad contents, such as pain or vice?

This last question indicates how the question about the value of mere living is related to the question about the conditions of a life worth living. Even if mere living does not have any non-instrumental value, a life can still be worth living; and even if mere living does have some non-instrumental value, that does not guarantee that a life is worth living. For it is not only the value of life *per se* that matters for a life worth living but also the value of its contents, that is, how well or badly one lives. The value of mere living, if any, can contribute to life's worthwhileness along with life's contents. If one grants that even mere living has some non-instrumental value to start with, then the mere fact of being alive already puts one closer towards reaching the threshold of a life worth living than if this value is denied. So the question about the value of mere living can be regarded as a sub-question of the question about the criteria for a life worth living.

From the distinctions among the value of happy life, life worth living and mere living, an axiology of life emerges that spans three different levels. On the bottom level, life may be good *per se*, independently of its contents. On a higher level, life can be valuable in the sense of being worthwhile or worth living. Unless the value of mere living is by itself sufficient to make a life also worth living, a life worth living will comprise the value of mere living – if any – *plus* the value of some good contents, or freedom from bad contents, that are sufficient to clear the threshold of a worthwhile life. Finally, the top level of the axiological hierarchy is reserved for happy lives, or lives lived well. Unless one maintains that what makes a life happy is wholly different from, or wholly identical with, what makes it worth living, happiness includes the value of whatever makes a life barely worth living *plus* the value of further good contents, or the freedom from bad contents, that is necessary for a happy life.

It is the top level of this hierarchy that is most explicitly discussed in the ancient texts and has deservedly received ample attention from commentators. The main contention of this project is that the ancient axiology of life is not exhausted by the theories of happiness. My main objective is to understand how ancient philosophers conceive of these three levels of value of life and the relationships among them. Throughout antiquity, we find philosophical accounts of a life worth living, as distinct from a happy life, as well as of the value of the mere fact of being alive. In contrast to the theories of happiness, these accounts often remain only implicit or, if explicitly set out, are stipulated rather than argued for. In such cases, my task is to reconstruct these accounts on the basis of the available evidence, and, in cases of stipulations, supply plausible arguments that justify these stipulations on the basis of other premises that these philosophers committed themselves to.

The most fundamental question about this three-level axiological hierarchy is whether it is a hierarchy at all. For that to be the case, all lower levels of value must be, in some way, contained in the top level. This containment is also presupposed by construing the relationship between a happy life and a life worth living in terms of threshold–target distinction.

If a life is worth living, but not happy, then it will have a part, or degree, of the overall value x that makes a human life happy. We shall see that this is indeed the mainstream position in ancient philosophy, endorsed by both Plato and Aristotle. In these cases, then, we want to understand what degree, or what part of x, is sufficient to make life worth living, and why.

Not everyone followed the suit, though. Perhaps the most influential dissenting voice are the Stoics, with their claim that being virtuous or vicious is irrelevant for life's worthwhileness. In combination with their view that virtue is both necessary and sufficient for happiness, they arrive at the conclusion that whatever makes a life worth living does not necessarily make it happy, and – more strikingly – that what makes it happy does not necessarily make it worth living. This points to an axiological conception where the top and middle level (a happy life and a life worth living) are constituted by two incommensurable orders of values, x and y, where x amounts to virtue and y to a value other than virtue. In that case, the threshold–target distinction collapses. But what good reasons did the Stoics have for allowing that a happy life may not be worth living?

Conversely, some cases of value commensurability can be intriguing as well. Consider Aristotle's views about the value of mere living. He notes that even 'mere living' (*zên monon*), as distinct from 'good living', has 'a share' of the 'fine' (*kalon*) (*Pol.* iii.6), the same term that describes the value of virtuous actions and a life lived well. *Prima facie* at least, this suggests that the value of mere living and the value of good living (the bottom and the top level of the axiological hierarchy) are different degrees of x, where x amounts to the 'fine', so that a happy life fully maximises the value already inherent in mere living. But what would such an account of the good life mean and would it be compatible with core commitments of Aristotle's ethical theory?

These preliminary interpretative queries indicate that the theme of life's worthwhileness, as distinct from life's happiness, has a potential to open up new angles on familiar themes and texts. This theme will also draw attention to texts and philosophers that have been less widely read, such as Plato's *Clitophon*, Aristotle's *Protrepticus*, the Cyrenaics and the later Peripatetics. Commentators have not entirely neglected the ancient views about the life worth living.[2] But the questions surrounding this broadly conceived axiology of life have not yet been addressed from the more panoramic perspective of ancient Greek and Roman philosophy as a whole.

---

[2] Brickhouse and Smith (1989) on Plato; Warren (2001) on Socrates and Plato; Echeñique (2021) on the Peripatetics; and Machek (2022) on Aristotle.

Besides happiness, another more familiar theme that lies in the vicinity of our questions relates to ancient views about the moral appropriateness or permissibility of suicide.[3] To the extent that suicide is appropriate when, or because, a continued life is not worth living, we can learn a great deal about ancient views about the life worth living by looking at the accounts of the appropriateness of suicide, and vice versa. Unsurprisingly, in some cases, as in Stoicism, some of the most important evidence about life worth living is embedded in the discussions about suicide. But we should not think that an account of a life worth living can be simply extracted from the accounts of the morality of suicide. One reason is that the appropriateness of suicide cannot be determined solely on the basis of whether a life is worth living or not: there are cases when staying alive would be worthwhile, and yet suicide is the appropriate option. Conversely, in other cases staying alive is not worthwhile, and yet one ought not to commit suicide, since there are intervening moral, legal or religious constraints; for instance, in the *Phaedo* Plato famously prohibits suicide on the grounds that it is against the divine law (*Phd.* 60c–63c). On the whole, views about life's value and worthwhileness are more fundamental than views about suicide; the former always rest on the latter. But precisely for this reason these views deserve more attention than they have so far been given.

Along with attempting to take a step towards filling a gap in the historical scholarship, this study also aims to benefit philosophers who work on questions related to life worth living from a contemporary perspective, such as in biomedical ethics and the ethics of procreation. First, it intends to serve as a point of reference for those who would like to make their work more historically informed. The possibility of formulating the above research questions in a way that is comprehensible both from the ancient and from the modern perspective indicates that there is a reasonable degree of continuity between ancient and modern approaches to defining a life worth living, but this common ground will also allow us to identify important differences and contrasts.

It is by bringing out these contrasts that this study can be useful in yet another respect, namely in promoting deeper, more fundamental reflection on modern views about the life worth living, and the assumptions behind them. Some influential ancient views about life worth living may, from the

---

[3] Christensen (2017) and (2020); Werner (2018); Cooper (1989) and Warren (2001) on Socrates and Plato; Papadimitriou (2007) and Zavalyi (2019) on Aristotle; Rist (1969); Seidler (1983); Cooper (1989); Brennan (2005) on Stoicism. Long (2019), ch. 7 has a comprehensive discussion of suicide in ancient philosophy.

modern perspective, strike one as harsh, unpalatable, even outlandish. It is easy to explain this by pointing to the different philosophical predicaments of the ancient and modern worlds, as well as to developments in the social, political and also scientific (particularly medical) conditions that inform these views. But one may also ask, more provocatively, whether these contrasts could prompt us to critically question certain influential modern ideas, such as the view that life is worth living if only one wishes to stay alive. Are not modern philosophers who hold views such as this, which are unparalleled in the ancient context, too deferential to unreflective popular sensitivities, in contrast to the ancients, who simply searched for the truth, often challenging widespread opinions? It is not my aim to defend a particular answer, but rather to present the ancient material in a manner that shows this question to be at least deserving of serious attention.

Finally, it should be noted that there is one question that could reasonably be considered to fall under the thematic ambit of a work such as this, but that this project does not systematically address, namely the question about the value of human life in comparison to the value of other forms of life. This question is central to contemporary environmental philosophy and animal ethics, and was also pursued with some vigour by several ancient philosophers, including Aristotle, the Stoics and the later Platonists. These discussions have also attracted significant attention from commentators.[4] I refer to these discussions only when they have immediate relevance for the questions on my agenda.

The remaining part of this introduction has the following structure. Section I.2 offers a selective overview of influential views about life worth living in early Greek non-philosophical literature. Insofar as philosophers were engaging with these views, in one way or another, they constitute the broader cultural background against which the motivation and significance of philosophical theories will stand out with greater clarity. Section I.3 outlines in more detail some terms and distinctions that make up the analytical framework of my interpretations. In Section I.4 I sketch contemporary philosophical discussions about life worth living and explain how the ancient discussions connect with these debates. Section I.5 discusses some important philosophical assumptions on which the ancient discussions rest, and sets out how they differ from the contemporary context. Finally, Section I.6 describes the general approach of this book.

---

[4] The most important studies include Rist (1983), Sedley (1991), Sorabji (1993), Osborne (2007) and Torres (2021).

I.2 Pessimistic Poets, Optimistic Philosophers?

The worthwhileness of human life was a pervasive theme in ancient non-philosophical literature.[5] As the epigraphs to this introduction attest, philosophical discussions of these questions were informed by this broader cultural context or even directly engaged views of the poets. The widely accepted cosmological dichotomy that underlies these views is that of powerful and immortal gods, on the one hand, and largely powerless human mortals, on the other. Insofar as godly interventions in the human affairs, if any, are not always benevolent, this prompts a fairly pessimistic outlook on the value of human life; not to be born is the 'first choice', as Sophocles puts it in *Oedipus at Colonus*. A similar statement can be found in Theognis: 'The best lot of all for man is never to have been born nor seen the beams of the burning Sun; this failing, to pass the gates of Hades as soon as one may, and lie under a goodly heap of earth' (425–428; trans. Edmonds).

It is possible that some human lives may be worth living, but this worthwhileness is heavily conditional upon the contents of those lives. This conditionality is inherent in the view that 'death is better than a miserable life' (Aeschylus, fr. 90), or that 'to die is better than to live in pain' (Euripides, *Troades* 636–7). Life must be of some quality if it is to be worth living. What makes the human predicament tragic is that the contents that make a life worth living are difficult to secure and, if they are secured, then they come at a significant price. Even more disturbingly, the bad contents that make life not worth living are difficult to avoid: 'no mortal can complete his life unharmed und unpunished throughout' (Aeschylus, *Choephori* 1018–20; trans. Smyth). This is why happiness is not within human reach: 'For no mortal ever attains to happiness (*eudaimonia*). One may be luckier (*eutuchesteros*) than another when wealth flows his way, but happy (*eudaimôn*) never' (Euripides, *Medea* 1229–30; trans. Kovacs).[6] The best mortals can hope for is a degree of good luck but not the state of happiness, or blessedness, which is regarded as the exclusive preserve of the gods. The difference between being lucky and being happy lies chiefly in the fact that the former condition depends on factors that are not within human control, and is thus generally unstable; rather, it is determined by chance, fate or the fickle will of the gods.

The tragic poets are fascinated by human characters who are not bad, or who are even good, and yet meet with utmost misfortunes because they

---

[5] Unless otherwise noted, the translations of the poets quoted in this chapter are my own.

[6] Cf. 'No mortal is blessed, but all whom the sun looks down upon are in a sorry state' (Solon, apud Stob. *Ecl.* iv. 34. 23).

cannot escape their fate. This inherent vulnerability of the human condition goes hand in hand with the fundamental epistemic limitations of humans. These limitations can be directly responsible for misfortunes, Oedipus' patricide being perhaps the most familiar and disturbing case. But they also prevent us from accessing knowledge that could make our lives somewhat less miserable. Consider the assessment of the nurse from Euripides' *Hippolytus*: 'But the life of mortals is wholly trouble, and there is no rest from toil. Anything we might love more than life is hid in a surrounding cloud of darkness' (189–95; trans. Kovacs). What we are inclined to cherish is our mortal life, but that life is, on the whole, rather miserable; whatever would be a more appropriate object of attachment is hidden from our sight.

Even if it were possible for at least some humans to remain quite lucky throughout their lives, their epistemic limitations and dependence on the mercy of gods would still prevent them from becoming happy. The occasional unpredictable strokes of good fortune are insufficient to make a life worth living. In fact, if one comes to lose whatever good things one happened to have, one is bound to be worse off than if one had not had them at all: 'The man who enjoys good fortune and then falls into misery is distraught in mind because of his previous prosperity' (Euripides, *Troades*, 639–40; trans. Coleridge). There is a short route from here to the conclusion not only that a human life cannot ever be happy but also that the condition of never having been born, or being dead, is preferable to that of being alive: 'For <one who is dead> feels no <more> pain <than those who have never been born> since he has <no> sense of his troubles' (ibid., 638). As the state without awareness of troubles, non-existence always comes out better.

This pessimistic view of the mortal condition in early Greek literature is not confined to tragedy. Perhaps the most characteristic Homeric expression is represented by the fate of Achilles. In Book IX of the *Iliad*, Achilles faces a momentous choice: 'Two fates bear me on to the day of death: If I hold out here and I lay siege to Troy, my journey home is gone, but my glory never dies. If I voyage back to the fatherland I love, my pride, my glory dies … True, but the life that's left me will be long, the stroke of death will not come on me quickly' (*Il.* ix.410–16; transl. Fagles). Eventually, Achilles chooses a short life and immortal glory over a long and inglorious life. For glory is the means to transcend, as far as possible, the fate of mortals and approximate to the immortality of the gods. And yet, as the dead Achilles tells Odysseus in Hades when the latter suggests that the immortal glory should be a sufficient reward for being dead, this choice comes at a considerable price and misgivings: 'No winning words

about death to me, shining Odysseus! By god, I'd rather slave on earth for
another man – some dirt-poor tenant farmer who scrapes to keep alive –
than rule down here over all the breathless dead' (*Od.* xi.555–7). This striking affirmation by a Homeric hero that it is better to be a slave in life than
a king in Hades does bring out a characteristically Homeric nod to the
value of life, its warmth and sweetness, but this nod exacerbates rather
than mitigates the tragic predicament of the mortals. Achilles did make the
right choice – he could not have acted otherwise: were he to have chosen
a long but inglorious life, he would have betrayed his character and made
his remaining life hardly worth living at all.

Moving from poetry to prose, an important figure that should be mentioned, given his influence on some philosophers, is the Athenian statesman Solon. Herodotus tells us about Solon's visit from Croesus, the rich
king of Lydia (*Hist.* i.30–33). Asked about the happiest men, Solon mentions Tellus, an Athenian statesman, who enjoyed a long life full of honours and a good death. Asked about the second-best life, Solon names
brothers Kleobis and Biton, whom the gods rewarded with an early and
painless death (i.31), expressing his view about the tragic nature of human
life. The fortune of Tellus is so extremely rare among humans, and hardships so inescapable, that non-existence can be regarded as a favourable
fate. Croesus is not on Solon's list at all. A happy life, according to Solon,
must be successful throughout – one cannot call anybody happy until they
are dead. But even that is not enough: to count as happy, one must also
have an honourable death and be favourably regarded by posterity. So
there is a whole lot of things that can go wrong and that one cannot control: 'man is entirely chance' (i.32.4, trans. Godley).

What about the philosophers? There is a well-established view in the
scholarship, one which goes back to Nietzsche and which has been more
recently espoused, in different versions, by Bernard Williams and Martha
Nussbaum, that it was a central contention of Greek philosophers to
affirm, in contrast to the poets, that happiness is, under certain conditions, within human reach. The strategy of the philosophers is to 'make
the goodness of a good human life safe from luck through the controlling
power of reason' (Nussbaum 1986: 3). Philosophers do not deny that some
external goods such as health, noble birth or good children are not fully
within our power; instead, they argue that human happiness is, to a significant extent, independent of those goods. For what makes our life happy,
largely or wholly, are goods that amount to or depend on the perfection
of our reason, and this perfection is – to some extent at least – impervious
to external misfortunes. It has been acknowledged that some philosophers,

particularly Aristotle, made significant concessions to the tragic outlook.[7]
Nor has it escaped the attention of commentators that some strikingly
pessimistic views on the human condition were adopted even by the philosophers: the Cyrenaic philosopher Hegesias maintained – like the tragic
poets – that happiness is 'entirely impossible' (DL ii.94) for humans.[8] Still,
in general, the ancient Greek philosophical mainstream has been regarded
as bringing good news about the human condition.

Can the shift of focus from the target notion of happiness to the threshold
notion of life worth living validate this contrast between pessimistic poets
and optimistic philosophers? Granted, the philosophers are optimists insofar as they argue that humans can aspire to happiness. But are they for that
reason also optimists when it comes to the question whether human life
is worth living, or whether life in and of itself has some non-instrumental
value? What if a life falls short of the target of happiness, as clearly the
vast majority of human lives do? Do unhappy lives ever have a reasonable
chance of passing the threshold test, according to the philosophers?

On the one hand, we shall encounter some philosophical views that
appear to be resoundingly optimistic. The passage from the epigraph in
which Epicurus explicitly rebukes the pessimistic outlook is a case in question. His attitude seems strikingly life-affirming: not only is human life
not to be rejected, but it is actually worth choosing, not least because of
'the pleasing aspects of life'. On this translation by Inwood and Gerson,
the phrase suggests that human life is worthwhile on account of some
of its characteristic good contents, in this case pleasant contents. But the
Greek original, *dia to tês zôês aspaston*, also allows for a slightly different
reading, as suggested by the rendering of Long and Sedley (1987: 150):
because 'life is something to be welcomed'. This translation lends itself to
a stronger and more controversial interpretation, on which life is worth
living in and of itself, simply because it is good to be alive. On this latter
reading, Epicurus would answer the question about the worthwhileness
of life by first answering the question about whether mere living is non-
instrumentally valuable: yes, life in and of itself is good, and this goodness
could perhaps be sufficient to make life worth living. This affirmation rein-
forces the perspective on philosophers as optimists by adding a new and
perhaps surprising facet to the optimistic outlook. What contributes to
life's worthwhileness is not limited to achievements such as reason, virtue

---

[7] Along with Nussbaum (1986), Aubenque (1963) is one of the best studies of Aristotle's ethics that
consistently emphasises this tragic dimension of his ethical theory.
[8] Hegesias will be discussed in detail in Chapter 4.

or other good things, but also extends to the more rudimentary level of the biological condition of being alive as a state that precedes any cultivation and that is common to all human beings without exception.

On the other hand, though, when it comes to passing the threshold test, we shall see that philosophers were, on the whole, not much more optimistic than the poets. Even if being alive is a good to start with, the prevailing view is that this goodness is insufficient to make life worth living. To pass the threshold test, some good contents, especially virtue, are indispensable. But these contents are hard to get. In fact, the majority of humans are excluded from any realistic aspiration to virtue due to their intellectual incapacity or low social status.[9] It does not seem disturbingly pessimistic if we say that these humans are excluded from happiness; after all, happiness is the highest ideal and we can swallow that only some fortunate humans can achieve it. But it is tougher to say that many among those who fall short of happiness also end up having lives that are not even worth living, or indeed that they would be better off dead. From the perspective of life worth living, then, the tenor of ancient philosophical texts will strike us as quite pessimistic, especially when compared with some modern and contemporary positions. In the view of some important philosophers, including Plato and Aristotle, passing the threshold of a life worth living is an uphill battle: it is easy to wind up having a life not worth living, but quite difficult to achieve the opposite. For others, such as the Stoics, the odds are at best even. So, the shift of attention from happiness to the life worth living will help to qualify the view that the ethical outlook of the philosophers is more optimistic, or life-affirming, than that of the poets.

I.3   The Analytic Toolbox

In comparison to theories of happiness, ancient views about the life worth living were subject to explicit theorising only to a lesser degree. This means that these views need to be reconstructed and interpreted on the basis of the available evidence. Some crucial terms and distinctions that make such a reconstruction and interpretation possible are supplied by the ancient texts themselves; others are supplied by me. In the following, I define and explain different elements of this conceptual framework and explore the logical space that they create.

---

[9] Epicureans would be a possible qualified exception; more about this in Chapter 4.

I.3.1 Life Worth Living and Life Worth Choosing

There are two Greek nouns with the meaning of 'life': *bios* and *zôê*. On the whole, these terms differ in that whereas *bios* tends to refer to a human life that can be shaped and narrated, *zôê* refers to biological life, not so much life understood as a temporal progression and whole, but as the activity of being and staying alive. Yet this distinction is not always strictly observed; for instance, Aristotle talks repeatedly about the *bios* of animals or even plants (e.g. GA ii.3, 736b13). *Bios* would seem to be the more natural option when being born is the object of choice, whereas *zôê* would be more suitable when staying alive is at stake. Indeed, we shall see that this is how these words are often used. In most cases, however, when the distinction between the value of being born and the value of staying alive comes into the picture, the distinction is made clear by the context and does not hinge on which of these two words is used.

There are three common words for valuing life: life can be *biôtos* ('worth living'), *hairetos* ('worth choosing') or just *axios* ('worthwhile'). Whereas the last term is an unspecific term for valuation, the first two terms have some noteworthy specific features. The word *biôtos* is ambiguous, and the ambiguity cannot always be resolved by attending to the context in which the word is used. This ambiguity is well documented by perhaps the most famous occurrence of this term in ancient philosophy, namely in Socrates' dictum from the *Apology* that 'unexamined life is not *biôtos* for humans' (*anexetastos bios ou biôtos anthrôpôi*) (38a). Grammatically, there are two equally legitimate translations of this phrase: one possibility is to gloss as the 'unexamined life ought not to be lived'; another as the 'unexamined life is not worth living'. In the first sense, the term refers to a norm – happiness – or to how one ought to live in the ideal case; in the second sense, it implies rather a comparative assessment of when a life is still good enough to pass the threshold test so that it is preferable to death. I shall discuss these options in more detail in Chapter 1 in this book. At this point, it suffices to note that in some contexts *biôtos* must be understood in the second sense. For instance, when Plato says that life with a corrupted body is not worth living, the idea is clearly that certain bad lives are not worth the bother. It is this second sense of the word *biôtos* that chiefly interests me in this book.

In contrast to *biôtos*, the term *hairetos* implies a certain distance from the life under evaluation in the sense that I can choose it or not. Also, the evaluative perspective implied by this term is not so much whether it is worth continuing to live but rather whether life is worth embarking on in the first place. The topos from the ancient texts that the word *hairetos* brings to mind is that of choosing among different alternative courses of life. Besides the choice of Achilles mentioned earlier, there is, in particular, the choice of Heracles between an easy but inglorious life of pleasure and a difficult but glorious life of virtue,[10] as well as Plato's myth from the last book of *Republic* in which disembodied souls have to 'choose' (*hairein*) one among the possible future embodied lives offered to them, some good, some mediocre and some bad (*Resp.* x, 614b–621b). What this perspective invites us to consider is not whether it is worth staying alive but whether I should choose this life or that one. What we should be considering when making this comparative choice, as Plato suggests, is not so much the threshold of minimally worthwhile lives but how much each among the lives on offer approximates to happiness.

Still, there are important contexts in which claims about life being worth choosing bear directly on the threshold notion. This holds, in particular, for views about when a life is *not* worth choosing; for then it is not worth living either. For instance, in the opening moves of Plato's *Philebus*, it is established that life reduced to the passive pleasures of a jellyfish is not 'worth choosing' (*hairetos*) 'for us' (*hêmin*), that is for humans (*Phlb.* 21d). The reason is, presumably, that such a life would not be worth continuing were one to happen to live it – as the dictum from the *Apology* may suggest, at least on one possible interpretation of it. We should also note, however, that there is one specific context in which life's choiceworthiness does not entail its worthwhileness. This occurs in some Stoic and Peripatetic sources that discuss the value of the bare condition of being alive (*zên*) and regard it as something 'worth choosing'. It is one thing to say that mere living has some rudimentary selective value, quite another to say whether a life, given its specific contents, is also worth living, all things considered.

I.3.2   'Life Worth Living' and 'Life Not Worth Living'

The opposite of life worth living, life not worth living (*ouk biôtos*), could mean simply life not worth living or not worth choosing. But it could also mean, more narrowly, that life is worth avoiding, or that living is actually worse than not having been born or being dead. In the latter sense, life is not only deprived of positive value but also has robustly negative value. The difference between these two senses of un-worthwhileness can have important implications for practical decisions about exiting life. If my life

---

[10] As reported by Xenophon (*Memorabilia* ii.1.21–34), who attributes the parable to Prodicus of Ceos.

is worth avoiding, this is a stronger reason to exit it than if it is just not worthwhile. This difference comes into the picture in several ancient texts, such as Plato's *Laws*.

There is also a question about the logical relationship between life worth living and life not worth living. Are they strict contradictories, so that your life is *either* worth living *or* it is not, or does the threshold have a certain latitude that makes it possible for some lives to remain neutral or indeterminate in terms of their worthwhileness? Whereas this question is nowhere explicitly addressed and settled, the default perspective shared widely by ancient philosophers seems to be that the terms are indeed contradictories.

I.3.3 Worthmakers, Worthbreakers and the Typology of Lives

What makes life worth living (or not) are different good and bad things in life. Contemporary philosophers have pointed out that what matters for the assessment of life's worthwhileness is not only the overall balance of good and bad things but also how these things are distributed over the course of one's life (e.g. Benatar 2006: 61–62). Since these distributional considerations were not generally taken into account by ancient philosophers, I shall put them aside in the following account. Still, one wonders whether the absence of a distributional perspective may not be a positive sign of a distinctly ancient way of determining the value of life. Rather than being aggregated from the value of specific, variable contents, the value of entire life derives from a lasting state of the soul that one has throughout one's adult life, and that is bound to fill life with some important contents rather than with others.

To be worth living, life must reach the threshold of a minimal value. In this sense, I shall be referring to some important good and bad things as 'worthmakers' and 'worthbreakers'. These terms are best defined in terms of sufficient conditions. Worthmakers are good things that are on their own, or in conjunction with other goods, sufficient to make a life worth living. Worthbreakers are bad things that are on their own, or in conjunction with other bad things, sufficient to make a life not worth living.[11] So, for instance, according to a hypothetical theory, virtue can be an unconditional worthmaker if it is alone sufficient to make a life worthwhile; it is a conditional worthmaker if it makes a life worthwhile only in combination with other conditional worthmakers, such as good health.

---

[11] If p is a worthmaker only in conjunction with q, and if there is p but not q, p does not count as a worthmaker.

There is a further question as to whether the mere *absence* of certain good or bad things can be a worthmaker or worthbreaker. In principle, this seems possible. So, for instance, it would be conceivable to say that (i) a life is worth living *insofar as* it is not vicious; on this view, the absence of vice could even be an unconditional worthmaker. Conversely, we can imagine the opposite constellation in which (ii) a life is not worth living *unless* it is virtuous. The worthwhileness conditions of these two hypothetical accounts would end up being identical if virtue and vice are contradictories, in which case the absence of vice entails the possession of virtue, and vice versa. But if there is an intermediate state of being not fully virtuous, or not fully vicious, then it is possible for a life to meet the conditions of (i) but not of (ii). The possibility that absences of goods and bads can be worthmakers or worthbreakers in a way that is not wholly derivative from the presence of their opposites plays an important role in some ancient accounts of life worth living.

Depending on the worthmakers and worthbreakers in them, lives can be categorised into four types. (1) If a life has worthmakers and is free from worthbreakers, it is worth living. (2) If it has worthbreakers and is void of worthmakers, it is not worth living. (3) If a life has neither worthmakers nor worthbreakers, then it is indifferent. Is there a further possibility that life (4) can have *both* worthmakers *and* worthbreakers? Yes, it can. For instance, it could be a virtuous life stricken by a chronic illness, insofar as the illness is regarded as a conditional worthbreaker. What is impossible, in contrast, is for a life to contain both an unconditional worthmaker and an unconditional worthbreaker.

A further question is whether it is possible, or even necessary, to determine whether an indifferent life is worth living or not, *all things considered.* If (i) every life necessarily has a status of positive or negative worthwhileness, and if (ii) life worth living and life not worth living are strict contradictories, then it seems that even an indifferent life must be either worth living or not. Should it be possible to determine this status, further criteria would have to be postulated for second-order, overriding worthmakers or worthbreakers. So, for instance, one could say that the overriding worthmaker of indifferent lives is the absence of unconditional worthbreakers in them. On this view, indifferent lives would be just barely worth living, all things considered.[12] I shall later propose that this option adequately captures the status of best possible life according to the pessimistic view of the Cyrenaic Hegesias.

---

[12] But if an indifferent life is worth living, it can be indifferent only in a qualified sense, namely in the sense of an absence of worthbreakers. This qualified indifference makes it worth living.

I.3.4 Axiological Monism and Axiological Plurality

Whether, or how, a philosophical theory distinguishes between the target notion of happiness and the threshold notion of a life worth living largely depends on the nature of the axiology that this theory is committed to. If an ethical theory rests on an axiology that espouses a single dominant good, then the distinction between a happy life and a life worth living is pre-empted, unless this dominant good can be acquired to different degrees. For instance, if there is a single good, such as virtue, and this is both sufficient and necessary for a happy life, then there will not be logical space left for an unhappy life worth living. That space will emerge only if (i) the dominant good allows for degrees, for example, if it is possible to be half-virtuous, which might be sufficient for having a life that is not happy but still worth living; or if (ii) the dominant good is a composite, so that it is possible to have a part of it, for example, just one virtue but not other; or if (iii) there are other, virtue-independent goods, such as bodily health, and it is on these other goods that life worth living depends, so that the life of a non-virtuous person with good bodily health will not be happy, but still worth living.

In general, the more 'pluralistic' axiological theories are – that is, the more kinds of value they recognise – and the more they allow for an intermediate or partial possession of these goods, the more scope and motivation there is for differentiating a life worth living from a happy life. Conversely, the more 'monistic' a theory is – that is, the more disinclined it is to recognise degrees of value and/or different kinds of value – the less space and appetite there is bound to be for this distinction. I shall argue that the Epicureans had the most monistically inclined axiology, and hence did not make much of the distinction between a happy life and a life worth living, whereas the Stoics had the most sharply dualistic axiology, and hence dissociated a happy life decisively from a life worth living.

I.3.5 Life and Its Contents

So far I have discussed how the worthwhileness of life is determined by the good or bad things in it, or its contents. But there is also a further possibility – that life could have some value, indeed non-instrumental value, in and of itself. The distinction between life and its contents was advocated in the modern discourse by Thomas Nagel (1970), but in this book I will not use the distinction in Nagel's sense; rather, I shall turn to two other distinctions that have an ancient provenance. In ancient Greece, to be alive as an individual typically means to have a 'soul' (*psuchê*) or to be a combination of a soul and a body. This is why, for instance, Plato defines death in the *Phaedo* as the separation of the soul from the body. But it is one thing to have soul, or to 'use soul', as Plato and Aristotle put it, and another thing to use it well or badly. The quality of a soul's use determines the quality of one's actions and psychological states or, in short, the contents of one's life. The very fact of having a soul and using it – that is, the bare fact of being alive – is a precondition for having these contents and as such is not identical with them.

Another ancient distinction that has a similar meaning is that between 'living' or 'mere living' and 'living well' (e.g. Aristotle, *Pol.* iii.6). 'Mere living' (*zên monon*) sometimes has disparaging connotations of an intellectually or otherwise impoverished life that falls short of living well, but in fact it should be distinguished from living badly, since it refers to the rudimentary condition of being and staying alive that underlies all assessments of life's quality. For some ancient philosophers, the definition of what it means to be 'merely alive' is indexed to the species of particular living thing: to be (merely) alive *qua* human may be something different than to be alive *qua* plant.

If even mere human living has some non-instrumental value, could this value be a worthmaker, or even an unconditional worthmaker? If the latter, it may even be the case that the value of being or staying alive is in itself sufficient to outweigh any and all bad contents in life: no matter how miserable, unfortunate and vicious you are, life *per se* is good to such an extent that any kind of life is better than non-existence. This sounds like a tall order for the value of mere living to fulfil. But perhaps mere living could turn out to be a conditional worthmaker, so that it could make a life worthwhile in conjunction with some good things in it.

I.3.6   *Non-Instrumental, Intrinsic and Contributive Value*

By default, to say that a life is worth living is to say that it is worth having, or choosing, as a non-instrumental or final good. In ancient Greek, this means that it is worth choosing 'by itself' (*kath'hauto*) or 'for its own sake' (*hautou heneka*), rather than for the sake of other things. Famously, this distinction plays a crucial role in Aristotle's distinction in the first book of the *Nicomachean Ethics* between happiness as the highest and final good, on the one hand, and all other goods that are chosen for the sake of happiness, on the other.[13] At least since the classic article by Christine Korsgaard

---

[13] In Plato, the *locus classicus* is *Resp.* ii. 357b–c.

(1983), philosophers have commonly distinguished 'non-instrumental' value from 'intrinsic' or 'unconditional' value.[14] Whereas the distinction between instrumental and non-instrumental (or: final) value is grounded in a distinction between ends and means, the distinction between intrinsic and extrinsic (or: unconditional and conditional) value concerns the difference between things which have the source of their goodness in themselves, or are unconditionally valuable, and things whose goodness depends on an external source.

Ancient texts do not explicitly distinguish between non-instrumental and intrinsic value, and indeed we do not find two pairs of distinct terms that would neatly capture the two pairs of modern distinctions. Does this mean that the ancients did not recognise the distinction between extrinsic and intrinsic value at all, or that they assimilated it to the distinction between instrumental and non-instrumental value? Neither appears to be the case. A recognisable case of the extrinsic–intrinsic distinction, as different from the instrumental–non-instrumental distinction, is at work in a passage from Plato's *Euthydemus*, where the point is precisely that conventional goods such as health or wealth are not good 'in themselves' (*kath'hauta*) (281d) but only on the condition that they are used well or wisely. In other words, we do choose these goods for their own sake; they have a non-instrumental value, but their value is extrinsic – that is, it is conditional upon wisdom. The distinction between non-instrumental and intrinsic value, while not always explicit, takes on particular significance in some ancient discussions of the value of mere living. This significance has been well documented in a recent study of a later Peripatetic theory of life's value (Echeñique 2021), where life has an intrinsic but not a non-instrumental value. With these caveats in mind, it is nonetheless the case in many ancient philosophical contexts that non-instrumental value also entails intrinsic value.

As for the relationship between life's worthwhileness and life's meaningfulness, there is another modern category of value that springs to mind, namely the so-called 'contributory' or 'contributive' value, that is, the kind of value that something has by virtue of being a part of a valuable whole (Lewis 1955). This contributive value must be a kind of extrinsic value, insofar as the value of my contribution depends on the value of the whole to which I contribute, and thus, arguably, is different from instrumental value (Bradley 1998: 110). This is consistent with the fact that the

---

[14] Some philosophers have argued for the possibility that value can be intrinsic *and* conditional (e.g. Kagan 1998), but this has been disputed (e.g. Bradley 2002).

relationship between a part and its whole is of a different logical nature than the relationship between a means and its end, insofar as the part participates in the whole and is contained in it. This participative relationship is suggestively brought out in some Stoic or Neoplatonic texts where every human life is said to contribute to the harmony of the universe, just as different notes, high and low, contribute to perfect harmony in the panpipes (Plotinus, *Enn.* iii.2.17).

I.4   The Contemporary Discourse and the Ancient Views

The notion of life worth living has been discussed in contemporary and recent philosophy from a variety of perspectives and with different objectives in mind. The more specific question whether life has a non-instrumental value, independently of its contents, has also been discussed. While I cannot do justice to the richness and complexity of these accounts, a brief overview is in order to enable me later to identify continuities, and contrasts, with the ancient approaches. The references to scholarship are mostly exemplificatory and far from comprehensive.

First, a basic conceptual disambiguation is needed. The notion of life worth living can be understood from a perspective that is internal or external to the person whose life it is. From the internal perspective, a life is worth living when it is worthwhile *for* the person who lives it, insofar as it is, on the whole, beneficial and thus constitutes an attractive or at least reasonable object of choice. It is this understanding of 'life worth living' that is operative in the following handbook definition: 'A life is worth living insofar as it has enough of the right sort of goods internal to the life to outweigh the bad in it, so as to make it sensible to exhibit positive orientations toward it such as being grateful for it, being glad about it, and sustaining it' (Metz 2014: 3602). This definition, which includes the more specific but intuitive idea that life's worthwhileness is determined by the overall balance of good and bad things in it, would be endorsed by many contemporary philosophers.

This notion of life worth living needs to be distinguished from the value of life in an external sense: instead of asking whether a life has worth for the person who lives it, we can ask what the worth of this life is from an external standpoint.[15] Within this external evaluative perspective, we can further distinguish three different kinds of value. (1) One type is the

---

[15] For slightly different versions of this distinction, see McMahan (2002: 240–241) and Wilkinson (2011).

economic worth of life – that is, the value that an individual human life contributes to the economic welfare of a state or community (e.g. Broome 1985). (2) Another type is life's meaningfulness – that is, the value that a life has by virtue of its significance and importance. Both these two types have an obvious overlap with 'meaningfulness' as I defined it, in contributory terms, in Section I.1. A third aspect is (3) the moral worth of life as the value that confers dignity and commands unconditional respect. The second and third types of external value call for further comments.

There is a range of views about the meaning of 'meaningfulness' in the modern discourse, but the common denominator is that a life is meaningful when it is somehow significant or important in terms of its contribution and achievements (Landau 2017; Metz 2012). The life of Mother Theresa or that of Albert Einstein was meaningful; the life of a 'Blob' who spends his days alone watching sitcoms and drinking beer is meaningless (Wolf 2015: 92). Some modern philosophers, such as Camus (1951) or Nagel (1971), understand meaningfulness not only in contrast to insignificance, but in contrast to absurdity, which they take to be a characteristic feature of the human condition. Since there is no transcendent entity such as God that would guarantee the meaningfulness of human endeavours, a human existence is inherently meaningless in the sense that there is no ultimate framework of value to which it could have recourse to justify itself (Taylor 1989, ch.1). This latter kind of worry does not seem to have a precedent in ancient philosophy, and this is why I defined 'meaningfulness' earlier in the sense that matters both in modern and ancient context, in terms of the making of a positive contribution to others or to the world at large. How precisely life's meaningfulness relates to its worthwhileness has been a matter of debate (Metz 2012; Matheson 2020). To what extent these kinds of value are interdependent depends largely on how precisely 'meaningfulness' is defined. In any case, several philosophers have thought it possible to have a life that is worth living for you, from the first person point of view, without therefore necessarily having a meaningful life, and vice versa (e.g. Trisel 2007; Metz 2012).

As to the third type of value that a human life may have from the external evaluative perspective, namely its moral worth, three strands have been especially prominent. Only one of these has remote antecedents in ancient philosophy; therefore, the moral worth of a life can be considered a modern contention. One justification for the moral worth of life is the theory, deriving from Kant, according to which all humans and their lives have an intrinsic worth and dignity (*Würde*), on the grounds that humans are rational agents (Rachels 1986; Kass 2008). Another is the doctrine known as 'sanctity of life' – the view that human life, or even life in general, has unconditional value, which is traditionally justified on religious grounds, and makes suicide or euthanasia problematic if not prohibited (Bayertz 1996; Barry 2002). This view has a long history, possibly going back to the ancient Greek Pythagorean tradition (Baranzke 2012). A version of this view is apparently also endorsed by Plato in the *Phaedo*, where suicide is prohibited on the grounds that human lives are the possession of the gods. However, this view never became dominant in ancient philosophy, and even in Plato there are dissenting views. Finally, the moral approach to the worth of life has also been prominent in recent environmental philosophy. The contention is that not only humans but also other or even all living things deserve unconditional respect by virtue of being alive (Taylor 1986; Agar 2001). Like meaningfulness, life's moral worth can also diverge from or even conflict with life's worthwhileness. Consider a murderer on death row: from his internal perspective, it may be best to die as soon as possible and find relief from unbearable distress; but from the external perspective of the sanctity of life, voluntary exit is prohibited – the life of the prisoner has a worth that nobody, not even the prisoner himself, ought to violate.

With this brief review of external evaluative perspective on the value of life in place, I now turn to modern views of what makes a life worth living, the proper theme of this book. There are two main areas of recent research in applied ethics in which the worthwhileness of life has been central: population ethics, or the ethics of procreation (Parfit 1984; Benatar 2006); and biomedical ethics, with its questions about life-extension and euthanasia (Foot 1977; Singer 1993; Harris 1985; Wilkinson 2011). These two areas correspond to the two different senses of life worth living: the ethics of procreation asks whether there are good reasons to bring humans into life; biomedical ethics is concerned with the circumstances under which it is worthwhile to stay alive. But the questions about life worth living and the value of life have also been discussed in more general terms with no explicit connections to these applied themes; a notable case is the debate about whether death is bad (Nagel 1970; Williams 1973; Raz 2001).

Broadly, recent accounts of life worth living have been preoccupied with three main challenges. The first problem is the qualitative threshold of a worthwhile life: does it suffice that the bads do not outweigh the goods, or does life have to be at least barely better rather than worse to be worthwhile (e.g. Wilkinson 2011)? The second problem is the aggregation and distribution of values across different temporal stages of life. So, for instance, there is a question whether the worth of life amounts simply to the sum of the negative and positive values of the atomistic conditions during one's life (Baier 1997), or whether the pattern – the way that this value is distributed over one's lifetime – is also important (Velleman 1991; Kamm 2003). Thirdly, and most fundamentally, there is a question about what things or experiences in my life count as truly good and bad in the first place. Insofar as good or bad are understood in the prudential sense of what is beneficial or harmful for me, the accounts of the value of life's contents coincide with theories of 'welfare' or 'well-being'. Two broad approaches have been distinguished to explain what makes my life good for me: subjectivist and objectivist.[16] Within these approaches, further positions have been differentiated.[17]

According to the subjectivist approaches, the value of life's contents is determined by a subjective judgement, feeling or attitude on the part of the person whose life it is. This view goes back to William James's contention that whether life is worth living for me depends solely on whether I regard it as worthwhile (James 1895). A characteristic implication of this view is that the possibility of erring about whether our own life is worth living is limited, for the value of our lives coincides with the value we ourselves give to our lives. The subjectivist approach has been articulated in two main positions, known as the hedonic and desire-fulfilment views. According to the hedonists, the criterion for the worthwhileness of life is the net balance of pleasure and pain (Feldman 2006; Benatar 2006). The desire-fulfilment view has been developed in several different versions (cf. Fletcher 2016), but the shared ground is that what makes being born or staying alive worthwhile is that our desires, or our informed desires, are satisfied rather than frustrated. The view that the fulfilment of our desires is generally good for us entails that the objects of our desires are good insofar as we desire them. This applies also to life; our life is worth living for us insofar as we desire it: 'what better evidence could there be [that one's] life is worth living [than the fact that one] wishes to go on living' (Singer 1993: 201).

One of the most powerful objections against subjectivist, and specifically hedonist approaches to well-being has been Robert Nozick's thought experiment with an experience machine. Imagine that you can plug into a machine that is programmed to give you all sorts of pleasurable experiences, including that of writing a great poem or being loved by your friends, for the rest of your life (Nozick 1974; 1989: 104–108). Would you

---

[16] Typically, there is a wide range of qualifications in these theories. There are also different 'hybrid' views that cut across this distinction.

[17] This is a standard classification that goes back to Parfit (1984).

choose the permanent prospect of such a life, without actually doing all those things that please you? No, you would not, because we do not care just about how things feel to us. What we want also is 'an actual connection with reality' (Nozick 1974: 106). We want the things we feel good about to 'actually hold and be so' (ibid.).

The recognition that our well-being depends on certain objective states of affairs is common to various objectivist approaches to well-being. What makes our life worthwhile, on these views, is not constituted by our subjective feelings and attitudes, and can be even independent of them; that is why it is possible to err about the worthwhileness of one's life, so that we may find out that we have wasted our life even though we have been quite satisfied with it (Kymlicka 1990: 202).[18] In general, the objectivist approaches maintain that 'lives are worth living if they are high in various objective goods and low in objective bads' (Smuts 2014: 711). Within the objectivist camp, several strategies can be differentiated. One broad strategy, known as the 'objective list' theory, seeks to determine the worthwhileness of life by the presence (or absence) of items from variously defined lists of objectively good things, such as achievement, friendship, autonomy or virtue (e.g. Parfit 1984; Rawls 1999). The other strategy, known as 'perfectionism' or 'developmentalism', identifies the objective goods by reference to the notion of human nature, so that well-being is defined as the perfection or development of certain cognitive and affective capacities that are essential or characteristic for us as human beings, such as practical or theoretical rationality (Hurka 2009; Kraut 2009; Bradford 2016). Yet another version of objectivist approaches – which is most directly inspired by ancient ethical theories – is 'eudaimonism', which defines well-being in terms of living well, understood as good or healthy functioning *qua* human beings (Russell 2012; LeBar 2013).

An objection to the objectivist accounts of well-being that is comparable in its suggestive force to Nozick's experience machine has been raised by Dan Haybron. Criticising eudaimonist theories of well-being, Haybron argued that these theories are unacceptably 'externalist', insofar as they understand what is good for an individual from an abstract standpoint of what it means to be a good human being (Haybron 2010: 157). If to be virtuous means to function well *qua* exemplar of the human species, then the goodness inherent in this functioning (or its opposite) is

---

[18] With the qualification that on some versions of the desire-fulfilment view, one can err as well, namely when one's desires are not appropriately 'informed', so that, in effect, one desires something that one does not really want.

too abstract to have any traction for my personal well-being. What makes me well or badly off is how I feel, rather than whether my life conforms to an external norm. Even in case of bodily harm, it is arguably not primarily the bodily dysfunction itself that diminishes my well-being but rather its consequences, such as pain or the inability to satisfy my desires. Arguing especially against the eudaimonist and perfectionist accounts of well-being, Haybron brings up the intriguing case of Genghis Khan. Although Khan's actions were morally repugnant, and he was hardly an examplar of perfect human being, it is difficult to deny that his life went well for him: he had a relatively long life, was well-respected in his community, and accomplished what he wanted (Haybron 2010: 159–160). If that is so, how can the objective perfection be the main criterion of well-being? Insofar as this objection also applies to some of the most influential ancient accounts of a life worth living, I shall return to it on several occasions as we proceed.

So far, I have been describing various approaches to defining the goodness or badness of life's contents – that is, of different things, events or activities that we do, have or experience. But philosophers have also discussed whether human life has a non-instrumental value independently of its contents – that is, whether it is good to be alive *per se* – and if so, what difference this value makes in the all-things-considered judgement about the worthwhileness of life. Thomas Nagel made the much-disputed claim that the activities that 'constitute life' such as 'perception, desire or thought' are 'formidable benefits in themselves'. These activities have intrinsic value 'despite the fact that they are conditions of misery as well as happiness, and that a sufficient quantity of more particular evils can perhaps outweigh them' (Nagel 1970: 74). The idea seems to be that the fact *that* we live – that is, that we think, desire or perceive – has an intrinsic value regardless of *what* we think, desire or perceive, or *how* well we do it. This view was rebutted, for instance, by Joseph Raz, who argued that life is 'not intrinsically and unconditionally valuable at all', since any value of life is conferred exclusively by its 'contents' (Raz 2001: 78).[19] Remarkably, Raz presents his rebuttal of Nagel as 'no more than a variant' of 'some ancient views' (ibid.: 77). This carefully vague reference exemplifies why a systematic treatment of ancient views about the value of life is desirable. Did some ancient philosophers indeed believe that mere living does *not* have any non-instrumental value for the person who lives it? And were there also dissenting views? Answers are forthcoming.

---

[19] Lee (2022) offers the most recent and sustained rebuttal of Nagel's thesis.

We have seen that both the subjectivist and objectivist approaches to well-being have had influential advocates and critics, and both are well established in the contemporary scholarship. However, when we move from theories of well-being to the more specific question of sufficient conditions for a life worth living, and especially to practical implications for biomedical ethics and the ethics of procreation, the subjectivist approaches prevail. It is a seriously entertained and contested proposition to say that your well-being depends on your being a well-functioning representation of the human species, but it is close to outrageous to say that poorly functioning or vicious humans cannot have a life worth living, and even to draw implications from this verdict for, say, biomedical deliberations about the right to life-saving measures. It is, rather, the desire of patients to stay alive, or their level of pain, that plays the decisive role in such contexts. This prevalence of subjectivist sensitivities may be a reason why ancient views about life worth living – in contrast to ancient accounts of happiness – have not been widely quoted. In fact, some of these ancient views may be rather difficult to swallow for a contemporary audience.

Let me give two characteristic examples. In Plato's *Apology*, Socrates famously claims that an 'unexamined life' – that is, a life involving no reflection about how one should live and why – is 'not worth living for humans' (*Ap.* 38a). Modern misgivings about this claim have been voiced by Fred Feldman, one of the most influential philosophers working on well-being. Finding Plato's view 'astonishing', he remarks: 'Surely there are plenty of unreflective, philosophically unsophisticated people who have been happy, and whose lives have been morally good, beneficial to others, and good in themselves for those who lived them' (Feldman 2006: 15). Even if we maintained that the worthwhileness of life depends, at least partly, on some objective goods, it is not at all clear why it should be conditional upon an objective intellectual perfection or aspiration of one particular kind. Such a criticism is perhaps not surprising from Feldman, who has himself developed a hedonist account of well-being, but even Nozick, who argued in favour of objectivist approaches, expresses reservations, finding Socrates' dictum 'unnecessarily harsh' (Nozick 1989: 15).

A further example is the view of Peripatetics, followers of Aristotle, that vicious humans should 'flee life' – that is, exit life voluntarily – even when the circumstances of their lives are otherwise favourable (Stobaeus, *Ecl.* ii.134.4–6). No matter how well off you may happen to be in terms of your social status, bodily health or other conventional goods, your life is harmful for you if you have a corrupt character and it is actually better for you not to live. Note that this is not, at least not primarily, the claim that vicious humans do not deserve to stay alive from a moral or legal point of view, but rather that their lives are not worth living for them from their own internal perspective. This view is unparalleled in contemporary discourse. Translated into contemporary terms, it implies that one's moral condition can and indeed ought to play an important role in the overall evaluation of one's well-being. But it is hardly possible to imagine that in current bioethical practice a patient could be legitimately prioritised for a life-saving intervention because they have a better character. In fact, it is an unchallenged view in modern biomedical ethics that considerations related to the moral quality of a patient's character, unlike considerations related to physical health or even psychological well-being, ought *not* to enter into the bioethical assessment of the patient's overall well-being (Harris 1985: 109). Not even those contemporary philosophers who, like the perfectionists, maintain that well-being depends on the presence of objective good in one's life, including moral virtue, would go as far as to argue that humans with a corrupted character would be better off dead even if they are otherwise well off.

By making the worthwhileness of human life conditional on intellectual richness or moral perfection, ancient views about the life worth living may seem on the whole too elitist, too dismissive of how subjectively content one is with one's life, and too inconsistent with the modern sense that all human lives have some intrinsic worth. We are ready to grant that one cannot live a truly flourishing life without a significant degree of moral and intellectual perfection that is accessible only to a few; but when it comes to judgements about whether human life is worth living, we are more reluctant to follow the ancients. Should we, then, conclude that some of the most influential ancient views about life worth living are no longer live options for us today? I shall try to offer a tentative answer to this question in the conclusion. But an early step towards such an answer must be an appreciation that ancient philosophers based their views on a set of assumptions and concepts that are not widely shared today, and that these may make their views, if not acceptable, at least intelligible to a contemporary audience. In the following sections, I address some of these assumptions that are particularly salient for our theme.

I.5   Some Background Assumptions of Ancient Theories

Consider again the striking claim that incurably vicious humans should, for their own sake, exit life. One important and potentially unsettling assumption behind this claim is that my moral excellences and flaws are necessarily beneficial or harmful for me. From the modern standpoint, this view appears to conflate two different kinds of practical reasons, or two different kinds of values, which have been distinguished at least since Kant: prudential value – what is good because it is beneficial for my personal welfare; and moral value – what is good because it is the right thing to do, given the valid normative demands or constraints.[20] Not only do these two kinds of value not entail each other, they may even conflict insofar as the pursuit of what benefits me personally may be at odds with what I ought to do from the moral point of view. Given this distinction, it is difficult to see why being a morally bad person should necessarily diminish my well-being, even to the point of making death preferable to life. In fact, is it not rather the case that possessing an unscrupulous character could actually make me better off in the purely prudential sense?

Philosophers such as Bernard Williams or Julia Annas have done a great deal to help a modern audience appreciate that what appears as a conflation may not necessarily be a shortcoming but rather a philosophically compelling feature of respectable ethical theories. The most characteristic feature of these theories is that all values and practical reasons ultimately derive their motivational and normative force from a single source, namely *eudaimonia*, as the chief prudential good. Whereas Williams (1985) regarded the ancient outlook as appealing on the grounds that it did without the modern notion of morality based on will and obligations, Annas argued that the ancients did have a robust notion of moral value, particularly other-regarding value, but that this value was integrated into the eudaimonist framework (Annas 1993, e.g. 322–325). One strategy to infuse moral value with a prudential dimension is to argue that the motivation to act morally has an important prudential component. So, for instance, Aristotle characteristically argues in the *Nicomachean Ethics* ix.8 that the good man will be eager to do 'fine' deeds because he is a 'self-lover'. He identifies himself with the rational part of his soul, and what this part is most gratified by is precisely the 'fine'. A different version of this strategy can be found in the Stoic view that the capacity to do what is appropriate, including fulfilling one's other-regarding duties, is a rationally cultivated extension of the rudimentary natural instinct for self-preservation (Annas 1993: 249–290). In both these cases, moral perfection is an achievement that does not necessarily presuppose the suppression or curbing of one's subjective pleasures and desires, but rather is conducive to their proper

---

[20] Crisp (2018) has a good overview of different aspects and levels of this distinction in contemporary thought.

fulfilment, on the condition that these desires and pleasures have been appropriately informed, developed and cultivated.

Whereas these strategies can explain how morality is conducive to happiness, they do not show in any straightforward way why a lack of excellence should make one unhappy. Yes, virtuous persons are pleased by acting virtuously, but vicious persons, according to Aristotle at least, are not necessarily pained by acting viciously, nor are their desires always frustrated; in fact, they may even be pleased by acting in the corrupt way they do – think of Haybron's Genghis Khan. So a different explanatory approach is needed to show that moral badness entails or guarantees prudential harm or unhappiness. When Plato or Aristotle maintain that vicious action is harmful for the agent, they appeal to the harm that this action inflicts on one's soul, and, more specifically, on its function. On this view, the harm is not to be primarily located at the level of one's subjective feelings, but rather at the level of objective functioning. This dysfunction may have, and sometimes necessarily entails, unfavourable felt consequences, such as emotional turmoil or frustrated desires, but these are derivative from the dysfunction. The soul of corrupted humans is thwarted in its functioning, and this is harmful for them. This is the logic behind Plato's repeatedly expressed view that if a life with a ruined body is not worth living, then a life with a corrupted soul is even less so.

In the recent scholarship, one popular strategy to defend the significance of virtue and vice for well-being has been to regard virtue as the 'safest bet' to achieve flourishing: whereas it is true that virtue is external to those psychological states that actually matter for well-being, it nevertheless reliably generates those states, some of which can be conveniently captured by the category of psychological health (Hursthouse 1999; Besser-Jones 2014). An alternative strategy takes issue with our understanding of who we are, or who, after all, is the subject of well-being. Whether something is good or bad for me always depends on a particular understanding of who I am. As Thomas Nagel (1970) and Jeff McMahan (2001) have pointed out, if we compare two persons with terminal dementia, one of whom previously had a rich intellectual life and another who had not, the dementia will make the former person worse off than the latter; in fact, one could even conclude that for the person with a rich intellectual history, a life with dementia may not be worth living at all, given her past condition, and death will be the preferable option. The reason is that well- or ill-being is always indexed to the broader context of our lives; it is measured by our losses. Our well-being cannot be assessed solely by reference to our present psychological states: the value of our present psychological states for our well-being depends on facts that are external to this present experience.

Now, it is arguably the case that the external context in which one's present well-being must be assessed is not limited to one's personal history. Consider an example inspired by later Peripatetic thought – that of a caged eagle that is reasonably well fed and taken care of. This bird does not suffer from any significant distress, and in some respects its life is easier than it would be in the wild. And yet many would think that such a life is not worth living for the eagle. The reason is that from the perspective of its natural constitution, this captive life is seriously impoverished. The bird is born to fly and hunt for its food, but all it can do is sit in the cage and passively wait to receive it. This assessment is relative to what eagles are supposed to do, or what their natural function is; in this sense, it is indexed to an external criterion. Still, what we feel pity for when looking into the cage is not the abstract species of eagles, but this particular bird. We feel pity for this bird regardless of whether it is distressed by its impoverished condition. Perhaps we can think of the condition of unfulfilled humans, such as those who live unreflective or morally unaccomplished lives, as comparable to that of caged eagles. Insofar as they cannot fully exercise the function that corresponds to the natural constitution of their species, as Plato or Aristotle argued, they are seriously incapacitated: they suffer a loss, their lives are wasted, they cannot be who, or what, they were meant to be.

The dementia and caged eagle examples indicate that, even from the contemporary perspective, the individual subject of well-being may, in some respects at least, be plausibly defined with regards to some criteria that are external to one's immediate subjective experience.[21] This holds all the more so for the ancient approaches. One could even say that the reason why the ancient accounts of what is good for p appear too externalist, in Haybron's words, is that p itself is understood in fairly externalist terms. As argued in the groundbreaking work of Charles Taylor (1989), the ancients envisaged the individual human self – in contrast to modern views – as fundamentally embedded in larger social, political and cosmic patterns. On this view, who or what we are is defined, from the start, by our role, job or function in the context of the wholes to which we belong, and which define our nature, be it our family, our city, the human species

[21] This is not to deny that the dementia case and the eagle case are not different in important ways. For instance, the poor quality of a captive eagle's life (assuming that it was born in captivity) does not depend on the manner of its prior life, but rather on its being contrary to an eagle's nature.

or even the universe; we cannot simply disown our functions without ceasing to be who we are. Perhaps the most suggestive expression of this idea is the Stoic notion of 'role' (*prosôpon, persona*). According to this view, each person has a multiplicity of different roles, including social roles in the family (e.g. brother, son), city (e.g. ruler, citizen) or the universe at large (the role of human being). Some of these roles we choose, but most of them are assigned to us by the providential god, similar to a director who assigns roles to different actors according to their individual aptitudes. As Epictetus makes clear, we do not have roles; rather, we *are* our roles: we are sons, brothers, citizens and, most importantly, human beings (*Diss* ii.10). Hence our flourishing is intimately connected with our prowess in, and capacity for, enacting these roles.

For all the emphasis on embeddedness and functioning within larger wholes, the ancients mostly did envisage individual humans as individual agents. That is, our function and roles are attached to an individual locus of the perception, thought and agency of an individuated living thing. What makes us who we are is the same thing as makes us alive, namely the 'soul' (*psuchê*).[22] We *are* our souls: it is to our souls that our functions and roles are attached. When Socrates' friends ask him in the *Phaedo* how he wishes to be buried, he answers: 'in any way you like, if you can catch me and I do not escape you' (116a). It is a mistake, Plato says, to think that what we are is our mortal body; rather, human beings are their immortal souls. The idea that our self is defined first and foremost by the soul was widely embraced by other ancient philosophers, whether or not they regarded the soul as immortal. The soul, too, has a function or functions, and at least some of these functions coincide with those social, biological or cosmic functions of human beings discussed earlier. The centrality of the soul for the ancient understanding of self helps us to appreciate why cognitive impoverishment or moral corruption should be harmful for the person who has it. When Plato says that a corrupted soul is even worse for the one who suffers from it than a corrupted body, the reason is simply that the soul is more constitutive of who we are than is the body. It is not the case that we are bodies that have souls; rather, we are souls that sometimes have, and use, bodies. If moral corruption amounts to a damaged soul, and soul is, as it were, more internal to us than the body, then this must be a devastating condition indeed.

---

[22] I discuss the importance of the 'soul' for the notion of self in more detail in Chapter 1. Noteworthy studies on ancient conceptions of the 'self' are Sorabji (2006), Gill (2006) and the collection of articles Remes and Sihvola (2008), as well as an accessible collection of essays by Long (2015).

I.6   The Approach

The book is structured in a straightforward way: each chapter is dedicated to a philosopher or a philosophical school, and the chapters are ordered chronologically. The selection of authors and texts is subservient to the goal of offering a representative overview of the main accounts of life worth living in the Greek and Roman tradition. Each chapter presents an interpretation of each account of life worth living, as well as connected views about the value of mere living and the relationship between worthwhileness and meaningfulness. The chapters do not have a fully uniform structure, since these themes do not always receive equal attention. For instance, the value of mere living is only marginally discussed in the dialogues of Plato, whereas it is a recurrent topic in Aristotle and the Peripatetic tradition; accordingly, two sections in the chapter on Aristotle are dedicated to this question, whereas no special section is assigned to it in the chapter on Plato. Still, all chapters follow a roughly similar structure. Typically, they begin with a formulation of the questions about the life worth living with regard to the specific context of each philosopher or school; in most cases, this question contains an interpretive puzzle that I try to solve. This puzzle bears on the accounts of happiness and their relationship to life worth living, and so this introductory section is followed by a sketch of these accounts of happiness. In the subsequent sections, questions about life worth living and the value of life are addressed, and always in an order that befits the discussions in the primary texts. Each chapter ends with a concluding section that (with the exception of that in Chapter 1) compares the views explored in this chapter with the views of the other philosophers discussed in the preceding chapters.

This project contains interpretations of difficult primary texts. The combination of linguistic distance, substantive background assumptions and philosophical sophistication, as well as (in some cases) the fragmentary nature of the evidence, makes these interpretations a task that often requires considerable patience. Characteristically for ancient philosophical texts, it is sometimes also necessary to inform the interpretation of issues in ethics and value theory by excursions into the philosophy of nature or metaphysics. The task is made all the more challenging since the existing secondary scholarship provides little guidance for addressing the texts from the vantage point of my questions.

Lest I strain the patience of non-historian philosophers, I shall limit the exegetical labours to the minimum necessary to establish informed interpretations of the ancient texts with regard to my questions. In some respects, this interpretation already presupposes an interpretation, or a commitment to an interpretation, of these texts at another level. Typically, views about life worth living and the value of life need to be expounded with some interpretation of theories of happiness in the background. In most cases, these theories are quite complex and some of their aspects have given rise to ongoing controversies in the secondary scholarship. In general, I try to settle on an exposition of theories of happiness that avoids addressing these controversies, and whenever this is not possible, I chart the different positions adopted in the scholarship and take sides with one of them. Occasionally, my interpretation provides additional support for one among the competing views. As befits the minimalistic approach to historical exegesis, my references to the secondary scholarship will be quite selective throughout. Typically, I cite the most influential works in the Anglophone scholarship in the last four decades or so, but it should be emphasised that this selection far from exhausts the vast high-quality scholarly work on ancient ethics done in past centuries both in English and other languages.

Finally, it should be noted that this project is interpretative in nature. My task is to contribute to a better understanding of ancient ethical theories. Whatever terminology and distinction I introduce, as it were, from the outside, this is strictly subservient to the interpretative project. For this reason, I also abstain from assessments of the merits and shortcomings of the different philosophical theories that I discuss. This is not to say that it would be inappropriate or misguided to adopt such a critical view, but it would have to be a part of a different project.

CHAPTER I

Plato on Making Life Worth Living by Doing One's Job

If I say that it is impossible for me to keep quiet because that means disobeying the god, you will not believe me and will think I am being ironical. On the other hand, if I say that it is the greatest good for a man to discuss virtue every day and those other things about which you hear me conversing and testing myself and others, for the unexamined life is not worth living for men, you will believe me even less.

(Plato, *Ap.* 38a)

When a carpenter is ill, he expects to receive an emetic or a purge from his doctor or to get rid of his disease through surgery or cautery. If anyone prescribed a lengthy regimen to him, telling him that he should rest with his head bandaged and so on, he'd soon reply that he had no leisure to be ill and that life is no use to him if he has to neglect his work and always be concerned with his illness. After that he'd bid good-bye to his doctor, resume his usual way of life, and either recover his health or, if his body couldn't withstand the illness, he'd die and escape his troubles.

(Plato, *Resp.* iii, 406d–e)[1]

1.1 Happy Life and Life Worth Living

All humans, according to Plato, desire to be happy, that is, to live well (*kalôs*).[2] But most of them have deeply misguided views about what living well amounts to. The main purpose of Plato's ethical theory is to expose these misconceptions and to offer his own account of what happiness and the truly good or beneficial things are. Commentators have noted that Plato sometimes refers to things that are conducive to the happy life as things that make a life 'worth living' (*biôtos*): 'The task is to give an account of happiness. This is understood in terms of specifying what makes life "worth living" as Plato sometimes puts it' (Sheffield 2018: 476). But the

[1] All translations of Plato's works, unless otherwise noted, follow translations in Cooper (1997).
[2] E.g. *Symp.* 204d–205a; *Men.* 77a–b; *Euthyd.* 278e–282d.

notion of a life worth living also carries implications that are absent from the notion of a happy life. In particular, it implies a comparative assessment: to say that a life is worth living means that there is enough reason to choose life *rather than* death. This is brought out by the fact that Plato typically mentions a 'life worth living' when he talks about lives that are *not* worthwhile, or lives that are even on the whole harmful for those who live them. From this comparative perspective, rather than defining the good life, the notion of a life worth living shows Plato's concern with defining when life is (still) a good, or at least not a bad. It may well turn out that, in his view, life is a good only if it is good; but this should not be presupposed from the start.

The idea that there is a philosophically significant difference between a happy life and a life worth living was floated, but not systematically pursued, by Christopher Bobonich: 'If happiness is a maximally good state including virtue and the possession of some other goods, then it seems reasonable to hold that some of these other goods might be subtracted from such a life while still leaving the person a life well worth living, although not one that attains happiness' (Bobonich 2002: 213).[3] If this suggestion can be backed by sufficient evidence, it would point towards the possibility that Plato construes the relationship between the best human life and a human life worth living in terms of the target–threshold distinction. This distinction would also be compatible with the possibility that happiness is a scalar notion, that is, that one can be happy to a greater or lesser degree; in that case, the threshold would be defined as a point on that spectrum.

The objective of this chapter is to consider what Plato says about the notion of a life worth living in its own right, rather than as a proxy for happiness, and on that basis to spell out his conception of the relationship between a happy life and a life worth living. To this end, the core body of evidence to be considered consists primarily of passages, and their broader contexts, where Plato explicitly talks about life being 'worth living' or 'not worth living'. These passages can be found in works that span all the traditional stages of the Platonic corpus – early, middle and late – but I shall focus on two texts in particular, namely the *Apology*, with its dictum that 'unexamined lives are not worth living', and the *Republic*, where Plato affirms that a life with an unjust soul is not worth living. The relationship between these two assertions raises questions about the compatibility of different claims about a life worth living across Plato's works.

---

[3] See also Bobonich (2002: 32). His view is that Plato does not grant this view in the *Phaedo* or the *Republic*, but that it is implicit in the *Laws*.

For the purposes of my interpretation, I shall give a privileged status to the theory in the *Republic* by making it explanatorily central and representative of Plato's views about life worth living more broadly considered. For the purposes of this book, Plato is primarily (though not exclusively) the Plato of the *Republic*. This is, of course, a controversial move; but given the diversity of the Platonic corpus, such choices must be made in a work of this kind, and the *Republic*, as arguably Plato's most influential text, is the obvious choice. It should be kept in mind, though, that a different picture of Plato's axiology of life, or one with different distribution of emphases, may emerge if other dialogues, such as *Phaedo* or the *Laws*, are given more central consideration.

The characteristic aspect of the ethical theory in the *Republic* is the centrality of the notion of 'function' (*ergon*). This includes an individual's social or professional function or job in the city, but also the function of one's soul. The good exercise of this function is what constitutes the excellent condition, or health, of the soul, which Plato also calls 'justice', and this health of the soul turns out to be the unconditional worthmaker. I shall also suggest that this account of a life worth living can accommodate, and further explain, the dictum from the *Apology*. But whereas all humans with healthy souls have lives that are robustly above the threshold for a life worth living, not all of them are equally happy. In particular, the lives of philosophers, or those who have lived examined lives in a particularly genuine or first-hand manner, are happier than the other citizens of Plato's ideal city.

1.2   The Unexamined Life Is Not Worth Living

No doubt the most familiar – and controversial – evidence on Plato's view about a life worth living is the dictum from the *Apology* that the 'unexamined life is not worth living for humans' (*anexetastos bios ou biôtos anthrôpôi*). Plato puts this claim in the mouth of Socrates, who defends himself against the charge that his public intellectual engagements have been corrupting the young. Socrates justifies his own philosophical mission by reference to his obedience to the command of god, who stationed him in the city to do the 'job' (*ergon*) of 'persuading and reproaching' its citizens (*Ap.* 30e). But this defence goes along with a more far-reaching normative claim, namely that a human life is not worthwhile unless it is itself subjected to rational examination, enquiry or scrutiny (*exetasis*). In other words, it is a life that is programmatically reflective about how one should live and why. The activity of examination may have some value in its own right,[4] so that we are invited to spend time in a continuous examination of our lives, but clearly it is also regarded as the instrument for taking 'care' (*epimeleia*) of the soul, that is, for bringing about the 'best possible state' of the soul and maintaining it (*Ap.* 29e). In this latter sense, we are encouraged to live not only a life that is *being* examined but also a life that *has been* examined.[5] To achieve this state, what one has to care about is not conventionally valued things, such as reputation or honour, but rather 'wisdom and truth' (*phronêsis kai alêtheia*) (ibid.; cf. 36c); this is why the rational examination is of paramount importance. An important part of this procedure is purgative, that is, cleansing the soul of unreflectively accepted convictions about what matters in life that do not stand closer scrutiny. This scrutiny typically has the form of dialectical refutation, the so-called *elenchos*, in which Socrates refutes his interlocutor's views by means of exposing contradictions among them.

It has been rightly remarked by commentators that Socrates' dictum is not about suicide.[6] When Socrates claims that an unexamined life is not worth living, his point is not that humans who cannot live up to that ideal should actively choose death, but rather that for him, in his specific situation, it is worth risking the death penalty because there would be no point for him in staying alive had he to denounce his current way of life. The appreciation of this point also has implications for the translation. Richard Kraut proposed that instead of the established version 'worth living', *biôtos* should be read as 'to be lived' (Kraut 2007: 231). On this reading, then, what Socrates really means to say is (only) that 'no human being should live an unexamined life': this is not a statement about the conditions of life's worthwhileness, but about how one ought to live. Grammatically this construal is possible, but it is not a good fit with the context of Socrates' speech.[7] Socrates' point is not only moral but also existential: for him, a continued existence deprived of public intellectual pursuits would be meaningless. This existential urgency of Socratic ethics is brought out perhaps most powerfully in the *Crito*, where Socrates defends his decision to remain in prison and to accept his punishment despite the chance to save his life by escape: if a life should be saved at the cost of acting unjustly, such a life would be not worth living anyway. On Kraut's reading, Socrates

---

[4] Cf. Bett (2010: 230): Socrates 'seems to regard the pursuit as itself a valuable and worthwhile exercise', even 'regardless of the prospects for actually finding the definitions he is seeking'.

[5] It is this latter sense (but not so much the former) that is the focus of the *Republic*.

[6] Warren (2001); Long (2019: 177–178).

[7] This duality of interpretive options emerges also in *Symp.* 211d. See Nehamas and Woodruff (1989: 59) for the translation of *biôtos* as 'should a person live his life'.

would be making the more impersonal claim that he would not do what humans in general ought not to do.

All the same, Socrates' claim does seem to express a more generally binding normative commitment. What he says is that an unexamined life is not worth living for humans in general, and not only for him in particular. If people don't critically reflect on their own lives, ever, do they have a life fit to be led? We have seen that the idea that an unexamined life is not worth living has alienated some modern commentators. One problem is the appearance of elitism: on the assumption that the examined life is the philosophical life, that is, the life lived exclusively by philosophers, this dictum seems to imply an 'extremely harsh attitude to one's fellow citizens' (Kraut 2007: 230) who do not have the privilege and leisure to lead a philosophical life. A related, but different issue, concerns the justification of this claim: why, precisely, should rational examination – regardless of its accessibility to different social classes – be the necessary condition for living a life worth living? In the introduction, I quoted this concern as voiced by Fred Feldman: surely there are people who lead respectable and rewarding lives even without engaging in any form of philosophical reflection (Feldman 2006: 15). In the later dialogue *Philebus*, Socrates easily gets his interlocutor Protarchus to agree that an extremely primitive and cognitively impoverished life, such as 'the life of a jellyfish or of one of those creatures in shells that live in the sea' is not 'worth choosing (*hairetos*) for us (*hêmin*)'[8] (*Phlb.* 21d).[9] Many would agree with this claim. But the requirement of living a reflective life may seem to set the threshold for worthwhile lives much higher, indeed too high. Also, the activity of theoretical philosophical reflection is narrow in its own way.

There are reasons to think that Plato himself made a concession to these objections in later works. In the passage from the *Republic* quoted in the epigraph to this chapter, he approves of the carpenter's view that his life is not worth living for him if he cannot do his job, but also that it *is* worth living if he can.[10] While the carpenter's life does involve some exercise of

---

[8] This qualification is important, since such a life is naturally worth choosing for a jellyfish (cf. Nussbaum 1995: 99–102).

[9] Interestingly, it is also established in the dialogue that a life of intelligence that is deprived of any kind of pleasure and pain and is 'insensitive' (*apathes*), too, is not worth choosing (21d–e). This is consistent with the conclusion that the good life includes *both* reason *and* pleasure. The view that a rational life of total insensitivity is not worth choosing seems also compatible with the theory from the *Republic*. For, as we shall see, only life of virtue is worth living, but virtue also brings about some pleasures, most importantly the pleasures of reason (*Resp.* ix).

[10] There is also an alternative and more pedestrian interpretation of carpenter's view, pointed out to me by Karel Thein, namely that he simply cannot afford not to work.

the rational capacities of the human soul, similarly to other crafts (*technai*), it is hardly an examined life in the sense of the philosophical life embodied by Socrates. Indeed, by Plato's own lights in the *Republic*, insofar as carpenters belong to the inferior social class of producers, they *ought* not aspire to a philosophical life in Plato's ideal city, and should leave this type of life to the philosophers – the rulers. And yet Plato does seem to think, or so I shall argue, that a good carpenter's life is robustly worth living for him. One possible explanation of this apparent discrepancy between the *Apology* and the *Republic* is that Plato's position has shifted, or, more precisely, that in the *Republic* he emancipates himself from the original Socratic view of the *Apology* and corrects it: 'Yes, says Plato [in the *Republic*], the examined life is the best available to a human being; but it is not good for everyone to try to live it' (Kraut 2007: 232). On this view, there are multiple paths to a life worth living, and not all of them presuppose rational examination in the Socratic sense. In fact, some humans are ill-suited to pursue such a life, and it would even be a mistake for them to aspire to it.

There are two alternative perspectives on the relationship between the *Apology* and the *Republic*, both denying that any significant shift takes place. One is that the position in the *Apology* is elitist, but so is the position in the *Republic*. On this view, Plato in the *Republic* does not in fact make any noteworthy concessions towards acknowledging the value of non-philosophical lives, and still maintains that a life worth living requires wisdom that is accessible only to philosophers (e.g. Bobonich 2002). Another possibility is that Plato's position in the *Republic* is not elitist, as suggested by the carpenter's case, but that nor is the position from the *Apology*. On an influential and rather attractive reading of the *Apology* by Gregory Vlastos (1991), Socrates' outlook there is far from elitist; rather, he is on a mission aimed at encouraging all citizens to lead an examined life. Not only professional philosophers but all citizens can and indeed ought to aspire to the examined life. Could this also turn out to be Plato's position in the *Republic*? *Prima facie*, this hardly seems to be the case, insofar as carpenters are not allowed to do philosophy. But it is perhaps also possible, or so I shall argue, that even in the *Republic* Plato thinks that all just citizens, including non-philosophers, do live an examined life, at least in a peculiarly qualified, second-hand sense.

Whereas the dictum from the *Apology* will never quite disappear from the picture, I shall also turn to other – relatively neglected – evidence about 'life worth living' found elsewhere in Plato's corpus. I begin in Section 1.3 by showing that, and explaining why, lives not worth living are consistently associated with the condition of having a corrupted or unjust soul. In Section 1.4, taking the *Republic* as the point of reference, I establish that all humans – including non-philosophers – can in Plato's view live a fully worthwhile life because their soul can be kept in a healthy condition insofar as they do their job, or function (*ergon*), well. In Section 1.5, I discuss a passage from the little-read dialogue *Clitophon* that espouses the view that those who do not know how to 'use' their soul would be better not living at all. The arguments in this passage further confirm and supplement the account from the preceding sections. In Section 1.6, I revisit the controversial dictum from the *Apology* and propose in what sense it is contained in, rather than superseded by, the account in the *Republic*. I conclude in Section 1.7 by summarising the main findings and anticipating what is to come.

1.3   Death Better than Life with a Corrupted Soul

The condition most commonly associated in Plato's dialogues with a life *not* worth living is not so much a failure to live an examined life, but a corruption (*diastrophê*) of the soul. There is good evidence for this view spanning Plato's early, middle and late works. Consider first the two following passages, one from the early dialogue *Crito* and another, later, from the *Republic*:

> Come now, if we ruin that which is improved by health and corrupted by disease by not following the opinions of those who know is life worth living (*biôton estin*) for us when that is ruined (*diephtharmenou*)? And that is the body, is it not? – Yes. – And is life worth living with a body that is corrupted and in bad condition? – In no way. – And is life worth living for us with that part of us corrupted that unjust action harms and just action benefits? Or do we think that part of us, whatever it is, that is concerned with justice and injustice, is inferior to the body? – Not at all. – It is more valuable (*timiôteron*)? – Much more. (*Cr.* 47d–48a)
>
> Even if one has every kind of food and drink, lots of money, and every sort of power to rule, life is thought to be not worth living (*ou biôton*) when the body's nature is ruined (*tou sômatos tês phuseôs diaphtheiromenês*). So even if someone can do whatever he wishes, except what will free him from vice and injustice and make him acquire justice and virtue, how can it be worth living (*biôton ara estai*) when his soul – the very thing by which he lives – is ruined and in turmoil (*tarattomenês kai diaphtheiromenês*)? (*Resp.* iv, 445a–b)

Before I analyse these arguments more closely, let me note that what Plato seeks to establish in these passages is that life with a corrupted soul lacks worthwhileness. But in other passages, one from the *Gorgias* and another from the *Laws*, which is traditionally considered to be Plato's last work, he also makes a stronger claim, namely that humans with a corrupted soul would be better off dead. This means not only that these lives are not worth living, in the sense that they lack what it takes to live a worthwhile life, but also that they are robustly negative and that death is the preferable option for those who lead these lives.

In the *Gorgias*, Plato argues against Callicles, an oligarchic hedonist, that the art of self-preservation cannot be the true purpose of rhetoric. To this end, he draws an analogy between the orator and the helmsman. A point is made that even a helmsman is rightly reserved about the value of his skill, since he cannot be certain that by saving lives, he actually benefits those whom he rescues:

> For he's [i.e. the helmsman] enough of an expert, I suppose, to conclude that it isn't clear which ones of his fellow voyagers he has benefited by not letting them drown in the deep, and which ones he has harmed, knowing that they were no better in either body or soul when he set them ashore than they were when they embarked. So he concludes that if a man afflicted with serious incurable physical diseases did not drown, this man is miserable for not dying (*athlios estin hoti ouk apethanen*) and has gotten no benefit from him. But if a man has many incurable diseases in what is more valuable than his body, his soul, life for that man is not worth living, and he won't do him any favor if he rescues him from the sea or from prison or from anywhere else. He knows that for a corrupt person it's better not to be alive (*hoti ouk ameinon estin zên tôi mochthêrôi anthrôpôi*), for he necessarily lives badly. (*Grg.* 511e–512b)

The idea of 'being miserable for not dying' also appears in a passage from the *Laws* which has received attention as evidence for the view that Plato regards suicide, in some circumstances, as permissible and even appropriate.[11] The following advice is addressed to those tempted by an 'evil impulse' to commit the most serious crime of robbing temples:

> When any of these thoughts enters your head, seek the rites that free a man from guilt; seek the shrines of the gods who avert evil, and supplicate them; seek the company of men who have a reputation in your community for being virtuous. Listen to them as they say that every man should honor what is fine and just – try to bring yourself to say it too. But run away from

---

[11] Cf. Cooper (1989). This raises questions about the compatibility of this view with a passage from the *Phaedo* (61c–62c), where Plato seems to endorse, or at least does not reject, a presumably Pythagorean prohibition on suicide on the grounds that we are to gods what slaves are to their owners (Warren 2001; Werner 2018; Christensen 2020). In any case, gods are the decisive presence in both cases.

the company of the wicked, with never a backward glance. If by doing this
you find that your disease abates somewhat, well and good; if not, then you
should look upon death as the preferable alternative, and rid yourself of life.
(*Leg.* ix, 854b–c)[12]

With the exception of the last passage, all the texts cited earlier contain
an argument based on a juxtaposition of, and a parallel between, soul and
body: (1) life is not worth living with serious incurable diseases in one's
body; (2) the soul is more important or 'valuable' than the body; and
hence (3) life with an incurably diseased or corrupted soul will be even less
worth living than life with a ruined body. This raises three questions. First,
is Plato's philosophically considered view expressed in (1), and if so, what
is the justification for it? Secondly, on what grounds does Plato think that
disease of the soul matters *more* than disease of the body? Thirdly, what
does disease of the soul amount to and why should it be so devastatingly
bad for the one who suffers from it? The first question is most conveniently
addressed jointly with the third; so I start with the second.

   This second question touches upon the much-discussed theme of the
soul–body relationship and its development in early Greek philosophy.[13]
Without delving into details, it suffices to say that Plato's valuation of soul
over body is motivated by an account of the soul that combines the standard, non-philosophical view in the Greek literature that the soul – and
not the body – is the life-conferring element,[14] with some distinctively
Socratic–Platonic innovations in the understanding of the soul. These
innovations evolved from a tendency in fifth-century BCE medical and
philosophical texts, particularly by Heraclitus and Democritus, to juxta-
pose body (*sôma*) and soul (*psuchê*) as two interrelated but different elements that are each subject to a special regimen of cultivation and care
(*epimeleia*).[15] Plato draws on these views, but further dissociates the soul
from the body, establishing a clear hierarchy between the two, putting soul
in the controlling position,[16] and even associating them, as in the *Phaedo*,
with two different metaphysical realms, that of immaterial, imperishable
entities on the one hand and material, perishable entities on the other.

---

[12] In a similar spirit is the following assessment from the *Republic*: 'But as for the ones whose bodies
are naturally unhealthy or whose souls are incurably evil, won't they let the former die of their own
accord and put the latter to death?' (410a).

[13] Among the most important studies are Snell (1946); Claus (1981); Holmes (2010). Lorenz (2003) is
a useful overview of ancient theories of the soul.

[14] As Plato puts it in the passage from the *Republic* quoted above, the soul is 'the very thing by which
we live' (445a).

[15] Nussbaum (1972) is the classic article on this theme.

[16] *Alc.* 130a; *Phd.* 80a; *Phlb.* 35d.

This hierarchical conception goes hand in hand with regarding the soul as the proper source and locus of individual agency or, if you like, the self.[17] The relationship between the notion of the soul as the ruling element and the soul as the self is explicitly affirmed in the *Alcibiades*.[18] From the premise that what uses (e.g. a lyre player) and what is being used (e.g. the lyre) cannot be the same thing, the conclusion is reached that what we are is our soul (*Alc.* 130c2–3). Since what one is is what rules (or: uses) the body (130a), what we are must be different both from the body and from the combination of soul and body; and this is the soul.

There are some important general implications of the Platonic view of the immortality of the soul for the question about life worth living. If I am my soul, rather than my body, and the soul is immortal, then it is not possible for me *not* to exist. So when Plato says that it is better for those with a corrupted soul not to be alive what he means is, presumably, that it is better for them to depart from the specific instance of the embodied existence that they are now having, that is, to separate their soul from this particular body. The myths at the end of *Gorgias* and the *Republic* specify in what sense the disembodied existence could be regarded as better for these humans: the appropriate punishments will be administered to the vicious souls so as to cure them of wickedness before they embark on another cycle of birth. According to the myth from the last book of the *Republic*, all souls after having been rewarded or punished also have a chance to 'choose' (*hairein*) their next life. This gives them the chance to choose for themselves a better life than the one they lived before. The souls that lived miserable lives and suffered from their punishments will be rather careful in making their choice. At the same time, Plato maintains in the *Gorgias* that some souls are wholly incurable even in the disembodied state; the punishments they have to suffer won't make them any better, and their suffering is nothing but punishment (*Grg.* 525b–d). This implies that the end of embodied existence is good news for all vicious souls, with the exception of these extreme cases.[19]

Turning to the question of why having a corrupted soul is worse than having a corrupted body, it should first be made clear that Plato's point is not just that your moral corruption makes your life worthless in a moral

---

[17] The classic formulation of this thesis is Burnet's (1916), but the claim that the notion of the soul as the locus of conscious personality was an ex-nihilo invention of Socrates has in important respects been qualified (e.g. Claus 1981).

[18] This dialogue is no longer regarded as spurious by the majority of commentators.

[19] So would it not be in everyone's interest to depart from embodied life as soon as possible? I discuss a Neoplatonist answer to this question in Chapter 6.

sense, but that life with a corrupted soul is bad *for* you, so much so that you would be better off dead. The reason why a ruined condition of the soul makes life insupportable should be understood in similar terms to the reason why life is unbearable when your body is ruined. It is a kind of disease: 'just and unjust actions are no different for the soul than healthy and unhealthy things are for the body' (*Resp.* iv, 444c).

But why, precisely, does a disease, whether bodily or psychic, make life not worth living? Perhaps the most obvious reason is pain. Just like bodily ailments, the disease of the soul can presumably be painful as well; and it has been argued that in the *Philebus*, for instance, Plato does characterise the condition of tyrants who suffer from *pleonexia*, or insatiable greediness for power, as inherently painful (Ionescu 2019: 111); we shall come to this point later in this section. But Plato nowhere says that it is the pain in and of itself that makes a life not worth living. Rather, the evidence suggests that the culprit is incapacitation or impaired functioning. This is clearly implied in the sick carpenter's case from the *Republic*: the disease is regarded as something bad because it impedes him in doing his job. Even bodily disease or injury appears to be bad not primarily because it is painful but because it thwarts the function of the body, and, as a consequence, and more importantly, thwarts those activities that fulfil the soul's function and that cannot be exercised unless the body is in a sufficiently good condition.

These considerations bring us back to the first of the earlier questions, namely whether Plato thinks that serious bodily ill-being can on its own make life not worth living. I do not think that the sources yield a conclusive answer. On the one hand, for the above arguments from *Crito* or *Gorgias* to work, the two branches of the comparison between bodily and psychic ill-being must have an independent validity. It is established, first, that life is not worth living with a corrupt body. This must be established without any reference to psychic ill-being, for only then can the move to psychic ill-being have real argumentative force. If the bodily corruption turns out to have been deemed bad only because of its dire consequences for the soul, then the whole argument is undermined. On the other hand, we do not find any evidence for the view that it is possible to have a well-functioning soul while suffering from such serious bodily corruption that this corruption would make life not worth living independently of, and indeed in spite of, the psychic functioning. Several scholars did find it to be Plato's view that even in the case of a philosopher, and not only a carpenter, extreme ill health can on its own be sufficient to thwart the psychic function and make even the life of a previously good person not worth living.[20] But this still does not make the bodily corruption a worth-breaker *per se*. It is also possible, as suggested by Betegh (2020: 233), that the very definition of what counts as bodily corruption is revisionist in the sense that it depends on the consequences for psychic functioning. Are you a philosopher with a disease that is quite painful, yet not painful enough to prevent you, on the whole, from doing your job? Then your bodily condition is not really quite wretched yet. But if this is right, the force of the arguments from the comparison between body and soul is still compromised, because bodily corruption is not a worthbreaker independently of its consequences for the soul.

In any case, Plato's perspective on physical diseases and life worth living seems to diverge, or even deliberately oppose, the position adopted in the medical literature of his time. According to different parts of the Hippocratic corpus, chronic bodily diseases should be treated even if they 'last seven or nine years' (*Diseases* 2: 49), and medical care ought to be provided even if prolonged suffering and death is the most likely outcome (*Glands* 14). Even those who have suffered life-threatening conditions such as amputation or gangrene were regarded as not entirely hopeless cases and were given the appropriate treatment (*Instruments of Reduction* 34; *On Joints* 68–69).[21] This starkly contrasts with Plato's stern views from the *Republic*. Even less compromisingly than the carpenter's case may suggest, Plato says that the judges in his ideal city will 'let die' those who have naturally deformed or dysfunctional bodies and – even more disturbingly – that they'll kill those who have ill-grown and irreparable souls (*Resp.* iii, 410a).

This brings us to the question of disease of the soul. Plato understands psychic disease in terms of a dysfunction and equates this dysfunction with the vice of injustice. The foundations for this account are laid in the first book of the *Republic*, where Plato defines what function is in general, and then specifies the function of the human soul in particular. The function (*ergon*) of each thing is defined as 'what it alone can do or what it does better than anything else' (*Resp.* i, 353a). So, for instance, the function of a pruning knife is pruning, since a pruning knife is better for pruning than other tools or even other knives; the function of eyes is seeing because there is no other part of the body with this capacity.[22] The soul has several interrelated functions, or functions which only the soul can do, namely

---

[20] Kraut (1984: 38), n. 31; Vlastos (1985: 8), n. 62.
[21] I owe these references to Levin (2014: 119–120), who addresses Plato's ambivalent relationship with the medicine of his time in a book-length study.
[22] Santas (2010); Keyt (2006).

'taking care of things, ruling, deliberating, and the like', but also, first and foremost, 'living'. But it is one thing to exercise function and exercise it *well*, for 'anything that has a function performs it well (*eu*) by means of its own peculiar excellence (*aretê*) and badly (*kakôs*) by means of its badness (*kakia*)' (353c). If living is the function of the soul, then the good exercise of this function amounts to living well, and bad exercise to living badly. It is the excellence or excellences of the soul that enable the soul to achieve its goodness. As becomes clear from later chapters of the *Republic*, it is when one lives well that the soul also exercises well its other, more specific functions, such as taking care of things and deliberating.

In the fourth book of the *Republic*, Plato fills out this preliminary account and articulates what living well and the excellence of the soul amount to. This theory rests on a structural account of the soul: the excellence of the soul turns out to be a harmonious arrangement and interaction among different elements within the soul. This harmony emerges when each of these elements is fulfilling its own peculiar function.[23] Here, again, the analogy between soul and body is deployed to bring out that the harmony within the soul is a kind of health which, like bodily health, is secured when a certain hierarchy and proportion among different elements is established as befits their natural affinities.[24] This healthy condition of the soul is called 'justice' (*dikaiosunê*):

> To produce health is to establish the components of the body in a natural relation of control and being controlled, one by another, while to produce disease is to establish a relation of ruling and being ruled contrary to nature. – That's right. – Then, isn't to produce justice to establish the parts of the soul in a natural relation of control, one by another, while to produce injustice is to establish a relation of ruling and being ruled contrary to nature? (*Resp.* iv, 444d)

The path by which Plato arrives at this definition of justice rests on a postulate of isomorphism between the city and the soul. This postulate posits a close correspondence between the different parts or 'kinds' (*eidê*) of the city, as well as their characteristic activities and functions, and the parts and functions of the human soul.[25] In mapping the different

---

[23] It has been common in the literature to refer to these elements as 'parts', though Plato's own vocabulary in referring to these elements is quite diverse. It has been debated in the scholarship whether these parts are to be understood as more or less independent agents, or merely as different aspects or faculties of a unified whole. Barney et al. (2012) is an excellent collection of articles on this theme.

[24] For an illuminating account of the analogies between bodily and psychic health in the *Republic*, including its indebtedness to ancient medicine, see Torres (2020).

[25] In the following reconstruction, I follow Santas (2010: 90).

parts, activities and functions of the city onto those of the soul, this isomorphism entails a much stronger and tighter analogy than the analogy between body and soul. For a city to be just, people of different 'natural classes' (*genê phuseôn*; 435b) must do the job that fits their natural aptitudes (443a–c). There are three main functions of the city: to rule; to defend; and to provide for the necessities of life (369b ff.; 428d ff.). Correspondingly, people in the city fall into one of three natural kinds, so that their natural aptitudes (intelligence, spiritedness and abilities for agriculture, crafts or trades) predetermine them to fulfil one of the three functions (435b): philosophers should rule; the military class or guardians should defend; and the producers should provide. A city is just when everybody does their job and does not meddle with the jobs of others (443c). The same structure can also be found in the human soul, and its justice precisely mirrors the justice of the city. There are three main sub-functions of the soul, and a human soul is just when each of its parts fulfils its natural function with the corresponding excellence (441e). The rational part should rule over the other two parts by means of 'wisdom' (*phronêsis*). The spirited part should be educated so that its capacity to feel anger is channelled towards helping the rational part enforce its commands by means of 'courage'. The appetitive part, which cares for the satisfaction of bodily needs, has no characteristic virtue of its own but does share in two other virtues that are common to all parts of the soul: 'temperance' or 'sound-mindedness' (*sôphrôsunê*), defined as an agreement (*homonoia*) about who in the soul/city should rule and who should be ruled (432a); and, of course, justice.

A just person establishes and preserves appropriate relationships among these parts, and thereby also establishes the health and 'well-being' (*euexia*) of the soul (444d) as a whole, by making sure that each part of the soul is doing its job and does not meddle with the jobs of other parts. Most importantly, the non-rational parts of the soul, the spirited and appetitive, must be governed by the rational part, because only the rational part 'has the knowledge of what is advantageous for each part and for the whole soul' (442c). Thus, the universally human excellence, justice, would be the psychological condition in which the *entire* soul can exercise its function well because each of its parts is doing own job, so that the three parts have been brought into a 'harmony' (*harmonia*) and what is 'many' has come to be 'one' (443d–e). In a diseased soul, there is a disharmony among its different parts, which causes a strife in the soul that is similar to civil strife in the city. In *Republic* viii and ix, Plato describes in detail the miserable condition of the unjust soul, and of the tyrannical soul as its worst case. In this soul, the lowest, appetitive part of the soul acquires disproportional strength and comes to rule over the entire soul. Insofar as the soul is ruled by the element that is to be ruled, and hence is naturally ill-suited to rule the soul, this soul as a whole is slavish and unfree (577d). What makes this condition robustly bad is the inversion, and perversion, of the hierarchy among the different parts of the soul, as determined by their natural aptitudes.

It is worth stressing, again, that the condition of the unjust soul is bad not only in the objective sense of dysfunction and vicious actions, but also in the sense that it is harmful, in a very palpable way, for those who suffer from it. After all, Plato's main contention in the *Republic*, as announced in the first book, is to prove, against Socrates' doubtful interlocutors, that being just is most beneficial not only for the city as a whole but also for the individual citizens, and that being unjust is harmful for them; the parallel between psychic and bodily health serves precisely this purpose. Accordingly, Plato offers a remarkably vivid account of the suffering of unjust humans. As a consequence of their objective psychological cor-ruption, their ill-being has two subjective dimensions that are remotely reminiscent of two contemporary subjectivist theories of well-being: the hedonic theory and the desire-satisfaction theory. First, the lives of unjust souls, taking the tyrannic soul as the worst example, are painful; it feels bad to live like that. The tyrant's 'waking life is like a nightmare' to him (576b); he is filled with 'regret' (577e) and 'fear' (579d); and he is full of 'convul-sions and pains throughout his life' (579e).

Plato's description of the tyrannical man suggests that this affective misery is largely a consequence of the second subjective dimension of ill-being, namely the frustration of one's desires. Such a person is 'least likely to do what he wants' (577d); he is 'far from satisfying his desires in any way' (579d–e).[26] This permanent frustration is due not so much to the unavailability of external resources as to the fact that his soul is 'unsatisfi-able' (*aplêstos*) (578a) or, as Plato puts it in the *Gorgias*, it is like a leaky jar (*Grg.* 493a–c). The dissatisfaction and unsatisfiability comprise two differ-ent levels, and at both levels they follow from the fact that it is the appeti-tive part, rather than the rational part, that is in the ruling position. On one level, the tyrant cannot effectively satisfy vicious desires for pleasure and power, since they are excessive and so prevent him from achieving the state of satisfaction. At another, more fundamental, level, the tyrant is not able to satisfy the universally human desire for happiness. This fol-lows from the view that what a tyrant desires is only what *seems* good to

---

[26] The idea that vicious humans necessarily fail to achieve, or even want, what they *actually* want is centrally discussed in the *Gorgias*, esp. 466a–468e (see below in this section).

him; this is not what actually *is* good for him, that is, virtue, which is the good for all humans (*Grg.* 466a–468e). For this reason, even if his vicious desires were to be securely satisfied, his desire for happiness would still be frustrated.[27] In the contemporary vocabulary, one could say that, in this sense, all desires of unjust humans are inherently misinformed.

To sum up, the fundamental flaw that necessarily makes life *not* worth living is the objective incapacity of the human soul to exercise its function, which amounts to the vice of injustice. This objective flaw is an unconditional worthbreaker in its own right, but it goes hand in hand with associated subjective disturbances. So much, then, for Plato's claim that life with an unjust soul is worse than death. With this account in mind, we can now proceed to the question about a well-functioning carpenter. On the elitist reading of the dictum from the *Apology*, it would follow that life is not worth living for him since it is an unreflective life. But it is also possible, as I shall argue in the next section, that in the *Republic* Plato regards the carpenter's life as robustly worthwhile, even though it may fall short of the highest happiness of the philosophical life. The reason is that a well-functioning carpenter has a healthy soul.

1.4 Why Is a Good Carpenter's Life Worth Living?

In the third book of the *Republic*, Plato exemplifies a commendable attitude to illness by the case of a carpenter. He contrasts the carpenter's attitude with that of other sick people who choose for themselves 'a slow death' by undergoing all sorts of medical treatments to extend their life as far as possible. The reason that Asklepios, the god of medicine, decided not to transmit his medical skills to further generations is that he knew that 'in a well-ordered city everyone has their own job to do, and that no one has the leisure to be ill and let oneself be treated all life long' (*Resp.* iii, 406e).[28] The carpenter's attitude is exemplary, since he lets himself be treated by

---

[27] There are two other notable attempts to explain why injustice is harmful for the agent that are compatible with my suggestions. One is Terence Irwin's view that 'without psychic justice other goods cannot have the value for us that we expect them to have' (Irwin 1995: 255). On this view, then, it is not about the weighing of a set of justice-unrelated goods against the badness of injustice; rather, the psychic disease cancels any goodness that these conventional goods may otherwise have, similarly to the way that chronic bad health does. Another possible strategy, suggested by Lloyd Gerson, is that living unjustly is a 'sort of self-deconstruction', or that committing an unjust act is a kind of suicide (Gerson 1997: 10). The justification for this claim combines the view that self is soul with the view that we have our 'identity' only insofar as reason remains in the ruling position. The subordination of reason to appetites 'deconstructs a self as an agent of effective rational activity' (ibid.).

[28] Cf. the relevant remarks in the preceding section about Plato's engagement with the medical views of his time.

a doctor only if there is a decent chance that the cure will enable him to carry on with his job, insofar as 'his life is no use to him (*ou lusitelei*) if he has to neglect his work' (406d–e) or 'if he doesn't do his job (*ergon*)' (407a). This indicates that carpenter's life is worth living for him, and rightly so, because, and in so far as, he can do his job. This is consistent with the claim that it is justice that makes life worth living and injustice that makes it not worth living. For the carpenter is doing his job, and that is precisely how justice is defined: doing 'one's own' job *is* justice' (*ta hautou prattein dikaiosunê esti*) (*Resp.* iv, 433a–b; cf. 434a).[29]

The fundamental idea behind this view is that if you do your proper job in the city, and do it well, then your soul necessarily also does its job well, that is, you live well. Before I consider some further evidence and justification for this claim, it is worth noting that this view bears on the bigger question about the relationship between life's worthwhileness and its meaningfulness. In Plato's view from the *Republic*, these two values appear to be fully coextensive and interdependent: you achieve your individual flourishing, or psychic health, to the extent of, and by means of, your contribution to the city of which you are a part. It is exclusively via specific professional and social roles in the city that each member of the city enacts, in a specific way, the function of the human soul in general and of their own soul in particular. Philosophers, guardians and producers can all have healthy souls, and thus live worthwhile lives, when, and insofar as, they do their jobs well, and, one could even add, *no matter what* these jobs are, if they contribute to the well-ordered society.

This view is premised on what Julia Annas (1981: 71–74) has called the principle of specialisation: to do a good job in any area of human action that is necessary to secure the city's needs, each citizen has to channel all their psychological resources into a single occupation; the best results will be achieved when each person 'does one thing, does it at the right time, and is released from having to do any of the others' (*Resp.* ii, 370c). This division of labour should take into account differences in individual constitutive natures, since 'we aren't all born alike, but each of us differs somewhat in nature from the others (*diapherôn tên phusin*), one being suited to one task, another to another (*allos ep' allou ergou praxin*)' (370a–b).[30] As Annas has pointed out, this view has to do less with valuing psychological attributes

---

[29] One may object to this claim that it rests on a conflation of political justice as the welfare of the city and psychic justice as the well-being of an individual soul: justice as 'doing one's own' could be political justice, but not necessarily psychic justice (cf. Kamtekar 1998: 317 against Vlastos 1978). For a compelling response to this objection, see Santas (2010: 147–148).

[30] 'It is right for someone who is by nature a cobbler to practice cobblery and nothing else, for the carpenter to practice carpentry, and the same for the others is a sort of image of justice' (*Resp.* iv, 443c).

that are unique and distinctive for an individual human being and more with acknowledging that 'people come in different types suited for different kinds of life' (Annas 1981: 74).

If each person contributes to the city in their own proper way, then they will, by so doing, also have a share in the city's flourishing, so that 'each class will partake of happiness in a way suitable to its nature' (*hekastois tois ethnesin hê phusis apodidôsi tou metalambanein eudaimonias, Resp.* iv, 421c). Supposedly, this means that the different classes will achieve their share of happiness by taking different paths. It is less clear, however, whether Plato also wants to say that the degree to which they are happy is different, too. I shall return to this question shortly. At this point, we should ask whether the non-philosophers indeed have excellences of the soul, as implied by the claim that they have a share in the city's happiness, and what these excellences are. Let me consider here only the lowest class of producers and leave the complexities attaching to the ethical status of the military class aside. The producers clearly do not have wisdom, since only philosophers are wise; they will also lack courage, the virtue of the military class. But besides justice, they may have a reasonable claim to 'sound-mindedness' (*sôphrôsunê*) insofar as they agree to be ruled by the philosophers, for sound-mindedness is defined as 'unanimity, agreement between the naturally worse and the naturally better as to which of the two is to rule both in the city and in each one' (432a).[31]

There has been significant opposition in the scholarship against the view that non-philosophers in general, and producers as the lowest class in particular, could be just – and therefore happy to any degree.[32] Two objections have been raised. One derives from the doctrine of the unity of the virtues defended in some of Plato's dialogues.[33] If producers lack wisdom, insofar as they remain in the Cave (*Resp.* vii, 516c–d), then, if all virtues are strictly interdependent, they cannot be just either. In its general form, this objection is weakened by the fact that it is not clear whether Plato means to uphold this doctrine in the *Republic*; some have argued that he does not (Devereux 2017: 52; 59–65). But a more specific version of this objection has more traction. If psychological justice requires the knowledge of what justice is, and this in turn requires wisdom that is accessible only to philosophers, then non-philosophers cannot be just (Bobonich 2002).

---

[31] For this view, see Kraut (2010) and Devereux (2017).
[32] Bobonich (2002, esp. 51–58) has been perhaps the most eloquent defender of the view in the recent scholarship that non-philosophers in the *Republic* cannot be happy to any degree.
[33] The strongest statement can be found in the *Protagoras* 333b.

Another kind of objection against the justice of producers is that the *type* of one's preoccupation, or what one does, does entail fatal constraints on the happiness and even bare worthwhileness of one's life. There are better jobs and there are worse jobs, and the quality or status of the job puts important limitations on one's flourishing.[34] So, Plato says that the souls of producers are 'cramped and spoiled by the mechanical nature of their work, in just the way that their bodies are mutilated by their crafts and labors' (*Resp.* vi, 495d–e). This is reiterated later in the *Republic*, where we read that 'the condition of a manual worker is despised' because the 'best part', being 'naturally weak', 'can't rule the beasts within him but can only serve them and learn to flatter them' (*Resp.* ix, 590c). This latter claim is especially disturbing. If indeed it is characteristic for these occupations that they weaken the rational part to the extent that it fails to rule the other parts, then these lives would seem to be unjust. In effect, the psychological condition of the producers would be no better than that of the corrupt rulers, the only difference being that they do not have the necessary resources at their disposal to act as they would like to. It is difficult to see, then, how these lives could be even barely worthwhile.

On a closer look, though, there are indications that Plato's assessment of producers' lives is less grim than it may seem.[35] As to the passage from the *Republic* ix, the broader argumentative context (589a ff.) indicates that Plato's point is not so much that it is the type of activity that is necessarily harmful *per se*, but that the non-philosophers need, for their own sake, to be ruled by philosophers, because their reason is 'naturally weak'. This claim indicates clearly that the weakness of the rational part is not a corruption, precisely because it is a natural condition. But this natural condition does make it necessary that the producers be guided by philosophers, lest their souls become corrupted, as with slaves who need to be guided by their masters: 'It isn't to harm the slave that we say he must be ruled ... but because it is better for everyone to be ruled by divine reason, preferably within himself and his own, otherwise imposed from without' (*Resp.* ix, 590d).

Thus, the inherent weakness of the non-philosophers' reason can, and ought to, be compensated for from outside. As regards the claim about

---

[34] Kamtekar (2001) raises this objection against the view espoused by Vlastos (1978) and Kraut (1973) that the producers' *ergon* can be their own good.

[35] A more optimistic view on the non-philosophers' condition was adopted by Vlastos (1991), Kraut (2010b) and Santas (2010, esp. 146–157). Santas also rebuts the objection raised by Bobonich.

the inherently distortive effect of the banausic occupations on the soul, it is worth noting that the words Plato uses – *sunklaô* and *apothruptô* – do not necessarily imply the kind of corruption and perversion that is characteristic of the unjust soul; the former means that the soul is cramped or stunted, the latter that its vitality is drained. These words could indicate that the soul of a manual worker is constrained in its flourishing in the sense that it cannot aspire to the other psychic virtues that are accessible to rulers, but this does not necessarily mean that banausic activities positively corrupt the soul. The virtues of the producers are clearly what Plato calls 'ordinary' or 'popular' (*dêmotikai*) virtues (*Resp.* vi, 500d), that is, those that are inculcated into their souls by the philosophers; but, as Kraut (2010: 58) notes, these are of a 'lower order of virtue', not just a mere 'appearance' or semblance of virtue, and, we can add, they are certainly different from vice.[36]

The idea that the producers can achieve and maintain a healthy condition of the soul on the condition that they willingly submit themselves to the rule of philosophers can help to mitigate other objections raised against the possibility that non-philosophers could be just. Most important among these is that psychological justice requires the knowledge of what justice is, and this in turn requires wisdom that is accessible only to philosophers. One might also point out that the lack of wisdom entails that non-philosophers cannot really benefit from any other good things they may have; in fact, without wisdom, they are bound to be harmed by them. This seems to follow from Plato's view that the goodness of things other than wisdom entirely depends on wisdom, which tells us how to use these things well (*Euthyd.* 278d–282b). But, as I shall argue in the next section, it is Plato's view that non-philosophers can in fact use things well on the condition that they follow the external wisdom of the philosophers. Their willing deference to this wisdom does not by itself remedy the cognitive impoverishment of their own souls, but is sufficient to compensate for it so as to establish that these souls are ruled by reason and therefore just.

Thus, from the account in the *Republic*, the lives of at least some non-philosophers in the ideal city, including the lives of producers, can be worth living without any reservations. But are these lives less happy than the lives of philosophers? And here I think the answer should be yes. Plato does say, repeatedly, that no part of the city should be 'outstandingly happy', but

---

[36] As in the *Phd.* 69b–c.

that the whole city should be happy 'as far as possible' (*Resp.* iv, 420b–421c; cf. also *Resp.* vii, 519e–520d).[37] These qualifications leave it open, and in fact imply, that there are necessary differences in the degrees of happiness among the different social classes. Besides the clear tendency in *Republic* vi and vii to regard philosophers as happy and non-philosophers as pitiable, Plato also makes an explicit comparison between the military class and the producers, saying flatly that the former lives are 'finer and better' (*kalliôn kai ameinôn*) than the latter (*Resp.* v, 466a), since they have a sense of what is 'fine' (*kalon*). The difference in the quality of life between the philosophers and the producers must, then, be even greater. This is consistent with the view that the producers can have only two virtues at best, sound-mindedness and justice, whereas the philosophers and guardians also have other virtues peculiar to them. Thus, as regards happiness as a target notion, the lives of just non-philosophers fall short of the supremely blessed philosophical life, owing to the nature of their activities and their psychological consequences. However, judged from the perspective of life worth living as a threshold notion, Plato's view may well be that just carpenters are as safely above the threshold as philosophers are. As long as they fulfil their *ergon*, no matter what that *ergon* is, their lives do qualify as worthwhile.

To support this interpretation, I now turn to a passage from the little-read dialogue *Clitophon*. This dialogue is no longer regarded as spurious by the majority of scholars,[38] though its standing and significance within the Platonic corpus remain unclear. For the purposes of the following interpretation, I subscribe to the hypothesis that the text is closely related to the *Republic* and in particular to its first book, where the character called Clitophon briefly appears. The *Clitophon* is possibly an introduction to this book (Altman 2011), possibly a missing part of it (Orwin 2004), or perhaps contains a speech to which the first book of the *Republic* is supposed to respond (Grube 1931; Annas 1981: 17). While this last hypothesis is controversial,[39] we shall see that in some important respects the claims espoused in the *Clitophon* are compatible, and indeed complementary, with those in the *Republic*; this compatibility in turn may be regarded as indirect support for this textual hypothesis. A particularly welcome contribution of the *Clitophon* for our discussion is that it integrates the topic

---

[37] Even the happiness of philosophers is curbed, insofar as they must return to the cave in order to 'share labours and honours' with the non-philosophers (*Resp.* vii, 519d); cf. Smith (2010) for a good discussion of the implications of this return.

[38] E.g. Annas (1981); Slings (1999); Kremer (2004).

[39] For a critical discussion of this hypothesis, see Bowe (2007).

of life worth living with an important Platonic topos of 'correct use' (*orthê chrêsis*). In so doing, it also comes to have important implications for the question whether mere living has a non-instrumental value.

1.5   Bad Use of the Soul and the Value of Mere Living

Clitophon is an atypical dialogue insofar as Socrates remains largely passive in the conversation and emerges in a critical light. Before criticising Socrates for offering insufficient instruction on what justice is and how it is to be achieved, Clitophon praises him for his views about the good and bad uses of the soul:

> When, Socrates, I hear you say such things time and time again, I'm very impressed and I praise you to the skies; and also when you go on to the next point, that those who discipline the body while neglecting the soul are doing something else of the same sort, neglecting that which should rule while busying themselves with that which should be ruled; and also when you say that it's better to leave unused what you don't know how to use (*mê epistatai chrêsthai*): if someone doesn't know how to use his eyes or his ears or his whole body, it would be better for him not to use it at all, whether for seeing or hearing or anything else, rather than use it in some haphazard way (*hôpêioun*). In fact, the same applies to skills; for someone who doesn't know how to use his own lyre will hardly be able to use his neighbor's lyre, nor will someone who doesn't know how to use the lyre of others be capable of using his own lyre, nor any other instrument or possession whatsoever.
>
> Your speech delivers a wonderful coup de grace when it concludes that someone who doesn't know how to use his soul is better off putting his soul to rest and not living at all (*to agein hêsuchian têi psuchêi kai mê zên*) rather than leading a life in which his actions are based on nothing but personal whim (*kreitton ê zên prattonti kath'hauton*). If for some reason he must live, it would be better for such a man to live as a slave than to be free, handing over the rudder of his mind, like that of a ship, to somebody else who knows that skill of steering men which you, Socrates, often call politics, the very same skill, you say, as the judicial skill and justice. (*Clit.* 407e–408b)

The argument has the following structure. (i) The explicit premise: rather than using a thing badly, one is better off not using it at all; (ii) the implicit premise: to use one's soul means to be alive; (iii) hence, combining (i) and (ii): if one cannot use one's soul well, one is better off not alive. The very notion of 'using one's soul' strikes one as somewhat unusual, because soul for Plato is something that itself uses other things, rather than something that is being used, and is something that we *are*, rather than something that we *have*. Two considerations come to mind that could explain this atypical use. One is that one part of the soul, namely the rational part of the soul, uses the non-rational part(s) of the soul. Another is that the soul as a whole is used by someone else, namely by the philosophers-rulers. This latter option is implied in the final section of the passage.

The notion of bad or harmful use echoes more familiar passages from Plato's other dialogues concerning 'correct use' (*orthê chrêsis*). It is in the *Euthydemus* that we find a passage that is most closely parallel to the *Clitophon*.[40] Socrates argues there that all things, including those that are conventionally considered good, such as health or wealth, but even virtues such as courage, are not 'in themselves good by nature', but rather that their value depends wholly on whether it is ignorance or wisdom that 'controls' them (281d). Consequently, and in addition to this, Plato argues not only that the use of these things is of benefit only when they are used wisely, but that they do harm whenever they are used badly, or 'in whichever way': 'There is more harm done if someone uses a thing in whichever way (*hotôioun*) than if he lets it alone – in the first instance there is evil (*kakon*), but in the second neither evil nor good' (*Euthyd.* 280e–281a). On this view, mistakes entail not only lack of benefit, but harm:

> Would a man with no sense (*noun mê echôn*) profit more if he possessed and did much or if he possessed and did little? Look at it in this way: if he did less, would he not make fewer mistakes (*hêtton hamartanôn*); and if he made fewer mistakes, would he not do less badly (*hêtton kakôs prattoi*), and if he did less badly, would he not be less miserable (*hêtton athlios*)? (*Euthyd.* 281b–c)

On the grounds of this understanding of mistakes, Plato in the *Euthydemus* counsels 'a kind of quietism' (McCabe 2015: 240). If you do not know how to use things, it is better for you to have fewer things and use them less, for you will cause yourself less harm. We could call this an idea of 'inverted value': if used badly, things that in most circumstances would be good become evil. The conditional goodness that health or wealth have does not disappear but is rather inverted into its opposite. We shall see in Chapter 5 that this notion of inverted value is adopted and further developed by the Peripatetics.

A premise at work in this argument of *Euthydemus* is that good use and 'whichever' use, as well as benefit and harm, are contradictories: whenever

---

[40] Another candidate is *Meno* (87d–88e) but the discussion there, in contrast to *Euthydemus*, does not echo the distinctive idea from *Clitophon* that all mistakes constitute harm, not just a lack of benefit. McCabe (2015: 237–247) has an illuminating discussion of the differences between the relevant passages in *Meno* and in *Euthydemus*.

you do not use a thing well, you use it badly, and whenever it does not benefit you, it harms you.[41] The harm itself does allow for degrees – that is, you can fare more or less badly – but this differentiation is clearly within the territory of harm, not just of a lack of benefit. So, along with maintaining that objects of use do not have any intrinsic value, Plato also maintains that they must have either positive or negative value whenever they are actually used.

It is precisely this Euthydeman perspective on the use of things and their value that is adopted in the *Clitophon*. A main difference is that in the *Clitophon* the objects of use are not putative goods such as wealth or health, but objects, including a body, bodily parts and in general possessions and instruments.[42] In a striking move, this list is extended to the human soul as well. Hence the quietistic perspective on life: just as in the case of using other things, when it comes to the human soul, no use is better than bad use, which means that not living at all is preferable to bad living or living in whichever way.

This account from the *Clitophon* usefully connects the topos of good use, characteristic of Plato's early or so-called Socratic dialogues, with themes that he expounds in more detail in the *Republic*. One such theme is whether non-philosophers can live a life worth living, and if so, under what conditions. The idea that those who do not know how to use their soul would do better to 'hand over the rudder of their mind' to experts in politics unmistakably echoes the view from the *Republic* that the producers should let themselves be ruled by the philosophers to make their lives worth living. In the *Clitophon*, just like in the *Republic*, the inferior but worthwhile lives of well-governed non-philosophers need to be distinguished from lives of corrupted humans, whether rulers or non-rulers, who use their souls badly. In fact, Plato's claim from the *Clitophon* that even the lives of non-philosophers can be worth living counts as an important piece of evidence to support the interpretation of the *Republic* on which even non-philosophers can be just: if life can be worthwhile only if it is just *and* the lives of non-philosophers can indeed be worthwhile, then it follows that the lives of non-philosophers can be just.

---

[41] There is no neutral, third option: if you do not use it at all, then you do not exist.

[42] The use of simple objects (lyre, gold) also appears in the *Euthydemus*. One might be puzzled why any incompetent use of these objects should be harmful rather than just deficient in benefit. Why, precisely, should my bad lyre-playing necessarily harm me? Presumably, the idea here is, as in the *Euthydemus*, that the value of use is ultimately assessed with regard to living well. To use a musical instrument well, on this view, is to use it in a manner that is conducive to the good life, i.e. to play the right kind of music, at the right time, for the right sake, etc.; to use it badly means to use it in a way that is conducive to a bad life. On the bad use of music in Plato, see e.g. *Resp.* iv, 424c–d.

Although an explicit link between good use from the *Euthydemus* or *Clitophon* and good functioning from the *Republic* is never established, the idea of the good or bad use of the soul sits well with the idea of good or bad functioning. To have a well-functioning soul means to live well; but living well also means to use one's soul well. To use a thing well, obviously, means to use a thing in accordance with its function and with skill and knowledge of how to optimise that function. To use a soul well, similarly, means to use it in a specific skilful, rather than haphazard, way, one that accords with the soul's constitution and function. If we read *Clitophon* from the vantage point of the *Republic*, this could mean, in particular, that the rational part of the soul rules over, and indeed uses, the non-rational parts of the soul.

Finally, the extension of the notion of right use to the specific case of using the soul has one remarkable implication that is particularly important for the topic of this book. This implication is that Plato regards the value of mere living, that is, the mere fact of using one's soul, as wholly instrumental. Whether being alive is something good or bad depends entirely on how the soul is used, that is, on whether one lives well or badly. This tallies with Plato's claim from the *Crito* 'that the most important thing is not living (*to zên*), but living well (*eu zên*)' (48b). Whereas this formulation leaves some space for the view that even mere living, while not most important, could still have some non-instrumental value, the passage from the *Clitophon* pre-empts this possibility: mere living, like other objects of use, has no non-instrumental value whatsoever.[43] Moreover, it is also the case that the fact of being alive, besides having only instrumental value, is never axiologically neutral: being alive always becomes either something good or something bad, depending on how well or badly you live. Either your soul is being used with knowledge, whether your own or another's; or it is being used without such knowledge, and hence 'in whichever way', which always inflicts net harm. In the former case, your life is worth living; in the latter, it is not.

1.6   The Unexamined Life Reconsidered

According to the account in Plato's *Republic*, what makes a life worth living is the exercise of one's job. If the job fits your 'nature' and your social role,

---

[43] Insofar as Plato's point is that the value of objects of use depends or is conditional on wisdom, their value is extrinsic rather than instrumental (McCabe 2015). But, of course, mere living also has an instrumental value, since it is a prerequisite for living well.

and if it is exercised well, then your life is worth living, no matter whether you live philosophically or not. Is this position compatible with the claim from the *Apology* that the unexamined life is not worth living? The option suggested by Kraut, namely that in the *Republic* Plato allows for alternative, non-reflective ways to achieve a worthwhile life, implies that it is not: human lives do not have to be reflective to be worth living. So did Plato change his mind on this point?

One possible strategy to square the *Apology* with the *Republic* is to argue that in the latter Plato is committed to a plurality of evaluative perspectives on human lives that enables him to contain, and preserve, the position from the *Apology* by linking it with one of these evaluative perspectives. This strategy was floated by Rachana Kamtekar in her suggestion that Plato may be differentiating between different social functions, on the one hand, and universal human function, on the other: 'carpentry is the carpenter's function *qua* carpenter, but *qua* human being, it must be justice, the excellence of the soul' (Kamtekar 2001: 199). On this view, then, we should dissociate one's specific job in the city from one's job *qua* human being, and assess their significance for life's worthwhileness on separate terms. This interpretation would make it possible to concede that even an unexamined carpenter's life is genuinely worthwhile, insofar as it is assessed from the perspective of his social role, and yet to maintain that it is *not* worth living from the more universal perspective of the human role.

However, the earlier discussion has indicated why a dissociation of these two evaluative perspectives is problematic. Plato seems to believe that you can achieve a healthy condition of the soul only *by means of* fulfilling your specific role in a well-governed city. In other words, you can only have a life worth living if your life is meaningful, that is, makes a due contribution to your city. There is no universal educational curriculum to become a perfect human being, but only specific curricula to acquire specific sets of excellences required for specific social roles: those of rulers, auxiliaries and producers. Plato explains in considerable detail that these curricula are quite different as regards the character and expertise they cultivate, as well as the means by which they do so, but ultimately they are all conducive to making the soul just. Learning to become a good carpenter is one of many paths to enacting justice as the excellence of the human soul.

There is a more promising strategy available to accommodate the dictum from the *Apology* within the account in the *Republic*, namely to show that even non-philosophers can, in a peculiarly qualified way, live an examined life, as indeed they can do in the *Apology*, at least according to some modern readings of it. They do not live an examined life in the sense of an ongoing engagement in the activity of rational examination, or a life that is being examined, but in the sense of a life that is conducted on the basis of a rational examination, or a life that has been examined.

The basis for this interpretation is the close connection between examination and self-knowledge. As the *Apology* itself indicates, the crucial objective of examination is not only to improve one's cognitive states about the good, wisdom or justice, but also to arrive at a better understanding of what or who you are, including your station within the cosmos (e.g. as a mortal being) and within society (e.g. as a philosopher or a carpenter), as well as of the prerogatives and constraints associated with this station (*Alc.* 124a–b). To arrive at this knowledge is precisely the objective of living an examined life. It is the achievement of self-examination that Socrates knows what he does not know, but also that he knows what he knows, for example, 'that it is wicked and shameful to do wrong, to disobey one's superior, be he god or man' (*Ap.* 29b). In the more specific sense of Socrates' own life, this entails an unwavering commitment to living a philosophical life and educating others, since this is Socrates' own 'function' (*ergon*) for which the god placed him in the city (*Ap.* 30e).

Now, the rationale for ascribing self-examination and self-knowledge to non-philosophers from the *Republic* is the fact that they possess the virtue of sound-mindedness (*sôphrôsunê*). It is in the *Charmides* that the definition of sound-mindedness as a kind of self-knowledge – more specifically, as self-knowledge in the sense of knowing one's place in the society (*Charm.* 171e–172a; 173a–d) – is seriously entertained (164d ff.).[44] This view is echoed in the definition of sound-mindedness in *Republic* iv, where it is defined in terms of a cognitive state, namely a 'correct belief' (*orthê doxa*) and 'agreement' (*homonoia*) about who should rule and who should be ruled (431d; 432a). Thus, insofar as even the producers can be sound-minded, they also have a claim to a sort of self-knowledge. This self-knowledge consists, first and foremost, in the acknowledgement of the serious limitations of their own cognitive capacities and the recognition that their well-being depends on the wisdom of philosophers. Thus, like Socrates' self-knowledge from the *Apology*, its chief achievement is a concession of one's own ignorance.

1.7   Retrospect and Prospect

Plato discusses the conditions of a life worth living in several dialogues spanning the early and late periods. While the question is nowhere tackled

---

[44] Cf. Annas (1985: 120–125).

in a systematic manner, and is addressed from different perspectives and in different argumentative contexts, the evidence adds up to a fairly coherent picture. The common denominator of Plato's discussions about what makes a life worth living is his concern with the function (*ergon*) of an individual soul. In most general terms, life is worth living whenever one's soul is healthy, that is, whenever it is under the rule of reason, whether its own or imposed from outside. This justice, or the health of the soul, is the unconditional worthmaker, and its absence – the vice of injustice and psychic disease – is the unconditional worthbreaker.

I have suggested that this account of a life worth living implies a gap between worthwhile lives and best possible lives. There is some evidence in Plato for the view that the lives of philosophers approximate, as much as is possible for humans, the lives of the gods, and are thus better and more desirable than the lives of non-philosophers. That does not mean, however, that they are more worth living in the sense of passing the threshold test. These lives may be happier than the lives of producers, but even the producers can have their fair share of happiness if they are just and sound-minded. When it comes to clearing the threshold of a life worth living, good carpenters are not any worse off than good philosophers; insofar as it exercises its function, the soul of a good carpenter is as healthy as the soul of a good philosopher. Since the good and bad uses of the soul are contradictories, there are no indifferent lives in Plato's picture: either your life is worth living or it is not.

From a larger axiological perspective, the distinction between the best human life and a life worth living is enabled by Plato's fourfold notion of the virtue of the soul. This notion warrants a degree of axiological pluralism that grounds this distinction. Virtue is necessary both for the best life and for a life worth living, but whereas the former requires justice and sound-mindedness, but also wisdom, justice and sound-mindedness alone are sufficient for a life worth living. If this interpretation is right, it serves as an indication in favour of the view that Plato no longer maintains in the *Republic* a strict version of the doctrine of the unity of virtues that he adopts in his earlier dialogues.

Plato also takes a position on the value of mere living, that is, the bottom level of the axiology of life. He understands the state of being alive as an activity of using one's soul. In itself this state is axiologically indifferent, as are all cases of the instrumental use of things. But because every use must be either good or bad, mere living is in practice always beneficial or harmful. We can say, therefore, that the value of mere living is both wholly instrumental, insofar as it is the prerequisite for living well, and wholly extrinsic insofar as its value depends on the particular mode of use. As for the relationship between life's worthwhileness and its meaningfulness, Plato regards these perspectives as interdependent and coextensive. The only path to the health of your soul is to exercise your job in the city. A good exercise of this function makes you just, not only in a political but also in a psychological sense, insofar as different parts of your soul are in a harmonious relationship.

We shall see in the next chapter that Plato's functionalist perspective on a life worth living, as well as the target–threshold distinction, was in its fundamental features adopted by Aristotle. But within this shared functionalistic framework, we shall identify two remarkable shifts. One is that Aristotle does attribute some non-instrumental value to mere living. Translated into Plato's terminology, Aristotle maintains that even the mere fact of using the soul is a good, regardless of whether it is used well or badly. While this position may seem to go against the grain of the functionalist approach, it is in fact motivated by it. The second shift concerns the relationship between worthwhileness and meaningfulness. In Aristotle's view, there are kinds of human lives that may be of genuine benefit for the city, and yet they may not be worth living from the internal perspective. So it turns out that the non-instrumental value of mere living cannot make up for the absence of some important contents that make life worthwhile.

CHAPTER 2

Aristotle on the Natural Goodness of Life

So does a carpenter or a shoemaker have certain functions and activities, while a human being has none, and is by nature a do-nothing? … What then, should we suppose this [human function] to be? For being alive (*zên*) is obviously shared by plants too, and we are looking for what is peculiar to human beings.

(Aristotle, NE i.7, 1097b28–35)

There is perhaps (*isôs*) some share of what is fine in the mere living (*ti tou kalou morion kai kata to zên auto monon*), as long as it is not too overburdened with the hardships of life (*an mê tois chalepois kata ton bion huperbalêi lian*).

(Aristotle, *Pol.* iii.6, 1278b25–27)

And yet living is distinguished from not living by perception, and living is determined by its presence and power, and if this is taken away life is not worth living (*ouk estin axion zên*), as if when you do away with perception you do away with life itself.

(Aristotle, *Protr.* 44.9–13)

2.1 Three-Level Axiology of Life

Aristotle is well known for his systematic account of the happy or flourishing human life (*eudaimonia*). He also says, unsurprisingly, that it is happiness that 'all by itself (*monoumenon*) makes life choiceworthy, and lacking in nothing (*aireton poiei ton bion kai mêdenos endea*)' (NE i.7, 1097b15).[1] More precisely, though, his claim is that happiness makes life *most* worth choosing, or most worth living. Aristotle notes that the virtuous person will be pained at the prospect of death, and the happier they are, the more pained they will be, since to someone like that 'life is most worth living'

---

[1] All translations from the *Nicomachean* and *Eudemian Ethics* follow Rowe and Woods, respectively, with occasional minor modifications. Translations from the *Protrepticus* follow Hutchinson and Johnson, those from the *Politics* follow Reeve.

63

(*malista zên axion*) (NE iii.9, 1117b11–12); and that 'being alive is choice-worthy, and especially (*malista*) so for the good' (ix.9, 1170b3–4). So there is a direct connection between the degree of happiness and the degree to which a life is worth living. There is a single axiological scale with happiness at the top and the threshold of a life worth living somewhere below that. But it is less clear where the threshold of a human life barely worth living lies and what the sufficient condition or conditions are to clear it.

The epigraphs suggest two broad options. Since Aristotle, like Plato, defines happiness as the good exercise of function, as the first epigraph makes clear, one option is that a life is worth living if one can exercise one's function to some degree, or in some respects. Insofar as the crucial prerequisite for this exercise is 'virtue' (*aretê*), perhaps some degree of virtue, or some approximation to virtue, would be sufficient to have a life worth living. Another option, suggested by the second epigraph, is that no degree of happiness – and virtue – is necessary to have a life at least barely worth living. Rather, the sufficient condition of a worthwhile life is a non-instrumental goodness of the mere human living combined with freedom from serious misfortunes or hardships. So perhaps the mere human living could be a conditional worth-maker. Surely, as the third epigraph makes clear, a life is not worth living if deprived of the activities of perception; such a life is not a human life at all. But could these perceptual activities in themselves possibly make a life human and therefore worth living? After all, Aristotle says that 'being alive is choice-worthy' (NE ix.9, 1170b3–4), not necessarily that only living well is.

Following the first option, Aristotle's views about life worth living would stay close to Plato. According to the second, Aristotle would radically depart from Plato: not only would he attribute some non-instrumental value to mere living, he would even make it a worthmaker. The quotations bring out that there are at least some indications in favour of this second account. But it is puzzling how Aristotle could, given his decisively teleological axiological commitments, justify the non-instrumental value of mere living on other than teleological, and thus functionalistic, grounds. While he does link the mere living with a kind of inherent pleasure, this pleasure is a good because mere living is a good, not the other way round. To resolve this puzzle, one might be inclined to cast doubt on the evidence from the *Politics* and *Protrepticus* as reliable statements of Aristotle's considered ethical views.

However, I submit that we should take this evidence seriously and that Aristotle is genuinely committed to the view that even mere human living has non-instrumental value. Surprisingly, perhaps, this view turns out to be fully compatible with – and indeed motivated by – his teleological axiology. Even mere human living is non-instrumentally valuable because it is an exercise of the human function, even if not a good exercise. All the same, Aristotle does *not* regard the value of mere living as a worth-maker. The mere fact of being alive *qua* human, even when combined with freedom from hardships, is not sufficient to make a human life worth living. At least some specific positive contents – in addition to freedom from hardships and from other negative contents – are needed to clear the threshold, and these largely coincide with the contents that are required for a happy life. Still, there remains a limited space for lives that never make it to happiness, or that cease to be happy after happiness has been achieved, and yet are worth living.

From the perspective of the three-level axiology of life, Aristotle's position could be summarised as follows. On the lowest level of mere living, all human lives are non-instrumentally valuable for those who live them. Taken on its own, however, this value is insufficient for reaching the middle level of a life that is at least barely worth living. In turn, if a life is at least barely worth living, that does not necessarily guarantee the attainment of the highest level of value: the happy life. These three levels of value do not rest, however, on three incommensurable orders of value; rather, the difference is one of degree. Happiness means to live 'finely' (*kalôs*), but even mere human living has a grain of the 'fine', while a life barely worth living has still more of it.

Neither Aristotle's views about the value of mere living nor his account of a life worth living have been the subject of sustained scholarly interpretation. Aristotle's views on these topics have to be reconstructed from scattered and fragmentary evidence. I start from an overview of Aristotle's account of happiness (Section 2.2). In the next two sections, I turn to the interpretation of material suggesting that mere living has non-instrumental value (Section 2.3) and argue that this view is compatible with Aristotle's account of the human function (Section 2.4). In Section 2.5, I discuss Aristotle's account of a life (not) worth living from *Eudemian Ethics* i.5, and on that basis propose in Section 2.6 that some unhappy lives may still be worth living on Aristotle's account. Next, I briefly consider the practical implications of this axiology for decisions about choosing life or death (Section 2.7), and conclude with a comparative assessment of life worth living according to Plato and Aristotle (Section 2.8).

The primary texts considered in this chapter are Aristotle's works on practical philosophy broadly construed, including the two main ethical treatises, *Eudemian Ethics* and *Nicomachean Ethics*, as well as his *Protrepticus* (or *Exhortation to Philosophy*), and the *Politics*. Potentially significant for our topic is also a fragment from the otherwise lost dialogue *Eudemus*, or *On the Soul*,[2] which is most likely a juvenile work by Aristotle heavily influenced by Plato's philosophy.[3] This appears to be a consolatory text, espousing the view that it is better to be dead than alive, as exemplified by the case of Eudemus, Alexander's general who died for a noble cause (Chroust 1966: 22). Without knowledge of the broader context, however, the axiological outlook conveyed by this fragment is too crude to be of any real help for the reconstruction of Aristotle's rather fine-grained axiology of life as it emerges from other texts.

While there are substantive thematic overlaps among the texts we shall discuss, each of them is chiefly relevant for a different reason. Whereas the *Nicomachean Ethics* is considered the primary reference point for Aristotle's account of happiness and his function argument, it is in the *Eudemian Ethics* that we find the most significant discussion of the criteria of a life worth living. Then, again, *Protrepticus* and the *Politics* contain the most important passages bearing on the value of mere living. All these texts probably originate from different stages of Aristotle's philosophical career and address ethical issues from a somewhat different angle. In some respects, this diversity indeed goes in hand with important shifts of focus or even tensions in the theory.[4] These shifts may also play a role in the present investigations, and indeed we shall encounter instances of such tension between *Protrepticus* and the *Nicomachean Ethics*. With these reservations, we can say that what will emerge from the following interpretations is a fairly coherent ethical theory about life worth living and the value of life.

2.2 *Eudaimonia,* or the Life Most Worth Living

Although some elements of Aristotle's account of happiness remain unclear or controversial,[5] the fundamentals can be summarised with some confidence. Aristotle undertakes his most systematic attempt to define happiness, or the human good (*anthrôpinon agathon*) (NE i.7, 1098a16), in the

---

[2] Preserved in Plutarch's *Consolation to Apolonius* 115b–e.
[3] For a recent interpretation of this text, see Segev (2022).
[4] So, for instance, the *Eudemian Ethics* vi contains a theory of pleasure that has been regarded as quite different from, though not necessarily incompatible with, the theory of pleasure in *Nicomachean Ethics* x.
[5] To the most debated topics belong the precise structure, scope and efficiency of the function argument in NE i.7 (e.g. Gomez-Lobo 1989; Barney 2008) or the question of whether Aristotle adopted an 'inclusivist' account of happiness, on which all other goods including virtue are contained in happiness (Ackrill 1974; Irwin 2012), or rather a 'monistic' account on which happiness, and specifically the life of contemplation (*theôria*), is the only good (Kraut 1989; Lear 2004). I shall briefly address some implications of my interpretation for the latter question in Section 2.4.

first book of the *Nicomachean Ethics*. After giving a formal account of the conditions that every compelling account of happiness must meet – the ultimate finality and full completeness – he sets out to define the actual content of happy lives. The underlying idea is that the human good can be defined by establishing what the function (*ergon*) of human beings is. This function must be something that is characteristic or unique (*idion*) of humans, in contrast to other things and living beings (1098a1). For this reason, the human function cannot amount to the mere fact of 'being alive' (*to zên*) (1097b34–35), since living in the minimal sense is defined by the vegetative functions of the human soul (nutrition and growth), and these are shared with all other living things. The life of perception (*aisthêsis*) is also insufficient, because humans share it with animals (1098a2–3). What remains is a life that involves the exercise of the rational part of the soul, and hence 'the function of a human being is activity of soul in accordance with reason, or not apart from reason' (*psuchês energeia kata logon ê mê aneu logou*) (1098a7–8); more specifically, this activity must be 'in accordance with excellence' (*kath'aretên*), that is, done 'finely' or 'well' (*kalôs*) (1098a15).

This account of happiness contains three different conditions that must be fulfilled if a life is to be happy. What matters is, first and foremost, *what* one does, or the type of activity. Life must consist of activities that involve rationality. Furthermore, as becomes clear from other parts of the *Nicomachean Ethics*, these activities must also belong to 'serious' (*spoudaios*) or worthwhile pursuits.[6] The best life is the life of 'contemplation' (*theôria*), dedicated to understanding things that 'cannot be otherwise' (NE vi.1), such as metaphysical truths. It is characteristic of this life that it is the most god-like among human activities, it is pursued for its own sake, and has the 'leisure' (*scholê*) that is necessary for these preoccupations (NE x.6–8).[7] The second-best life is the life of political pursuits (NE x.8, 1178a9–10). Whereas this life lacks the god-like character of the contemplative life, being engrossed in the realm of contingent things, it is still a respectable alternative insofar as it exercises the deliberative element of the human soul and aims at doing fine actions for their own sake.

There are humans who are deprived of access to either of these lives due to the natural constitution of their souls, their social position or both. Women, for instance, can make rational decisions, but the deliberative

---

[6] For a discussion of Aristotle's axiology of 'activity' (*energeia*) in general, and the notion of activity's 'seriousness' (*spoudê*) in particular, see Machek (2021).

[7] On leisure as the prerequisite for happiness, see NE x.6, 1176b16–17; NE x.7, 1177b4; *Pol.* 1337b33–34.

part of their souls 'lacks authority' (*akuron*), which is necessary for political life (*Pol.* i.13, 1260a12–13).[8] As for the lives of craftsmen, merchants or other 'vulgar' (*banausoi*) workers, these do not even 'enter the contest' for happiness (EE i.4, 1215a25). One reason is that these lives make the character ignoble and corrupt (*Pol.* vii.9, 1328b38–40); another is that they have a slavish quality insofar as they are typically not chosen for their own sake but 'under compulsion of need' (*biaios*) (NE i.5, 1096a6; EE i.5, 1215a27).[9] Then there are natural slaves, humans who are by nature suited to become the property of others because their soul lacks the deliberative element entirely (*Pol.* i.2, 1252a31–34), which is just one of the reasons why they cannot be happy (*Pol.* iii.9, 1280a32–34).

The second condition is *how* one does what one does – that is, well or badly. Here, the notion of 'excellence' or 'virtue' (*aretê*) enters the account. It does not suffice that one dedicates one's life to reason-involving and serious activities that are chosen for their own sake; it is also required that these activities are exercised well (NE i.7, 1098a15–16). There are two kinds of virtues that correspond to two main kinds of serious pursuits, namely the ethical virtues needed for the practical life of politics, which consist of the virtues of character and 'practical wisdom' (*phronêsis*), and the theoretical virtues, the best of which is 'theoretical wisdom' (*sophia*). Since these virtues are by definition tied to the domain of serious activities, whoever has these virtues automatically also clears the first condition of engaging in intrinsically worthwhile preoccupations. While Aristotle himself does not explore these options, we can note that his theory leaves space for the possibility of a life of worthwhile activity pursued without excellence (e.g. that of a mediocre philosopher) or of a life of perfection or excellence (*aretê*) in a relatively un-worthwhile preoccupation (e.g. that of an excellent cobbler).[10] In the following discussion, I shall reserve the English term 'virtue' for excellence in serious activities so as to distinguish it from excellence in other activities (such as crafts).

The third condition of happiness is *whether*, or to what extent, one does what one is capable of doing, in the sense that activities must be

---

[8] Cf. Connell (2015) for the view that this lack of authority is not a biological given but a result of the social segregation of women.

[9] This agrees with the discussion in the *Politics* where Aristotle makes it clear – in a striking contrast to Plato in the *Republic* – that craftsmen are 'certainly not happy' (*Pol.* ii.5, 1264b23–4), and that 'the citizens should not live the life of a vulgar craftsman or tradesman' (*Pol.* vii.9, 1328b38–40). Similarly to the lives of farmers, these lives lack leisure, 'debase the mind', are 'unfree' and have a slavish character, since they engage in purely instrumental activities that are not chosen for their own sake (*Pol.* viii.3, 1337b10–14).

[10] Aristotle mentions the phrase 'excellence in a craft' (*aretê technês*) at NE vi.7, 1141a12.

free from inhibitions or impediments. Whereas the first two conditions are familiar, in different guises, from Plato, this last requirement reflects the characteristically Aristotelian emphasis on the actuality or actualisation (*energeia*) of psychological capacities, in contrast to their mere possession (e.g. NE i.7, 1098a5–8). The full actualisation of capacities requires some external goods, 'for it is impossible, or not easy, to perform fine actions if one is without resources' (NE i.8, 1099a32–3); thus, for example, generosity requires wealth. The unimpeded actualisation of a soul's capacities also needs freedom from serious and repeated misfortunes that 'bring on pains, and impede many sorts of activities' (*empodizei pollais energeiais*) (NE i.10, 1100b29–30).[11]

The acknowledgement that external goods play a significant role in achievement of happiness has been regarded in the scholarship as a qualified concession on the side of philosophers to the tragic outlook of the poets. Indeed, the combination of Aristotle's emphasis on the value of actualisation with the common-sense orientation of his ethical outlook has made it difficult to deny that happiness is not wholly impervious from external fortunes. But how far Aristotle actually goes in this concession has been a controversial issue. He does admit that 'many major misfortunes' – like those of Priam, who lost most of his sons – will 'spoil and oppress blessedness' (*thlibei kai lumainetai to makarion*) (NE i.10, 1100b28–29). Some commentators have argued that Aristotle strictly distinguishes between 'blessedness' (*makariotês*), the highest, god-like condition of utmost self-sufficiency and freedom from disturbances, and 'happiness' (*eudaimonia*), which is the good life that humans can reasonably hope for.[12] This distinction enables him to concede that external misfortunes can indeed deprive virtuous persons of the most desirable state of blessedness, while not having enough weight to prevent them from being happy. But others have pointed out that Aristotle uses these terms rather interchangeably and that his concession is more substantial: many major misfortunes can make even the good person unhappy.[13] In fact, while Aristotle says that the good will not be 'moved' (*kinêthêsetai*) from *eudaimonia* easily, and that even amidst misfortunes their fine character will 'shine through' (*dialampei to kalon*) (NE i.10, 1100b30–31), he admits that moved he will be and a 'return to happiness will take no short time' (1101a11–12). This does

---

[11] See also NE x.8, 1178b34–35 on the necessity of health and bodily provisions for the life of contemplation.

[12] E.g. Joachim (1951: 59–60).

[13] E.g. Nussbaum (1986: 329–335).

seem to indicate conclusively, I think, that happiness is vulnerable to some extremely adverse twists of fortune.

If any of these three conditions – worthwhileness of pursuits (the 'what'), virtue (the 'how') and freedom from major misfortunes (the 'whether') – fails to be met, life falls short of happiness. Various kinds of shortcomings and their combinations are possible. There are good and healthy cobblers, for instance, who nonetheless fail to be happy due to the low status of their occupation. There are politicians who are active, fortunate but corrupt, or excellent philosophers who are plagued by extremely painful, chronic disease. None of these lives is happy in Aristotle's eyes. But could they be worth living, whether in the sense of staying alive, or in the sense of having been born? Or are perhaps only some of these lives worth living, while others are not? I return to this question in Section 2.5 of this chapter. At this point, I start from the bottom level of the axiology of life, namely from the question whether Aristotle assigned some non-instrumental value to life quite independently of whether these conditions of happiness are cleared. If so, then all human lives would have something good in them to start with.

2.3   Life Is Fine

The evidence attesting to Aristotle's view that all human lives have some non-instrumental value is fragmentary but robust. Presumably the earliest bits can be found in his *Protrepticus*, a work extant only in reconstructed fragments. The text is woven from the speeches of different characters, two of which are relevant in the context of this chapter: one is the voice of Aristotle himself; the other is, presumably, the voice of Heraclides Ponticus, a fourth-century BCE Academic philosopher with distinctly Pythagorean leanings. There is some latitude concerning the relationship of Aristotle himself to the views he puts into the mouths of other characters, including Heraclides. On the one hand, the voice of 'Aristotle' at times critically engages some of the views expressed by other characters; on the other, other voices sometimes seem to express elements of Aristotle's own view, and this works well for his dramatic strategy.[14]

In their interpretation of passages bearing on the value of life in Chapter 8 of the *Protrepticus*, Hutchinson and Johnson, the authors of the latest (and ongoing) reconstruction of this work, regard the views expressed by voices of 'Heraclides' and 'Aristotle' as contrasting. Heraclides' outlook on

[14] I am grateful to Doug Hutchinson and Monte Johnson for helping me to navigate the polyphony of the *Protrepticus* in an e-mail communication.

the value of life is 'dark and pessimistic' (Hutchinson and Johnson 2017: 41), since he holds that 'nobody would choose to live' (*oudeis an eloito zên*) (*Protr.* 45.7) when 'some disease ruins his intelligence' (*nosôn tôi phronounti*), which includes conditions such as mental illness, or being drunk or juvenile to the end of one's life (*Protr.* 45.18–25). Such conditions are unconditional worthbreakers, for such a life would 'not be worth choosing' (*ouk hairetos*) even if one had all other goods, including property, power and pleasure; for without intelligence – and this strikes one as a distinct echo of Plato's *Euthydemus* – 'none of these goods would be of any benefit' (ibid.). This pessimistic view is taken to stand in 'stark contrast' with the 'relatively life-affirming' view adopted by Aristotle himself (Hutchinson and Johnson 2017: 41). This life-affirming view is, they suggest, contained in Aristotle's idea of 'degrees of life' (ibid.), which eventually allows him to attribute even to unperfected human lives a share of the same non-instrumental value that is fully maximised in perfected human lives.

In the following, I support, unpack and qualify the view that Aristotle's view is, in contrast to Heraclides' pessimism, relatively life-affirming. The qualification rests on a distinction between two perspectives on life's value, a distinction that coincides with the distinction between the bottom and the middle level of our axiology of life. On the one hand, Aristotle's outlook is indeed life-affirming, insofar as he grants that all human lives have some non-instrumental value; on the other, he is far less optimistic when it comes to the question under what conditions different kinds of human life are worth living. This position is internally consistent: it is one thing to maintain that all human lives are non-instrumentally valuable, and another to grant that, considered on its own, this value is sufficient to make a life good enough to be worth living. All human lives have some value, but that alone does not necessarily make them worth living. From the latter perspective of what it takes to have a worth living, Aristotle's own position may well be closer to the pessimistic view of Heraclides than the assessment of Hutchinson and Johnson suggests. From this twofold perspective on life's valuation, Aristotle's position on the value of life from the *Protrepticus* turns out to be largely consistent with what we find in the two *Ethics*. The remaining part of this section unpacks Aristotle's idea of the degrees of life and non-instrumental value of mere living.[15] The different issue of what it takes to pass the threshold of a worthwhile life will be addressed later in Sections 2.5 and 2.6.

---

[15] The following two sections present a compressed version of my interpretation of Aristotle's account of the value of mere living in Machek (2022).

The *Protrepticus* reveals Aristotle's clear commitment to the naturalistic teleology that is articulated in more detail in his later works.[16] In general, the products of the workings of nature are non-instrumentally valuable: 'everything that has come to be in accordance with nature (*kata phusin*) at any rate has come to be well (*kalôs*)' (*Protr.* 50.15–19). *To kalon* ('beautiful, noble, fine') and its adverbial form *kalôs* ('beautifully, well, finely') belong among the key terms of Aristotle's philosophy and value theory. Virtuous actions are *kala* and the virtuous person, who has a highly developed sense and appreciation of what is truly *kalon*, chooses them for precisely this reason: 'what makes actions fine is also (in part) what makes them worth choosing for their own sakes' (Lear 2006: 117). 'Fine' is thus the non-instrumental value *par excellence*.[17] Whether a human action or a natural process, what makes each of them fine is their finality or end-likeness, which again is defined in terms of fulfilling a specific function (*ergon*).[18] As Aristotle makes clear in the continuation of the above passage, everything that comes into being 'correctly' (*orthôs*) and 'well' (*kalôs*) comes into being 'for the sake of something' (*tinos heneka*), and this is precisely what makes it fine. For instance, the eyelid has come to be 'in order to be of help to the eyes, so as to provide them with rest and prevent things from falling on them in front of their vision' (*Protr.* 50.22–24).[19] This goal-directedness is characteristic of natural processes in general, as captured by Aristotle's famous dictum that nature 'does nothing in vain'.[20]

Human life, too, is a product of nature, and hence also comes to be for the sake of some end and function. In the *Protrepticus*, Aristotle defines the human function, or more precisely the function of the human soul, as 'only' (*monon*) or 'most of all' (*malista*) 'thought and reasoning' (*dianoesthai kai logizesthai*) (58.3–4). Consequently, he claims that it is those who exercise this function well, that is, those who 'contemplate correctly' and 'most tell the truth', who live well or 'perfectly' (*teleôs*) (58.9). So far, this account is roughly familiar from the *Nicomachean Ethics*. The peculiar feature of the account in the *Protrepticus*, as correctly noted by Hutchinson and Johnson, is Aristotle's view that those who live perfectly are also 'most alive' (*malista zên*). In contrast to the NE i.7, where being

---

[16] Johnson (2005) and Leunissen (2010) are the most comprehensive studies of Aristotle's teleology in general, and natural teleology in particular.

[17] E.g. NE ii.4, 1105a32; iii.7, 1116a12–15; NE iv.2, 1123a24–6; *Rh.* i.9, 1366a33–4.

[18] 'When the natural function (*ergon*) of each thing is brought to perfection and is said to be most beautiful not by coincidence but in itself, that is when one should say that it is good' (*Protr.* 42.6–7).

[19] There is a wealth of other examples in Aristotle's works on natural philosophy, e.g. PA i.1, 640b32–641a4; GA i.23, 731a24.

[20] E.g. DA iii.9, 432b21; GA ii.6, 744a37–8; *Phys.* ii.9.

alive is wholly excluded from the account of human function, here the degree to which one lives well is coextensive with the degree to which one can be said to be alive at all. One important implication of this view is that even unperfected human lives – insofar as they qualify as human lives – could have a portion of the non-instrumental goodness of perfect lives. So Aristotle operates here with 'living' in a strongly normative sense, in which living entails living according to one's nature. This value comes in degrees, with only the best lives fully instantiating a human life in its proper and best form.[21]

The argument in the *Protrepticus* by which Aristotle establishes that living better is coextensive with living more recalls the account of life's worthwhileness from Plato's *Clitophon* and can be usefully compared with it. There, too, life is understood as the use of the soul. Aristotle postulates a correlation between 'more' and 'better' by saying that 'someone who uses a thing correctly is using it more' (*mallon chrêsthai kai orthôs chrômenos phateon*) (58.1–2); for example, we say that a good flute player uses a flute more, or gets more out of a flute, than a poor flute player, where 'more' is understood as a greater degree of actualisation (*energeia*) of corresponding flute-player's capacities (57.10–23). The justification for this view is that 'the natural objective and mode of use belong to someone who uses a thing precisely and well' (*to gar eph'ho kai hôs pephuken huparchein tôi chrômenôi kalôs kai akribôs*) (58.2–3). The qualitative attribute of using a thing 'well' is, as it were, not an accidental but an essential attribute of use: it is the defining feature of what it means to use something. In subscribing to this premise, Aristotle's notion of correct use is rather different from Plato's, who makes the essence of use independent of its goodness: whether you use your soul well or badly has no bearing at all on how much or little you use it. You can use a thing badly *and* use it much; that is why unwise persons are *worse* off the *more* they use the things at their disposal. Not so for Aristotle in the *Protrepticus*. Here, goodness of use is built into the definition of what use is.

Rather than the binary contrast between the good and the bad use, what we see in the *Protrepticus* is the idea of different degrees of falling

---

[21] Aristotle's notion of degrees of life, and, more generally, degrees of being, has been a much discussed and controversial theme in the scholarship (Owen 1960; Strycker 1968; Morrison 1987). For our purposes, it suffices to note that Aristotle's discourse about living more or living less operates with conceiving 'more' and 'less' as a difference in degree of ontological or teleological priority (*Protr.* 57.12–19). Thus, living in the proper or primary sense is an activity, or the actual use of the soul's capacities, and in that sense those who are awake and act are 'more' alive than those who are asleep.

short of the best possible use, where the bad use is nothing but a privation of the good use. The life of intellectual excellence is life in the fullest degree, but even those who fall short of this ideal can still be said to use their soul, albeit to a lesser extent. But that means that their lives do have a share in the natural goodness of life. What is not clear is the status of extremely bad lives, or the lives of those who 'have a corrupted and sick intelligence' (45.18–19): do they count as 'lives', strictly considered? If living well means to live to the full, are those who live extremely badly 'merely alive' at all? If living better means living more, does 'life' itself fade away entirely if it lacks quality altogether? Or can we specify a minimal sense in which all human lives, included corrupted lives, count as lives? In the *Protrepticus*, Aristotle gestures in this direction when he says that a life without perception would not be a life at all. I shall argue in the next section that such a definition of human life in a minimal sense is established more clearly in later works.

Let us now turn to other evidence from Aristotle's works that life in itself has a non-instrumental value. This idea from the *Protrepticus* seems to be echoed in the following passage from the *Politics*:

> But human beings also join together and maintain political communities for the sake of life by itself (*tou zên heneken autou*). For there is perhaps (*isôs*) some share of what is fine in the mere living (*ti tou kalou morion kai kata to zên auto monon*), as long as it is not too overburdened with the hardships of life (*an mê tois chalepois kata ton bion huperbalêi lian*). In any case, it is clear that most human beings are willing to endure much hardship in order to cling to life, as if it had a sort of joy inherent in it and a natural sweetness (*hôs enousês tinos euêmerias en autôi kai glukutêtos phusikês*). (*Pol.* iii.6, 1278b 24–30)

Aristotle is somewhat reluctant to grant this ('perhaps'),[22] and he makes an important reservation ('unless one's life is too overburdened with hardships'),[23] but it seems that he means to attribute some non-instrumental value also to mere living, rather than exclusively to living well. Mere living is worth choosing precisely because it has a portion of the non-instrumental value of the 'fine'. Along with, and because of, having a share

---

[22] Note that *isôs* can also mean 'indeed' or 'doubtless'; the latter is the rendering of this passage by Rackham. This would strengthen my case.

[23] This qualification is important insofar as it applies not only to the all-things-considered choiceworthiness of a life but also to the value of mere living. There are extreme hardships that deprive human life of any non-instrumental value whatsoever. Aristotle does not spell out what these extreme hardships might be. I proceed on the assumption that this qualification still leaves space for lives that are properly unhappy but not quite wretched.

of the fine, mere living also has qualities that make it worth choosing from the internal evaluative perspective: there is an inherent 'joy' and 'natural sweetness' in the activity of living.

The idea that even mere living has a 'share of the fine' fits the account from the *Protrepticus* perfectly. The idea of degrees of life can, in turn, explain why Aristotle in the *Politics* attributes to mere living a portion of the 'fine'. If indeed living well is a gradation of living *per se*, mere living is already bound to have a degree of the same value that is contained fully blown in living well. The notion of 'natural sweetness' further supports the parallel by referring to nature as the source of life's goodness and sweetness.[24]

The network of interconnections among life, nature and the fine is bolstered in a difficult passage from the *Nicomachean Ethics* ix.9 where Aristotle says that 'being alive is something that is good and pleasant in itself (*to de zên tôn kath'hauto agathôn kai hêdeôn*), since it is definite (*hôrismenon gar*) and the definite is of the nature of the good (*tês tagathou phuseôs*)' (1170a20–21), and that 'being alive is naturally good (*phusei gar agathon zôê*)' (1170b2).[25] The link between the 'definite' and the 'fine' is attested most explicitly in the *Metaphysics* xiii.3, where Aristotle lists the 'definite' as one of the attributes of the 'fine', along with 'symmetry' (*summetria*) and 'order' (*taxis*) (1078a36–b1). Being alive is said to be good 'naturally' because the attribute that makes it good – the 'definite' – belongs to the 'fine', which, as we know, is the quality that generally characterises things that come to be through nature. The 'definite' (*hôrismenon*) is cognate with the 'definition' (*horismos*), and what defines what each thing is its end or function;[26] and so we come full circle, since what is 'fine' is fine by virtue of fulfilling its specific function.

This link between definition and the fine explains why in the same passage Aristotle feels the need to qualify the claim that life is non-instrumentally good. Not all lives exemplify the natural goodness of life equally well: 'But one should not take as example a life that is bad and corrupted, or lived in pain (*mochthêran zôên kai diephtharmenên oud' en lupais*), since such a life is indefinite (*aoristos gar*), as are the attributes (*huparchonta*) that belong to it' (NE ix.9, 1170a22–24). Vice and pain are both indefinite,

---

[24] Yet another piece of evidence in favour of the view that life itself has non-instrumental value appears in *Rhetorics* i.6, where we find 'life' as an item on the list of intrinsic goods: 'for even though no other good should result from it, it is worth choosing itself' (*kath' hauto haireton estin*) (1362b26–27). We can assume that Aristotle is referring here to mere living, rather than good living, since the latter option would render the claim that 'no other good should result from it' odd: good living is the highest good, and hence whether or not another good should result from it would be irrelevant.

[25] I offer a detailed interpretation of this passage in Machek (2022).

[26] E.g. *Pol.* i.2, 1253a22–23; *Mete.* 390a10–13.

and inflict this indefiniteness on the life to which they belong. Aristotle explains the indefiniteness of vice in his theory of virtue: there is an unlimited and hence indefinite number of different ways of missing the right mean between deficiency and excess, whereas there is only one definite way of hitting it, which is virtue (NE ii.6, 1106b29–35). Vice and pain make life indefinite because they prevent it, in different ways, from reaching its optimal form, or from achieving the end that makes this life definite and fine. Vice ruins the quality of activities, and pain impedes their full realisation or, as Sarah Broadie has put it, 'blurs' them and makes them less distinctive (Broadie and Rowe 2002: 427). But does this qualification not amount to a concession that there are some human lives that do not have any non-instrumental value at all? This conclusion does not necessarily follow from this passage, for even vicious or painful lives still can have at least *some* degree of definiteness, and indeed it is blocked by Aristotle's definition of human life to which I shall attend more closely in the next section.

So there is significant evidence scattered across Aristotle's treatises for the view that not only living well but also mere living has a non-instrumental value by virtue of being a fine product of nature. But if indeed Aristotle means to attribute non-instrumental value to living in general, rather than to good living exclusively, we are faced with a puzzle: how is this claim compatible with Aristotle's view that goodness is conferred by end or function? Why should even the human lives that fail to fulfil the human function be non-instrumentally valuable? After all, it is precisely for this reason that in the *Nicomachean Ethics* i.7 Aristotle excludes 'life' from the account of human function, and indeed seems to deny, like Plato, that life in and of itself has any non-instrumental value whatsoever.

The solution looks as follows. When Aristotle attributes a share of the fine to life he does not think of life in the minimal sense common to all living beings, namely the life of nutrition and reproduction. This life is the end for plants, but for humans there is nothing fine whatsoever in living this kind of life, because this life does not achieve the human end to *any degree*. Rather, he is talking about life in an essence-sensitive sense – in this case about the specifically human life.[27] Metaphysically considered, one

---

[27] Is this compatible with the idea of degree of lives from the *Protrepticus*? Yes: a clear indication that Aristotle's discussion of degrees of life in the *Protrepticus* excludes the vegetative life is that he defines this life by the activity of 'perception' (*aisthêsis*): 'if you do away with perception you do away with life itself' (*Protr.* 44.12). And according to the definition of human life that Aristotle offers in the *Nicomachean Ethics* ix.9, the life of perception could be sufficient to satisfy the definition of the specifically human life. So, in the *Protrepticus*, any degree of 'life' can be regarded as a degree of 'human life'.

can be alive only in the essence-specific sense, for what exists in the primary sense are individual things, or 'substances' (*ousiai*) (*Met.* iv.2), and what defines substances are the primary essences (or definitions) that belong to them, such as the essence of 'human' (*Met.* iv.4). This means, in effect, that whatever exists (and in the case of ensouled things, whatever lives) does so, in the primary sense, *qua* a specific, definite essence. As a concrete thing, or substance, you can only be alive *qua* member of a definite species (e.g. *qua* an apple tree, *qua* a horse or *qua* a human being); in each case, you are alive insofar as you fulfil the specific function that defines each of these living things. It is precisely for this reason that Aristotle says in NE ix.9 that life is something 'definite', or something that has a definition: it is always the life of a definite substance.

If indeed the unperfected 'living' from the *Protrepticus* or the 'mere living' from the *Politics* is not living in the most general and minimal sense of vegetative life, but living in the more specific sense of 'mere *human* living', then we could see why Aristotle may find himself justified in attributing to it a share of the fine. Insofar as this life satisfies the definition of a species (i.e. in this case, the human species), it has the finality that is characteristic of the works of nature; in contrast to some overwhelmingly indefinite creatures that do not have their natural form or essence, such as a man-headed calf, unperfected human lives fit a definite box in the natural teleology.[28] But this view rests on an important premise, namely that the human end – happiness – does not strictly overlap with the human definition or essence. In the next section, I explain why, and on what grounds, such a gap is possible.

2.4 The Good versus the Mere Exercise of Function

We have seen that there are three criteria that a human life must meet in order to be happy. It must consist of certain kinds of activities, namely those that involve reason but which also pertain to worthwhile or serious pursuits; further, these activities must be exercised with virtue or excellence; finally, they must be free from major impediments or inhibitions. All these are needed for happiness, or for the good exercise of the human function. But are they also needed for the exercise of the human function *simpliciter*, whether good or bad? If it is possible to fulfil the human

---

[28] The example of the man-headed calf appears in *Phys.* ii.8 (198b32). Such indefinite creatures come to be whenever the 'formal nature has not mastered the material nature' (GA iv.4, 770b16–17), i.e. when the underlying matter has not been actualised into a definite form.

function without necessarily fulfilling it well, then there is logical space to preserve the link between goodness and function *and* to claim that all human lives can be non-instrumentally valuable even though they fall short of the human good. On this view, then, there is something like a mere exercise of human function, an intermediate finality, which falls short of the good exercise, but is sufficient to define even unhappy human lives as recognisably human, and thus naturally fine to some extent. So the idea of degrees of human life can be supported by the corresponding idea of degrees, or levels, of human function: the level of good exercise of the human function, and the level of mere exercise.

I shall reconstruct this view in two steps. I start by establishing that Aristotle's definition of human life, or human essence, is more inclusive than his definition of the human good. Next, I show that this broader inclusiveness dovetails with the view that even unhappy humans exercise the function that defines the human species. A useful starting-point is Aristotle's definition of human life in *Nicomachean Ethics* ix.9:

> Now people define (*horizontai*) being alive in the case of animals by capacity for perceiving (*dunamei aisthêseôs*), and in the case of human beings by capacity for perceiving or thinking (*aisthêseôs ê noêseôs*); but the capacity carries a reference to the activity, and the primary level is that of the activity; being alive in the full sense (*kuriôs*) seems (*eoike*) to be perceiving or thinking. (NE ix.9, 1170a16–19)

This definition has not received much scholarly attention. This lack of attention may be partly due to Aristotle's quick dismissal of 'living' (*zên*) as a candidate for the human function in *Nicomachean Ethics* i. But one should not overlook the fact that in the context of this passage Aristotle is not talking about life in the most general and minimal sense – the activity of the nutritive soul – but specifically about *human* life.[29] What we are given here is a definition of what it means to be alive *qua* human, rather than, thinking of Plato's *Philebus*, *qua* jellyfish.

As befits the announced shift to a more naturalistic mode of explanation in this passage, the definition of the human life in NE ix.9 is consistent with the accounts of human psychological capacities in Aristotle's biological works and in *De anima*. In DA iii.9, 'perception' and 'thought' are the capacities of the animal soul that have to do with 'discrimination' (*krisis*), in contrast to locomotion or nutrition (432a16–17). Insofar as the 'faculty of understanding and thought' (*to dianoêtikon kai nous*) is distinctive

---

[29] This account presumably also includes what Aristotle notoriously considers to be defective humans, such as women (GA ii.3, 737a28) or natural slaves (*Pol.* i.4, 1254a14–16).

of humans or other rational beings (DA ii.3, 414b18–19), we can see why Aristotle chooses perception and thought as the basic defining attributes of the human life.[30] This definition is already familiar from the *Protrepticus*, where Aristotle mentions intellection as the most characteristic attribute, and perception as the sufficient attribute, of the recognisably human life.

According to the definition of the human life from *Nicomachean Ethics* ix.9, perceptual activity comprises two levels of psychic life. There is a first-order perceiving or thinking, and there is also a second-order perception or awareness (*aisthêsis* or *sunaisthêsis*) of these first-order activities: perceiving that one sees, perceiving that one hears, perceiving that one walks, perceiving that one thinks and so forth (NE ix.9, 1170a29–b6). While Aristotle does not state this explicitly, the way he describes these activities suggests that the definition of the human life refers equally to activities at both levels, and that the first-order activities are typically accompanied by second-order perceptions of these activities. We are alive insofar as we think or perceive, but also insofar as we are aware of these activities.

Several commentators[31] have proposed that instead of 'perceiving *or* thinking' the text should read 'perceiving *and* [*kai*] thinking' – as it appears in the parallel version of this definition in *Eudemian Ethics*[32] – since the capacity for perception is shared by humans *and* animals. One so far overlooked consideration in favour of sticking to the text is that the phrase 'perceiving or thinking' could well reflect Aristotle's definition of the human function as the 'activity of the soul in accordance with reason, *or* not apart from reason' (*psuchês energeia kata logon ê mê aneu logou*) (NE i.7, 1098a7–8). These two kinds of activity might refer, according to a well-established reading, to two different parts of the soul: a strictly rational part which possesses reason, and a non-rational but reason-responsive part.[33] But it is equally possible that this definition of human function refers to the definition of human life as consisting of activities of thought or perception. In neither *Nicomachean Ethics* i.7 nor *Nicomachean Ethics* ix.9 does

---

[30] In the biological works, perhaps the most useful parallel is the account of *scala naturae* in PA ii.10, 655b37–656a9. Whereas plants are alive in the minimal sense defined by nutrition and reproduction, animals have, in addition, a capacity for perception. Even more complex are humans, 'whose nature partakes not only of living but, in addition, of living well', since 'mankind most of all partakes of the divine'. This is a clear reference to the activity of thought. For 'thought' as the essentially divine capacity, see PA iv.10, 686a26–32; GA ii.3, 736b27–29; for humans as thinking, see PA iv.10, 686a25–19; GA i.23, 731b1–2; DA ii.3, 414b18. The idea of humans as rational animals, i.e. animals endowed with the capacity for speech, appears in *Pol.* i. 2, 1253a7–18.

[31] Michael of Ephesus (2001: 195–6); Gauthier and Jolif (1958–1959: 756).

[32] To be alive means 'to perceive and to know' (*to aisthanesthai kai to gnôrizein*) (EE vii.12, 1244b24–25).

[33] See NE i.13. Broadie and Rowe (2002: 277); Irwin (1999: 184).

this amount to a concession that even a merely perceptual life, or a life devoid of any rational activity proper, could qualify as human, but rather that the characteristically human activities are of two different kinds, owing to the peculiar composition of the human soul. Given this composition, even the purely perceptual activities of the human soul, or at least some of them, may be qualitatively different from the perceptual activities of non-rational animals, insofar as they are transformed by the cohabitation with the rational part of the soul.[34]

So, looking at the three conditions of happiness above, we come to the conclusion that one can still live a recognisably human life while falling short of happiness on one or several fronts. Actually, only one sub-condition must be met, namely that one's vital activities must involve reason, whether directly, by exercising rational capacities, or indirectly, by exercising perceptual capacities that are, in some way, informed by reason. Excellence, types of pursuits and freedom from major impediments do not seem to play any role. You can live a distinctly human life even if you lack excellence and spend your life on trivial pursuits, and probably do so even when your life involves a great deal of hardship. Life can remain a definitely human life, and thus have a grain of non-instrumental value, not only when it lacks goods, but also when it contains bads. This comes out most clearly in the case of vicious lives, for these lives not only do not conflict with having a rational capacity, they presuppose it; vicious activity is in fact possible only within the characteristically and distinctly human *modus operandi*.[35] The clearest indication for this is that vicious actions, just like virtuous actions, spring from a 'decision' or 'rational choice' (*prohairesis*). In contrast to virtuous and self-controlled persons, who make good choices and act on them, and in contrast to akratic persons who make good choices but fail to act on them, vicious persons make bad choices, because vice 'distorts' (*diastrephei*) their character, makes them to be 'deceived' about the 'starting-points' (*archai*) of practical reasoning (NE vi.12, 1144a34–35), so that their practical reasoning rests on a wrong conception of the end of human action. Nonetheless, even these defective decisions are decisions in the full sense, insofar as the procedure that results in them is rational, including both rational desire and practical thought. 'Decision is not possible without understanding and thought' (*aneu nou kai dianoias*)

---

[34] For recent versions of this 'transformative' reading, see Rabbås (2015: 100–101) or Cagnoli Fiecconi (2019: 64–65).

[35] This point was well made by Barney (2020: 298–299).

(NE vi.2, 1139a33–34); it is not only acting well that requires thought, but also acting badly (*eupraxia kai to enantion*) (NE vi.2, 1139a34–35).

To appreciate the extent to which vice presupposes rationality, it is perhaps useful to compare it with the state of 'brutishness' (*thêriotês*). In NE vii.1, Aristotle distinguishes three defective conditions of character: lack of self-control, vice and brutishness. Just as there is a superhuman condition that exceeds virtue, embodied by heroes such as Priam, there is a subhuman condition that exceeds vice, namely brutishness. This is a condition caused by an originally bad nature (*phusis mochthêra*), disease or bad habits (NE vii.5, 1148b17–19), and is characterised psychologically, in particular, by taking pleasure in things that are not pleasant 'by nature' (NE vii.5, 1148b15–19). Aristotle offers a fairly heterogenous catalogue of brutish states: ripping open pregnant women and devouring the infants, homosexuality and fearing the squeak of a mouse (NE vii.5–6). What is important in the context of our argument is that he sharply distinguishes brutishness from vice: it is a 'different kind of state from vice' (*heteron ti genos kakias*) (NE vii.1, 1145a27). One important reason for this distinction is that Aristotle associates at least some kinds of brutish – but not vicious – conditions with the absence of rationality: 'and of mindless people those who by nature are lacking in reasoning powers and live by their senses alone are brutish' (NE vii.5, 1149a8–10).

If essence is defined by function, and if vicious humans fulfil the definition of humans, it follows that even vicious humans fulfil the human function. Of course, they do not exercise it well – yet they still exercise it, albeit barely. The distinction between the mere and the good exercise of function is implied in Aristotle's analogy between the function of practitioners of arts and the human function in *Nicomachean Ethics* i.7:

> If the function of a human being is the activity of the soul in accordance with reason, or not apart from reason, and the function, we say, of a given sort of practitioner and a good practitioner of that sort is generically the same (*to d'auto phamen ergon einai tôi genei toude kai toude spoudaiou*), as for example in the case of a cithara-player and a good cithara-player, and this is so without qualification in all cases, where a difference in respect of excellence is added to the function (*prostithemenês tês kata tên aretên huperochês pros to ergon*). (NE i.7, 1098a7–11)

Note that the function of a human being or of a cithara-player is at first defined without any reference to excellence. Both a cithara-player and a good cithara-player play the cithara, and thus exercise their function as cithara-players. Their activity is identical, insofar as it belongs to the same genus. The excellence of the good player's playing does not make it an activity of a different kind; rather, the excellence is an *addition* to the bare exercise of function. This indicates that, in order to fulfil one's function in a rudimentary sense, the exercise of that function does not necessarily have to be impeccable. Even a poor cithara-player exercises her function insofar as she meets certain basic conditions that define what cithara playing is, which is why she can justly be called a cithara-player.[36] This is consistent with Aristotle's careful formulation that the human good 'resides in the function' (*en tôi ergôi*) (NE i.7, 1097b27), rather than that it is identical with the function.

The distinction between the mere and the good exercise of human function implies a distinction, attributed to Aristotle by Christine Korsgaard, between descriptive and normative rationality. Making a bad rational decision is clearly a rational failure, but this is a failure of rationality in the normative sense; as for the very fact of having made that decision, this is an achievement of rationality in the descriptive sense. This distinction also seems a good fit with Aristotle's discussion of 'cleverness' (*deinotês*) as a rational capacity that is importantly different from 'practical wisdom': whereas cleverness can be used to deliberate effectively towards a vicious end, and thus exemplifies rationality in a purely descriptive sense, practical wisdom requires good ends (NE vi.12, 1144a25–30). According to Korsgaard, Aristotle is using rationality in the descriptive sense, rather than the normative, in his account of human function (Korsgaard 2008: 144).

Thus, all human lives, insofar as they fulfil the definition of human life in terms of exercising the distinctively human-reason-related capacities of the soul, have a grain of non-instrumental value. This value derives from the fact that these lives, even when they are unperfected lives, actualise – if in some cases just barely – the natural form that is characteristic of the human species. From the perspective of Aristotle's division of goods, this means that the mere living of a human life belongs, along with pleasure, honour and virtue, to the category of intermediate goods that have both instrumental and non-instrumental value: they are chosen both for the sake of something else – happiness – and also for their own sake (NE i.6, 1096b13–25).

There has been a debate in the scholarship about whether these intermediate goods are included in happiness as its component, or whether their value, while non-instrumental, depends on one single final good: the life of contemplation. If life indeed belongs to the category of these goods, what does this imply for this debate? While it is difficult to see how living

[36] A detailed interpretation of this passage along these lines was defended by Gomez-Lobo (1989).

can be a component of living well, we can more easily explain the non-instrumental value of life on the monistic reading – or at least on a version of this reading espoused by Gabriel Richardson Lear. On her proposal, all non-instrumental goods 'imitate' or 'approximate' happiness, just like mortal creatures approximate the immortality of the gods (Lear 2004: 81–8); so, for instance, virtuous actions approximate the highest value of contemplation. The relationship between the mere living and the good life would fit this account: the mere living could approximate to the good life in the sense that the rudimentary finality of the former aspires to, or emulates, the perfect finality of the latter.

In the special case of the relationship between mere living and the good life, this approximation can be combined with the maximisation model (Section 2.3), so that the value of the mere living, when increased, increases towards the value of the good life. This is the account familiar from the *Protrepticus*: an imperfect human life is a lower degree of the perfect human life, and the value of the latter is a degree of the value of the former. But this maximising version of the approximation model does not fit as well with the distinction implied in the *Nicomachean Ethics* between two kinds of rationality, descriptive and normative. One worry raised by this distinction is that rationality can drift from goodness: 'a bad man who pursues wrong ends may be just as rational in his pursuit of them: just as logical, intelligent, sound in his calculations and grasp of empirical facts' (Broadie 1991: 48).[37] If rationality makes your life a human one, then living more, *qua* human, does not necessarily mean living a better human life. In fact, just as in Plato's *Euthydemus* or *Clitophon*, living more – living longer or exercising your agency with greater external resources and free from inhibitions – can be all the worse for you.

Rather, the distinction between descriptive and normative rationality points in the direction of two incommensurable orders of value: the mere fact of exercising your rational agency has a value x, while the virtuous exercise of rational agency has a value y; but you will get no amount of y by having a lot of x, and vice versa. In fact, the rational villain could even argue that x and y are two potentially competing goals: either your end is to y, that is, to live *well*, or your end is to live *much*, that is, to maximise x in the sense of being active more often, for longer periods of time and without inhibitions. Could these not even be two legitimate and possibly competing life-projects? To live well; or to have, so to speak, the

---

[37] But cf. Barney (2020) for the view that the reasoning of the vicious is not sound because it is biased.

abundance of life. In the latter case, you will aim at longevity and freedom from external impediments, that is, at having plentiful, unimpeded vital activities, but not necessarily at virtue or perfection, unless a compelling case can be made that virtue promotes or is indispensable for *x*. Recall Haybron's Genghis Khan. As ruthless and primitive as he was, he arguably had a rich or abundant life, without having ceased to be a recognisable member of the human species. Even though the value of mere living could, by virtue of its finality, be regarded as a sort of approximation to the value of the good life, it cannot be conceived in terms of the maximisation model as conceived the *Protrepticus*. What you achieve by maximising the non-instrumental value of mere human living is not the good life but rather an abundant life; this is a kind of maximisation, but not the one that approximates to the good life.

Insofar as both the distinction between descriptive and normative rationality (*Nicomachean Ethics*) and the approximation-maximisation account (*Protrepticus*) do seem to have a non-accidental foothold in Aristotle's ethics, the tension between them may well reflect a genuine structural tension in his ethical theory. In contrast to Plato, Aristotle does attribute non-instrumental value to mere living but, in contrast to the Stoics, as we shall see, he does not assign it to an order of value that would be incommensurably different from the value of virtue and good life. So while the non-instrumental value of mere living can plausibly be justified on teleological grounds, it remains puzzling how precisely this value is contained in the value of good life, or indeed whether Aristotle could provide a compelling account of such a containment within the framework of his theory. In Chapter 5, I shall argue that the potential for this tension between the value of life's abundance and of life's perfection comes to light sharply in later Peripatetic thought.

We are now ready to turn to the question of how the natural goodness of life matters for the assessment of life worth living. We have seen that there is indeed some textual support for the claim that Aristotle's perspective is relatively 'life-affirming'. But does it follow from this that Aristotle also adopts a correspondingly optimistic view about what does it take to live a life worth living? For it is one thing to affirm that all lives have some non-instrumental value, and another to specify whether, or under what conditions, this value is sufficient to clear the threshold of a worthwhile life. We shall see that Aristotle does not mention the value of mere living in his discussions of life worth living, and that what he does say about life worth living implies that the value of mere living is not a worthmaker.

2.5   Lives Not Worth Living

The earliest Aristotle's discussion of what makes a life worth living, or rather what makes it *not* worth living, can be found in the *Protrepticus*. In one of the passages quoted in the epigraph to this chapter, we read that 'living is distinguished from not living by perception, and living is determined by its presence and power, and if this is taken away life is not worth living (*ouk estin axion zên*), as if when you do away with perception you do away with life itself' (44.9–13). In principle, this allows for the possibility that all human lives are at least barely worth living, insofar as the defining attribute of life, namely perception, is the attribute that also makes them worth living. But this is not a view that Aristotle seems to adopt in the *Protrepticus*. One indication to this effect is a disdain for those who cling to mere living (40.7). Other evidence from the *Protrepticus* also implies a fairly high-threshold account of a life worth living, but its standing is complicated by the fact that the main discussion of the life worth living is, presumably, put into the voice of Heraclides; thus, we cannot be certain about the extent to which it represents Aristotle's own position. Therefore, I first note some elements of Heraclides' speech that are without a clear parallel in Aristotle's later ethical works; as for the material from the *Protrepticus* that is echoed in later works, particularly in the *Eudemian Ethics* i.5, I refer to it later as I proceed with the discussion of these works.

The most striking element of Heraclides' speech that we do not find in Aristotle's later works is the uncompromising view that philosophical life is the only way of life that can ever make a life worth living. This view is embedded in the familiar tragic contrast between the inherent misery of human lives and the blessedness of the gods. Only philosophy can make a human life preferable to non-existence because it alone adequately engages that divine and immortal aspect of our souls that makes our life 'manageable':

> So nothing divine or happy belongs to humans apart from just that one thing worth effort, as much intellect and intelligence as is in us for, of what's ours, this alone seems to be immortal, and this alone divine. And by being able to such a capability, our way of life, although by nature unfortunate and difficult (*athlios phusei kai chalepos*), is yet so gracefully managed (*ôikonomêtai charientôs*) that, in comparison with the other animals, a human is like a god. ... So one should do philosophy or say goodbye to living and depart from this place (*ê philosophêteon oun ê chairein eipousi tôi zên apiteon enteuthen*), since everything else at least is, in a way, like much trash and nonsense. (*Protr.* 48.9–20)

Aristotle is clear in the *Protrepticus* that intellectual excellence in general, and philosophy in particular, is the way to reach the full maximisation of life and its value. But the passage here expresses a stronger and more controversial claim, namely that philosophical studies are necessary even to make a life worth living, and that a life deprived of philosophical pursuits would be better not lived at all. The thought that philosophy is the necessary condition of a life worth living was adopted, from different perspectives and for different reasons, by other thinkers in the tradition: Socrates' dictum from the *Apology* comes readily to mind; we shall see that the Epicureans, too, hold that at least some level of philosophical progress is the *sine qua non* of a life worth living. But this stance does not really resonate with other views about the life worth living found elsewhere in the Aristotelian corpus. A related claim from the above passage that may seem to sit uneasily with Aristotle's views is that the human way of life is 'by nature unfortunate and difficult'. Aristotle's remark in the *Politics* iii.6 that mere living has a share in the fine unless a life is overwhelmed by hardships implies that human lives are unfortunate incidentally rather than inherently.

This still pessimistic but more concessive outlook pervades the most sustained discussion of the conditions of a life worth living in the Aristotelian corpus from *Eudemian Ethics* i.5. This chapter is a continuation of the inquiry into happiness begun in the preceding section. Aristotle frames the chapter as a discourse about 'which of the things in life is worth choosing' (*ti tôn en tôi zên haireton*), but this quickly evolves into a discussion of things that make life itself worth choosing or, rather, not worth choosing. More precisely, the question becomes what the things are 'on account of which it would have been worth choosing not to be born in the first place' (*dia tauta to mê genesthai haireton*) (EE i.5, 1215b21–22) or the things that 'make not existing at all preferable to being alive' (*to mê einai kreitton tou zên*) (1215b26). What we get here is, effectively, a list of unconditional worthbreakers. The significance of this chapter for the distinction between happiness as the target notion and life worth living as the threshold notion was well captured by an *ad loc* remark in Michael Woods's commentary: '[A] life which is satisfactory enough not to warrant suicide, or the thought that it would have been better ... not having been born in the first place, is not the same as the good life' (Woods 1982: 58).

Two preliminary remarks about this list are in order. Aristotle's formulations point towards the notion of a life worth living in the sense of never having been born, rather than staying alive. At the same time, those things that make not having been born preferable are at once said to be things that 'induce people to abandon life' (1215b19), which again refers to life worth living in the sense of staying alive. So we may assume that in Aristotle's eyes nothing important hinges here on the distinction between the two senses of life worth living. Another thing to note is that these formulations imply, similarly to Plato, but unlike the purely privative account of imperfection from the *Protrepticus*, that some lives are not only not worth living, but are actually *worse* than being dead or never having been born. This indicates that there are things in life that are robustly bad, or have a net negative value.

So what are these unconditional worthbreakers? They can broadly be categorised into three kinds, which correspond to the three kinds of conditions for a happy life: types of activities (the 'what'), excellence (the 'how') and freedom from impediments (the 'whether'). The first set of worthbreakers on Aristotle's list corresponds to the third kind: here belong things like 'disease, extreme of pain, storms' (1215b20). These are misfortunes arising through external circumstances, rather than flaws of the soul. This list recalls the claim from the *Politics* that mere living has a share of the fine as long as it is not too overburdened by the 'hardships of life'. It also echoes the remark from the *Nicomachean Ethics* that extreme pain can break or diminish the natural goodness or 'definiteness' of life. But one cannot help wondering how this claim fits with Aristotle's discussions in the first book of the *Nicomachean Ethics*. Aristotle acknowledges there that many major misfortunes, presumably including serious diseases or extremes of pains, could make even a virtuous life unhappy. But here an even stronger claim is suggested, namely that these unfavourable external conditions prevent life from being worth living at all. Is this claim compatible with what he says in the *Nicomachean Ethics*, and does this apply equally to virtuous and non-virtuous humans? I shall return to this question in Section 2.6.

The second kind of worthbreaker has to do with types of activities, particularly those that are absent from one's life. This absence makes some lives not worth living because they are seriously and permanently impoverished in terms of their cognitive contents. Here belongs a life entirely deprived of pleasures of knowledge and perception, such as 'life solely for the pleasure associated with nutrition and sex' (1215b31), or a life of sleep, which amounts to the life of a plant (1216a5). The text suggests that a life might have a reasonable claim to being worth living on the condition that it is not wholly reduced to non-cognitive pleasures but has the 'pleasure that knowledge or sight or any other senses provide people with' (1215b32–33). This sounds like a fairly low-threshold account of life worth living, one that falls squarely within the possibility suggested in the *Protrepticus* that all recognisably human lives are worthwhile because they include perceptual activities along with pleasure in these activities.

But the broader context of Aristotle's discussion does not suggest that he believes that a life worth living can have such a low threshold. Echoing Socrates' view that unexamined lives are not worth living for *humans*, Aristotle has an unfavourable view of cognitively impoverished lives that are human only in name but not in essence. There is something fatally wrong with your life if you are born as a human, but eventually fail live up to the human essence, and instead end up living a life that is fit for grazing animals (cf. NE 1095b20–21), like those who only care about the gratification of their appetites. A special case of such an impoverishment is 'the life which men lead while they are still children': 'no one in his right mind', says Aristotle, 'would tolerate a return to that sort of existence' (EE i.5, 1215b22–24). This claim is paralleled in the *Nicomachean Ethics*: 'no one would choose to live with a child's level of thought for his whole life' (NE x.3, 1174a2–3); and also in the Heraclidan speech from the *Protrepticus*: 'not even one of us would put up with being either drunk or a little child to the end of our lives' (45.24–25).

This dismissive stance seems surprising insofar as the life of children is arguably rather rich in cognitive activities, for it includes, at the very least, various activities of perception. To understand this stance, it might be useful to distinguish between the value of the cognitive state of children, while they are still children, and the state of a life-long childhood. It is true that Aristotle characterises the cognition of children in terms of 'ignorance', which is not quite dissimilar to the ignorance associated with drunkenness or madness (EE iii.3). What is characteristic of a child's ignorance, in contrast to the temporary ignorance of the drunk, is that it is due to the absence of a firm conception of the good, or well-established starting-points for moral reasoning. This is an important reason why children, like animals, do not have the capacity for rational 'decision' that would allow them to choose fine actions for their own sake (NE iii.2, 1111b8–9). But this cognitive impairment is a natural phase of human development, and becomes pathological ('sickness of intelligence', *Protr.* 45.19–20) only when it settles into a life-long condition. Those humans who never attain the moral perspective of normally developed adult humans are like eagles who never learn to fly.[38]

---

[38] By 'normally developed' I mean all humans who have healthy 'starting-points', i.e. including the akratics, in contrast to the vicious humans, who have corrupted 'starting-points'. The state of vicious humans, i.e. of those who exercise activities characteristic of their species, but do so in a perverted rather than merely imperfect way, does not seem to have a parallel elsewhere in the biological realm but is rather a peculiar feature of the human condition.

Aristotle mentions a further, more general precondition for a life worth living that adds a further perspective on the case of the life-long childhood, namely voluntariness of life's contents: 'all things that everyone does, or undergoes, but "not voluntarily" (*hekontes*)' are insufficient to make life worthwhile (EE i.5, 1215b26–29). The voluntariness and involuntariness of actions is an important theme of Aristotle's ethics and crucially informs his account of moral responsibility. He dedicates to this theme several sustained – but not always neatly converging – treatments in different parts of his corpus. In general, voluntary actions are caused by desires and beliefs in the agents themselves, rather than being imposed on them by external 'force', or caused by ignorance of some relevant circumstances (NE iii.1). But in the discussion in EE i.5, Aristotle further specifies what he means by 'not voluntarily' in this particular context: things done or undergone involuntarily are those that are 'not done or undergone for their own sake (*mêthen autôn dia to mêd' autou charin*)' (EE i.5, 1215b28–29). This indicates that voluntariness is understood here in an unusually narrow sense of actions or passions that spring from 'rational choice' (*prohairesis*) and, even more narrowly, those that are chosen for their own sake.[39] That would explain why living a whole life like a child might amount to living a life full of involuntary actions or passions, for children are not capable of rational choice.

This special, narrow sense of voluntariness yields a broad range of actions that are *not* voluntary. The breadth of this range provides a key for understanding Aristotle's unfavourable assessment of other kinds of lives, such as the lives of slaves or *hoi polloi*: craftsmen, peasants, merchants or, collectively, the lives of moneymakers. Aristotle apparently thinks that moneymaking lives have something involuntary in them insofar as they are 'somewhat forced' (*biaios tis*); as Aristotle himself specifies, they are 'not [chosen] for their own sake (*allou charin*)' (NE i.5, 1096a7).[40] The qualification 'somewhat' implies that these actions are 'mixed'; they combine elements of voluntariness and involuntariness, perhaps in a way similar to throwing cargo overboard in a storm (NE iii.1, 1110a9–12), insofar as they result from a rational decision, but are forced or involuntary 'in a way' (*pôs*) (EE ii.8, 1225a12–14). Not having any other existential choice, those who embark on moneymaking lives are acting voluntarily in one

---

[39] The realm of voluntary actions is broader than the realm of actions done from choice: 'what is chosen is all voluntary, but what is voluntary is not all chosen' (EE ii.10, 1226b 34–35).

[40] But could not possibly even these banausic lives be chosen for their own sake? Aristotle would likely respond that if you were to make that choice rather than choosing, say, a life of philosophical pursuits, that in itself would show that you had a poorly developed sense of the fine. This shortcoming limits the extent to which your life is worth living for you.

sense, namely that they make a choice to live like that, but involuntarily in another, namely that they could have hardly made a different choice with good sense. Their lives are not worth living because they are, in a way, not *their* lives, but lives that were imposed on them by their circumstances.

The same holds also for the lives of natural slaves, which appear to have even more involuntary content, in the narrow sense from EE i.5, than the vulgar or moneymaking lives, since the slaves have no capacity to make 'choices' whatsoever. In this respect, they can no more have lives worth living than those who experience life-long childhood. At the same time, the lives of slaves are a special case insofar as their quality depends on the goodness of their masters. If slaves are 'sort of part of his master' (*Pol.* i.6, 1255b10–11), and a master's life happens to be worth living, should not this slave's life, too, be worth living?

Finally, the third kind of worthbreaker has to do with excellence or, rather, its opposite – vice or the corruption of character. This is implied by the claim that pleasure of a 'reprehensible sort' (*hêdonê mê kalê*) might in some circumstances be 'enough to make not existing at all preferable to life' (EE i.5, 1215b25–6). In the *Nicomachean Ethics*, Aristotle notes that the great-souled person 'does not risk himself for small things, or often, because there are few things he values, but for great things he does, and when he does he is unsparing of his life, as to whom there are some conditions under which it is not worth living (*ouk axion on pantôs zên*)' (NE iv.3, 1124b8–9). Aristotle does not make clear what these conditions are, but there are roughly two options, both of which align with the discussion in the *Eudemian Ethics* i.5. One is that they are conditions in which one's voluntary agency is seriously inhibited, as in captivity. Another is that saving one's life by foregoing an opportunity for a fine deed – such as a heroic death in a battle – entails doing something shameful – in this case, a cowardly desertion – and this shameful action would make life unbearable.

What Aristotle says here, precisely, is that there are conditions under which life is not worth living *for* the great-souled person. Her character is such that she would not tolerate the sort of impoverished or shameful existence just described. Does this not imply that even a shameful life might still be worth living for a petty-souled person, and that, in general, judgements about life's worthwhileness are always relative to the specific moral level of individual lives? Aristotle's view seems to be that these judgements are relative only insofar as they concern specifically human lives, rather than lives in general. The list of worthbreaking conditions is clearly supposed to apply to humans in general. Aristotle says that for a man who would choose for himself a life filled only with passive pleasures, it would actually make no difference if he were born a beast or a man (EE i.5, 1215b35–36). But once you are a human, there are objective, universal criteria of what is good or bad for you. The claim that a shameful life is not worth living for a great-souled person in fact implies that such a life is not worth living for any human, regardless of their level of moral perfection.[41] For virtuous humans set the criteria of what is truly good, pleasant and so on for humans in general. For instance, in the *Nicomachean Ethics* x.5, Aristotle says that what counts as truly pleasant for humans is what is actually pleasant to the virtuous person: the virtuous person is the 'measure' (1176a18–28).

At base, all these conditions amount to a failure to exercise the human function well, and correspond quite neatly with the three major ways of falling short of a happy life, as discussed in Section 2.2. Diseases or other misfortunes correspond to impediments or inhibitions of activities. Different forms of cognitive impoverishment correspond to the requirement to engage in the right sort of activities, that is, those that involve the rational capacities *and* count as serious or worthwhile pursuits. And the life filled with reprehensible pleasures or shameful actions corresponds to the life of vice.

However, this account does not necessarily imply that *all* unhappy human lives are not worth living. Most worthbreaking conditions mentioned in the *Eudemian Ethics* i.5 are extreme ways of failing to meet the conditions for the happy life. These conditions do not make lives just unhappy; they make them miserable. Thus, there could still be, in theory at least, a space for human lives that are lacking in the attributes necessary for the happy life but that are still worth living, as long as they stay clear of some fatal flaws. I explore this space in the next section.

2.6 Unhappy Lives Worth Living

For Aristotle, all happy lives are worthwhile and many unhappy lives are not worth living. But are there some unhappy lives that are worth living? In particular, at least those lives that fall short of happiness only in one of the three relevant respects ('what', 'how' and 'whether') could perhaps have a reasonable claim to a life worth living. Aristotle nowhere discusses this question explicitly, which may well indicate that this was not a

---

[41] This is compatible with the notion offered earlier in Section 2.3 that all human lives have some non-instrumental value. For this non-instrumental value of mere human life is not necessarily sufficient to make a life worth living.

burning issue for him. Still, it is tempting to approximate an Aristotelian answer to this question, and this is what the following reconstruction seeks to achieve.

Consider first the life of a good and healthy carpenter. In Aristotle's view, the chances of this life being worth living are, I think, better than in the case of natural slaves but also more uncertain than in the case of the carpenter from Plato's *Republic*. On the one hand, this life is certainly not as worthless as a life deprived of any perceptual and rational activities. The exercise of 'skill' (*technê*) involves, after all, the exercise of the rational part of the soul (NE vi.4). Unlike natural slaves, the carpenter can in principle make rational decisions. On the other hand, the scope and scale of his moral agency, or exercise of virtues, is seriously limited by the lack of access to good education as well as by the daily grind of his job. These lives are inherently such that they do not allow a full, free expression of human nature at its best, and that is why nobody with good sense would ever choose them if better alternatives were available. As to whether Aristotle regarded these limitations as too serious to make such a life not even worth living, the available evidence does not allow us to arrive at a conclusive answer.[42]

A remarkable consequence of the relatively deprecative view of the value of banausic life is a discrepancy between the internal and external evaluative perspectives on life. For the lives of carpenters or slaves typically still have a contributive value: Aristotle does not deny that a well-functioning city cannot do without the work of peasants, merchants and craftsmen, just as it cannot do without the work of slaves. This makes their lives meaningful. But, in contrast to Plato's view from the *Republic*, this meaningfulness does not necessarily translate into life's worthwhileness: a good carpenter's life is worth living from the point of view of the city, but perhaps not from the point of view of the carpenter himself. Aristotle does not suggest, like Plato, that workers would have a share in the city's happiness.

There are two other kinds of unhappy human lives that seem to pass the threshold of a worthwhile life more securely. One is otherwise perfect but unfortunate lives. On the one hand, Aristotle makes a blanket

---

[42] This can also be said about the life of women. But it seems that at least some women can, according to Aristotle, generally aspire to a degree of rationality that makes their lives worthwhile for them. They can be better off than those humans who spend all their life at a mental level of children, for they have some degree of deliberative and decision-making capacity. For the magisterial treatment of the cognitive and deliberative capacities of females in Aristotle's philosophy, see Connell (2015).

claim in the *Eudemian Ethics* i.5 that a life fraught with extreme hardships is not worth living; this is echoed in the *Politics* iii.6 and *Nicomachean Ethics* ix.9. Without further qualifications, this would mean not only that a virtuous person living amidst misfortunes is not happy, but also that his life is not even worth living. But the discussion in the *Nicomachean Ethics* i.10 appears to supply a qualification that blocks this consequence. While misfortunes may remove the good man from happiness, he will not ever be 'miserable' (*athlios*), since he will not ever do anything shameful, and even in those cases of suffering misfortune, 'what is fine shines through' (1100b30–31). This implies that virtue is not sufficient for happiness and does not provide sufficient protection against unhappiness; however, it does provide sufficient protection against the collapse of a happy life into a life not worth living. The same misfortunes are likely to have a more damaging impact on a not fully virtuous person, and possibly might move her to doing shameful deeds, thereby making her life not worth living.

The last case of unhappy lives worth living are non-vicious lives that are free from major misfortunes. Clearly, lives that are unhappy due to vice are not worth living, even though they involve the exercise of reason. But matters are less clear when it comes to the lives of humans who are neither virtuous nor vicious. Aristotle allows for a broad scope of human conditions that fall short of virtue but are better than vice, with the condition of akratic humans as the most familiar case. The akratics make good decisions but fail to enact them, like cities that pass good laws but fail to implement them (NE vii.10, 1152a20–21). These lives are free from vice and corruption, since even akratics have healthy 'starting-points' (*archai*) for ethical deliberations – they decide for the sake of the good (NE vii.8, 1151a25). In the absence of any evidence to the contrary, the lives of akratic humans could also, in Aristotle's view, be worth living on the condition that they contain worthwhile pursuits *and* are free from major hardships.

To sum up, there are three kinds of unhappy lives that could be nonetheless worth living: 1) lives which are unhappy on account of the inferior status of their activities, such as the lives of moneymakers, but which are free from other conditions of unhappiness; 2) lives which are unhappy on account of external misfortunes, but which are free from other conditions of unhappiness; and 3) lives which are unhappy due to a lack of virtue, but which are free from other conditions of unhappiness. Only vice and serious cognitive impoverishments are unconditional worthbreakers; other conditions, such as bad health or the absence of virtue, are conditional worthbreakers.

2.7   Practical Implications of Choosing Life

If indeed we can reconstruct from Aristotle's works an account of life
worth living, one wonders what implications this would have for practical decisions concerning staying alive or for bringing other human beings
into life. Since Aristotle has views about the appropriateness of suicide,
one might expect that these simply draw practical consequences from his
axiology of life. As a matter of fact, though, the two discussions have little
in common. Aristotle's most explicit discussion of suicide in *Nicomachean
Ethics* v.11, or the voluntary act of killing oneself, treats suicide chiefly as
a legal problem. The question is not so much under what conditions one
would be better off exiting life, but rather under what conditions suicide
is just, or, more precisely, whether suicide could ever *not* be an act of
injustice. The worth of life does not seem to play any role whatsoever in
this assessment.

Still, Aristotle makes some relevant remarks about the issue of abandon-
ing or risking one's life. But this connection does not work the way we
would expect, such as that having a life worth living would always be a
reason to stay alive, while living a worthless life would always be a reason
to choose death. As for humans who do not live worthwhile lives, the lack
of worthwhileness cannot be cited as a legitimate reason for exiting life.
Rather, such an act in their case is a sign of 'softness' (*malakia*): 'to die to
escape from poverty or love or anything painful is not the mark of a brave
man, but rather of a coward; for it is softness to fly from what is troublesome, and such a man endures death not because it is noble to do so but
to fly from evil' (NE iii.7, 1116a12–15). Paradoxically, those who *can* choose
death on legitimate grounds are precisely those for whom their life *is* worth
living. In an unmistakable reference to Achilles' choice between life and
glory, Aristotle says that the good person will choose a year of living finely
over many years of indifferent life' (NE ix.8, 1169a22–23) and 'die for others in order to achieve the fine for himself' (ibid., 1169a25–26). On the one
hand, we know that the prospect of death is painful for the good, considering how good their life is. But the pleasure in accomplishing a grand, fine
deed by choosing death trumps this loss. The heroic death, while cutting
life short, also crowns it; it is a way of bringing life to a grand conclusion.
On the negative side, avoiding such a death may taint life with cowardice.
This is not to say that such a heroic sacrifice does not come at a price: a
valuable life has been lost.

There is less evidence concerning Aristotle's views about the implications
of the life worth living for procreation. But in comparing the 'friendship'

between father and child to the relationship between a king and his subjects, Aristotle notes: 'Fatherly friendship is also like this, but the scale of the benefits conferred is different; after all, a father is responsible for his son's existence, for which there seems no greater benefit, and for bringing him up and educating him' (NE viii.11, 1161a 16–18). The implication is that, besides the obvious benefits bestowed by parents, such as a good upbringing and education, even the mere fact of bringing children to life is a real benefit for the children. This agrees with the view that life is non-instrumentally valuable, but is of no real consequence for whether this benefit makes the life of the children worthwhile for them. Rather, in light of the above considerations, we would expect upbringing and education to be far more decisive, insofar as they are crucial for securing some of the necessary contents of lives worth living.

2.8 Jellyfish and Humans: Plato and Aristotle on Life Worth Living

There are some important general lessons to be drawn from looking jointly at Plato's and Aristotle's views about life worth living. Perhaps the most important premise in the background of their discussion is that worthwhileness of a human life is always judged with regard to the normative standards inherent in its being a representation of the human life. This suggests a more general principle – that no life can be evaluated on absolute terms, but always relatively to a general kind of species that it instantiates. To establish whether a jellyfish has a life worth living, and whether a human has a life worth living, two different sets of criteria must be applied. One difficult question that this principle raises is whether the relativity of evaluation implies also evaluative incommensurability: given the different standards, is it the case that we cannot compare at all which lives are better for those who live them? In that case, there would be no way to tell whether a life of a well-functioning human is better for this human than a life of a well-functioning jellyfish is better for this jellyfish.

Now, there is little doubt that Plato and Aristotle regard a human life at its best as better than a jellyfish life at its best. Surely, if you were able to choose whether you would rather be born as a good jellyfish or as a good human in your next life, you would rightly choose the latter. Only humans can achieve *eudaimonia*, whereas none of plants or animals can. Thus, the species-relativity of evaluation does not seem to entail an interspecies incommensurability of life's value. But how do we handle, then, the following trickier question: if you had that choice, would you choose to live as a well-functioning jellyfish or as a vicious human? From the inter-species perspective, there seem to be reasons to choose the latter; after all, even a vicious human life is more rational than the life of a jellyfish, and hence cognitively richer and more rewarding. But from the intra-species perspective, one would be advised to choose the former, since to live viciously is worse than not being alive at all, whereas the life of a jellyfish may not be (we are not really told); if it is not at least barely worth living, it might well be an indifferent life, and thus still less bad than a vicious human life.

So there are two aspects of life's value, one that concerns a species in comparison with other species, and another which concerns a flourishing of whatever species that is. We can call the former the 'value of complexity': the more complex an organism is, the more rational and capable of cognitive discrimination, the more valuable its life.[43] The latter can be called the 'value of perfection': the better an organism fulfils its natural function, whatever that function is, the more valuable its life. The life of a well-functioning jellyfish would score well in the value of perfection, but poorly in the value of complexity; for the life of a vicious human, this would be the other way round.[44]

Does this distinction of value allow us to arrive at a judgement about which of these two lives – that of a good jellyfish and that of a vicious human – is better, *all things considered*? One sensible way to approach this problem is to point out that both of these lives are *not* worth choosing, for Plato and Aristotle at least, and hence the question about which one is 'better' is moot. Still, when pressed to make a comparative judgment, a relevant consideration, repeatedly voiced by Plato, would be that the vicious life is harmful for those who live it (whereas the life of jellyfish is not); and in that sense the vicious life is worse. This gives us a hint to grasp how the value of complexity and the value of perfection could combine to yield the all-thing-considered evaluative comparison. The value of life is like a vector, where the degree of complexity determines the magnitude and the degree of perfection determines the direction. Being born as a human, there is a chance that your life may end up being more worth

[43] In Aristotle's case, the value of complexity could rest on 'definiteness' which, as we know, confers goodness (see Section 2.3). Complex organisms are more definite insofar as they fulfil a higher degree of hypothetical necessity: they must meet a greater number of specific conditions in order to function in the complex way they do.

[44] The distinction between the value of life's perfection and the value of life's complexity does not coincide with the distinction proposed in Section 2.4 between the value of life's perfection and the value of life's abundance. The former enables to compare the value of life across different species, whereas the latter bears on different dimensions of life from an intra-species perspective.

living for you than if you were born a jellyfish, but there is also a greater risk that you may wind up having a life that is very bad for you – worse for you than the life of a jellyfish is for the jellyfish – if vice gives the value of your life a negative direction. Your rationality is a potential that can be fully developed but also mis-developed (in the case of vice) or wasted (in the case of cognitively impoverished lives). If the former, all the better for you; if the latter, all the worse.

Unlike Plato, Aristotle counts rationality not only as a potential that has an instrumental value but also as an actuality that is non-instrumentally valuable, insofar as it constitutes the (mere) exercise of human function.[45] For this reason, Aristotle could in principle maintain that all human lives, on account of their rationality, are already more worth living than lives of jellyfish. But he does not assign to rationality *per se*, or rationality in a descriptive sense, such a high value, and eventually his view about the all-things-considered value of vicious human lives, in comparison with the lives of jellyfish, seems similar to Plato's. We shall see that this insistence on vice as the unconditional worthbreaker is retained in later Platonic and Peripatetic traditions and exerts a strong influence on other major schools.

While Plato and Aristotle make any life worth living depend on a degree of objective perfection of the rational capacities, they also allow for a gap between the best possible human life and life (barely) worth living. In particular, life worth living does not require a completely virtuous soul. The carpenter in Plato's *Republic* has virtues of justice and sound-mindedness, but not courage and wisdom. Aristotle, for his part, grants that even intermediate state between virtue and vice, including *akrasia*, could be sufficient to warrant life a worth living, when combined with the absence of some conditional worthbreakers. Another kind of life worth living that falls short of the happy life is instantiated by completely virtuous persons who suffer from non-psychic evils, such as Aristotle's virtuous person facing extreme misfortunes. Some passages from Plato suggest that a ruined body alone might be sufficient to make life not worth living, but the evidence is inconclusive.

Aristotle can be regarded as a life optimist, insofar as he, unlike Plato, attributes a grain of non-instrumental value to all human lives that satisfy the definition of the human species. This value is a portion of the same

---

[45] In other words, by virtue of having the kind of complexity that defines the human life, every human life also automatically has a degree of perfection. Following the notion of value of life as a vector, we could say that by having its axiological magnitude every human life also has a marginal direction towards goodness.

kind of value that characterises the perfected actions of virtuous humans. Both good living and mere living are 'fine', or non-instrumentally good, by virtue of achieving some definite degree of finality. The rudimentary finality of the mere human living is conferred by nature; the complete finality of good living is a full actualisation of the characteristically human capacities by means of moral training and education. On the one hand, this account can secure that all human lives, regardless of their perfection, have a non-instrumental value on account of having a share in rationality in a descriptive sense; on the other hand, it raises worries about whether or how this kind of value can be neatly integrated into the overall value of the good life.

But regardless of how compelling Aristotle's life-affirming stance is, it clearly has its limits; in some respects, Aristotle's perspective is even more pessimistic than Plato's. Whereas Aristotle's naturalistic perspective motivates him to value mere living, he does not regard this value on its own as sufficient to make human life worthwhile. In addition to being free from vice, a life worth living for a human must be filled with some particular preoccupations rather than others. Banausic lives, regardless of their contribution to the city and of the affinity to different types of human nature, are just barely worth living, if at all. In this respect, Aristotle's outlook is more elitist than Plato's. When Aristotle says that slaves are better off under the authority of their master's reason, this echoes Plato's view that the non-philosophers can have lives worth living if they agree to be ruled by the philosophers. But in contrast to Plato, Aristotle is less willing to affirm that this subordination is sufficient to make the life of a slave worth living for a human.

Although there is not a strict overlap between happy lives and lives worth living, the things that make life worth living broadly coincide, for both Aristotle and Plato, with those that make it happy. If there are unhappy lives worth living, these lives are worth living by virtue of having a share in those goods that are abundant in happy lives. In the later development of ancient Greek thought, this premise is challenged head-on by the Stoics. The Stoics follow Aristotle in adopting a decisively naturalistic perspective on the value of life, and on those grounds likewise regard mere living as non-instrumentally valuable. However, instead of locating the value of mere living and the value of good living on two different levels of a single continuum of value, they assign them to two fundamentally different and incommensurable axiological domains: the domain of good and bad on the one hand; and the domain of indifferent things on the other.

CHAPTER 3

Decoupling Happy Life from Life
Worth Living in Stoicism

As you know, life is not always something to hang on to. Our good does not consist merely in living (*vivere*) but in living well (*bene vivere*). Hence the wise person lives as long as he ought to (*debet*), not as long as he can. He considers where he will be living, and how, and with whom, and what he will be doing. He is always thinking about the quality of his life, not the quantity (*qualis vita, non quanta sit*). If he encounters many hardships that banish tranquility, he releases himself.

(Seneca, *Ep.* 70.4–5)

Attacking Plato, who said that for those who have learned nothing and do not know how to live it is beneficial not to live, Chrisyppus said literally the following: … 'Even the bad ought to (*kathêkei*) stay alive.' And then, word for word: 'For in the first place virtue quite on its own is no reason to stay alive, nor is vice a reason to our needing to depart.'

(Plutarch, *De st. rep.* 1039d–e)[1]

3.1 Two Ways of Doing Well

In Plato's *Crito*, Socrates explains that escaping from prison is not an option for him, for doing so would corrupt his soul and make his life not worth living. In the same spirit, Socrates says later in the dialogue that it is not 'living' that is 'the most important thing' but 'living well'. Seneca, a Stoic philosopher, subscribes to this claim almost verbatim. On his view, our good does not lie in whether we are alive, or how long we live, but in the 'quality' of life, or how well we live. To be worth living, our life must be good. In the second passage, however, we find an important early Stoic scholarch, Chrysippus, in disagreement with Plato: whether you are

---

[1] Throughout, translations of the Stoic sources follow the anthology of Long and Sedley (1987), sometimes complemented by a later anthology of Inwood and Gerson (2008). Cicero's *Fin.* is rendered according to Annas and Woolf, *Off.* according to Atkins and Griffin. For Seneca's *Letters*, we use the translation of Graver and Long.

99

virtuous or vicious has no bearing on whether it is worthwhile for you to carry on living. This view indicates a radical break from both Plato and Aristotle, but also appears to sit uneasily with Seneca's claim: if even the bad may have reasons to stay alive, how can it be that life's worth-whileness should depend on its quality? If (i) the worth of staying alive should depend on the quality of that life, and if (ii) virtue and vice make a momentous difference to that quality, we would expect that the virtuous have strong reasons to stay alive whereas the vicious have strong reasons to choose death.

Several strategies may come to mind to reconcile these two passages, and it will be useful to take two of these options off the table right away. (1) One possibility is that the Stoics do not commit to premise (ii), and maintain that virtue or vice have no bearing on how well or badly we live. But this will not help. Among Greek philosophers, the Stoics most emphatically affirmed the importance of virtue for living well: not only is virtue a necessary condition for happiness, it is even a sufficient condition (DL vii.127). All virtuous persons are always happy; all vicious persons are always unhappy; and everyone who is not virtuous is vicious. (2) Another possibility is that there is a distinction at work between a prudential and a moral perspective. When Chrysippus says that the vicious 'ought to' stay alive, what he possibly means is that they have, for some reason, a moral duty to stay alive even though their life is not worth living from them.

This second option does have some *prima facie* plausibility in light of the Stoic view that the cosmos is the creation of a providential god, in which all humans – including the vicious – have a role to play and thus contribute to the harmony of the whole. All lives are meaningful, though not necessarily worthwhile. Does this inescapable meaningfulness entail a duty to stay alive in all kinds of circumstances? Clearly not, for then it would make no sense to say that in some circumstances the virtuous ought to depart. More fundamentally, any such distinction between moral and prudential reasons clashes with the core commitments of the Stoic ethics, and particularly with the view that doing what I ought coincides with doing what is beneficial for me, at least in some sense of that word. An explicit statement of the inseparability of the prudential and moral per-spectives can be found in Cicero's account of the Stoic ethics in *On Duties*: 'When men separate benefit from virtue (*cum utilitatem ab honestate sei-ungunt*) they subvert the foundations of nature' (*Off.* iii.101). We all have a natural tendency to pursue what is beneficial, Cicero further explains, but this desire does not conflict with our other-regarding commitments; if the natural desire for benefit is properly cultivated and fully developed, doing what we ought just becomes the most effective way of fulfilling the desire for benefit. So whereas the distinction between worthwhileness and meaningfulness may well be real and important, it does not map onto the distinction between prudential and moral reasons.

There is yet another strategy, a more promising one, available. What we need is a distinction between two different senses of quality of life, or between two ways in which my life can go well for me. In one sense, life can go well for me because I live well, just as Socrates did even on the last day before his execution. There is only one thing needed for such a good conduct of life, namely virtue. In another sense, life can go well for me not because of my conduct of my life, but because of the possession of certain other things besides virtue that are worth having. Things such as being free from physical pain, not living in poverty and having one's body intact are obviously reasonable objects of choice. The Stoics call these things 'preferred indifferents' (*proēgmena*) or, more broadly, things 'in accordance with nature' (*secundum naturam*): they are in some sense good to have, but they are irrelevant for your happiness in the strict sense of that word. Now, it is possible that the criterion of life's worthwhileness – *not* of life's happiness – is this second sense of the quality of life; that would explain why the possession of virtue, the sufficient condition for happiness, has no bearing on whether one has good reasons to stay alive. When you decide whether to stay alive, you should consider not virtue but the balance of the ordinary, common-sense values and their opposites in your life. This fits the quotation from Seneca well: when he mentions 'many hardships' and 'tranquility', these do not refer to a bad conduct of life, but to things that make life go well or badly in the latter sense.

We shall see that this is indeed how the Stoic position on life worth living needs to be understood: virtue makes your life happy, but not worth living; naturally valued things may make your life worth living, but not happy. What makes this position difficult to accept, or even understand, is the Stoic insistence that it is virtue and happiness, and *not* these other naturally valued things, that is the 'end' (*telos*) of human life. Like Plato and Aristotle, the Stoics hold that all human strivings are ultimately motivated by a single, overarching end, namely happiness. There are two puzzles here. First, how is the idea of two ways of doing well compatible with the commitment to a single end of human life? If happiness and virtue is the only end, where is the space for the second way of doing well? Secondly, if happiness has a higher or more privileged standing in making our life good, why should decisions about staying alive – apparently the matter of utmost importance – be referred not to happiness but to some inferior or subordinate ends? If it is happiness that matters in the first place, should it not be the unconditional worthmaker?

I try to answer the first question in Section 3.2 by offering a summary of Stoic ethics and value theory. It turns out that postulating two normative perspectives on the quality of life within the eudaimonistic framework, where happiness remains the only end, is a defensible move. The second question is addressed in Section 3.3. Happiness is indeed not the worthmaker; rather, the worthmaker is a favourable balance of preferred and dispreferred indifferents. The reason for this is that staying alive or departing from life is likewise a matter of indifference and as such should be measured by other indifferent things. While the Stoics were chiefly interested in life worth living in the sense of the worth of staying alive, we also find a discussion in Seneca's works of whether it is worth being born at all; this discussion is addressed in Section 3.4. I suggest that the general principles of the deliberations about staying alive should also apply to decisions on whether human beings should be brought into the world. In Section 3.5, I discuss Stoic views about the value of mere living. Mere living is a preferred indifferent, and thus non-instrumentally valuable. This value always contributes, along with the value of other preferred indifferents, to life's worthwhileness, but remains preserved even if life happens not to be worthwhile. Section 3.6 briefly addresses the question of the relationship between life's worthwhileness and its meaningfulness. In the Stoic picture, all lives have a contributive value from the external standpoint, but this makes no difference for their worthwhileness. I conclude in Section 3.7 by comparing the Stoic approach to the life worth living and the value of life with that of Aristotle.

Before I start, a brief note about the scope of the textual material and the history of the Stoic school is in order. The school had a history spanning about five centuries, running from the Hellenistic (ca. third century BCE) to the Roman Imperial period (ca. second century CE). It was developed, and practised, in different political contexts, by philosophers of different social standings, and in two different languages, Greek and Latin. This raises the question whether it is possible to speak of Stoicism as a unified phenomenon and whether Stoic philosophy has a doctrinal unity. The matters are further complicated by the fact that the textual material from the early Stoic period has been preserved only in the form of fragmentary testimonies by non-Stoic philosophers, some of whom were hostile to the Stoics. The prevailing view among the commentators about the relationship between the early Stoicism of Zeno or Chrysippus and the later Stoicism of Seneca or Marcus Aurelius has evolved: whereas several decades ago there was a widespread view that the later Stoics departed on philosophically substantial points from the early Stoic 'orthodoxy',[2] most contemporary commentators gravitate to the view that there is considerable doctrinal unity across the different stages of the school's development, and that what were earlier regarded as substantive shifts in doctrine are more appropriately understood in terms of a plurality of different approaches within a single theoretical framework, or in terms of shifts of emphases. Following this view, I shall take the liberty throughout the chapter of quoting evidence from early Stoicism alongside material from the later Stoics.

3.2   Happiness, Virtue and Indifferent Things

Several different definitions of the end of human life emerged during the history of the Stoic school. Perhaps the most famous is that happiness is 'living in agreement with nature' (*homologoumenôs phusei zên*), which is the same thing as 'living in accordance with virtue' (*kath'aretên zên*) (DL vii.87).[3] But some other definitions do not refer to virtue but rather to the 'preferred indifferents', or things 'according to nature'. So, for instance, according to a definition attributed to the middle-Stoic scholarch Antipater, the end 'is to do everything in one's power continuously and undeviatingly with a view to obtaining the predominating things which accord with nature' (Stob. *Ecl.* ii.76.9–15). If we can see why living in agreement with nature is the same as living in agreement with virtue, and why both these definitions converge with doing everything in one's power to attain preferred indifferents, we shall arrive at a basic understanding of Stoic ethics and value theory. I start with nature, then turn to virtue, and finally link the two with the selection of preferred indifferents.[4]

The Stoics had an expansive notion of 'nature' (*phusis*), regarding it as synonymous with the totality of all existing things, and so also with 'God', 'reason' or 'fate' (DL vii.148–9). Nature is a 'tenor which achieves everything methodically', literally 'in a specific way (*hodôi*)' (Olympiodorus, *On Plato's Gorgias* xii.1), which matches the view that god is 'intelligent,

---

[2] A good example is John Rist's important study of the Stoic account of suicide in Rist (1969).
[3] Throughout, translations of the Stoic sources follow the anthology of Long and Sedley (1987), unless otherwise noted. This is sometimes complemented by the later anthology of Inwood and Gerson (2008). For translations of passages not included in these anthologies, I quote from recent English translations of these works, as given in the references.
[4] For more detailed introductions into the Stoic ethical theory that likewise focus on the relationship between virtue and nature, see Gill (2013) and Bénatouïl (2013).

a designing fire which methodically proceeds towards the creation of the world', or a 'breath pervading the whole world' (Aetius i.7.33). Owing to the intelligence of its creator, the world 'has nothing missing and is equipped, from every point of view, perfect and complete in all its measures and parts' (Cicero, DND ii.37). The universe is a single unity of interrelated things that spontaneously function according to their peculiar natural tendencies, and these tendencies are conducive to a rational order that has been designed by a providential god for the good of this whole. The characteristic organising principle of this well-ordered world is teleology: so, for instance, Chrysippus reportedly argued that even bed-bugs and mice are created for some reason, specifically for the sake of humans: 'bed-bugs are useful for waking us, mice encourage us not to be untidy' (Plutarch, De st. rep. 1044d). As befits the emphasis on methodical and teleological structuring, the pervasive imagery used to characterise the creative intelligence of nature or god is that of craftsmanship.[5]

The striking feature of the Stoic account of nature is the emphasis on adverbial attributes or its *modus operandi*: it operates methodically, consistently, in a craftsmanlike way – in sum: rationally. To live in agreement with nature means, then, to live in agreement with this rational *modus operandi* of the cosmos, or simply 'in agreement', so that one's actions and decisions in the course of one's life add up to an internally consistent, harmonious pattern, which is comparable with the rationality of a well-ordered speech: 'Orderliness must be imposed upon our actions (*ordo actionum*) in such a way that all the parts of our life, as of a speech that has internal logical consistency, are fitted to one another and in agreement (*omnia sint apta inter se et convenientia*)' (*Off.* i.144). Just as the universe at large is 'in agreement' on account of its logical consistency, so an individual life is a good one if it agrees with itself, and in so doing is in agreement with the cohesive rationality of the universe.[6] Another Stoic definition of happiness characterizes this internal consistency in terms of a flow: happiness is a 'good flow of life' (*eurhoia biou*) (DL vii.88). A characteristic aspect of the Stoic philosophy that these different definitions of happiness bring out is the interpenetration of logical, ethical and physical perspectives on rationality.[7] The logical consistency manifest in a good speech *is* the physical force of nature that arranges all existing things into a harmonious whole,

---

[5] E.g. DL vii.137, vii.148–149; Cicero, DND ii.57–58, ii.87.

[6] For further references to 'consistency' (*homologia, constantia*), see also DL vii.89; Cicero, *Academica* ii.30–31; Seneca, *Ep.* 92.3.

[7] Hence the Stoic conception of philosophy as a unity of logic, physics and ethics (e.g. Sextus Empiricus, AP vii.19).

which again *is* the consistency of a pattern of actions that makes a human life good. In all cases, consistency is what confers cohesion: in the logical sense, rationality holds together a consistent argument; in the physical sense, rationality holds together a living body or the universe; in the ethical sense, rationality holds together a human life.

Thinking of the distinction from the preceding chapter between *what* one does and *how* one does it, one ethical implication of the Stoic notion of rationality as a *modus operandi* is that *what* one does, or the type of one's actions, is of lesser importance, whereas *how* one acts, in the sense of the consistency of one's actions, as well as the disposition from which one acts, becomes all-important. This relative indifference of the type of activities is perhaps brought out most suggestively in the imagery of acting and roles. The Stoics adopted this imagery from the school of the Cynics and developed it into a sophisticated theory. The wise man is like a good actor. It does not matter what social role you play, whether that of king or beggar, and it is not up to you to choose one; what matters, and what is up to you, is your skill – how well you play the role that has been assigned to you by fate (Epictetus, *Ench.* 17). According to a later account attributed by Cicero to the Stoic scholarch Panaitios, there are some roles, such as our profession, that we can choose. But in so doing we should always make sure that our choice fits our individual natural talents and aptitudes – which again is a 'role', namely our *persona propria* – because that match is bound to promote consistency in our actions (*Off.* i.111–14), and that we avoid 'introducing any discordancy into our actions and into the whole of our lives'. Again, the most important thing is not what job one does: even if 'other pursuits may be weightier and better' (*Off.* i.110), we should primarily consider whether what we do allows us to achieve a smooth flow in our lives.

To live in such an ordered, craftsmanlike way, one needs the right craft. This craft is 'virtue' (*aretê*), sometimes also called the 'craft of living' (*technê peri ton bion*) (Sextus Empiricus, AP xi.201). Insofar as the exercise of this craft guarantees that one's actions match the cosmic patterns, living in agreement with virtue is living in agreement with nature. This follows also from the claim that living in agreement with nature means living in agreement 'with the nature of oneself' (DL vii.88). For humans, this means living in agreement with reason (*logos*); for reason is the 'end' of humans as rational animals (Seneca, *Ep.* 76.20), and virtue is the perfection of reason. The characteristic attribute of the Stoic notion of rationality is reflectivity, or, as Epictetus puts it, the capacity of 'attending' (*parakolouthein*) to one's own thoughts so that, in contrast to animals, human action is not an automatic response to external stimuli, but always results from a reflection, whether explicit or implicit, on what one ought to do and why (*Diss*. i.6.12–14). There is a close link between the rational constitution of humans and their function, one of which is to be both 'student' and 'interpreter' of god's works (ibid. i.6.16–22). This is not only a privilege of humans but also their predicament: unlike plants or animals, who infallibly do what they ought to, humans cannot but attempt to figure this out on the basis of their interpretation of the cosmos and their place in it.[8]

Stoic virtue is excellence in the thoughtful interpretation of the godly design of the world. Everything that happens is determined by the providential god, all the way down to the minute details of individual lives. Humans ought to strive to meet their fate by aligning their individual will with the will of god: if I knew that I was now fated to be ill, says Epictetus, I would even choose to be ill (*Diss*. ii.6.9). As a matter of fact, though, most humans, including sages, do not know what is going to happen, and so even sages sometimes choose to do things that later turn out not to be a part of the divine plan. What is important is that this does not make them act contrary to nature.[9] For what determines whether they live in agreement is not the type of their actions, but rather *how* they act and deliberate. The sages will always be able to provide a perfectly rational explanation of why they decided the way they did and why that was the best possible decision in the circumstances, or one that has the most plausible claim to approximate the divine plan. This explanation will be informed by their virtue, 'wisdom' (*sophia*) or 'knowledge' (*epistêmê*) – which again are synonymous terms – that is, a coherent and irrefutable set of cognitions in the three main disciplines of the Stoic philosophy, namely logic, physics and ethics.[10]

The consistency of this set of cognitions, again, matches the cosmic 'right reason' (*orthos logos*) and is continuous with it (Stob. *Ecl*. ii.66.14–67.4). The consistency of a sage's actions throughout her life results from the firmness and consistency of her cognitions. Here, again, the importance of *how*, rather than *what* one does, is affirmed. The Stoics even

---

[8] It is debated in scholarship to what extent the interpretation of nature is necessary for the acquisition of virtue; Annas (1993) is perhaps the most influential proponent of the view that core Stoic ethical doctrine stands independently of references to universal nature.

[9] This is possible because the impulses of the sage are with 'reservation' (*hupexairesis*, *exceptio*): one can avoid conflict with the will of god by making a reservation, e.g. that one pursues health with the reservation that this is what one selects unless something comes along to interfere (cf. Inwood 1985: 120; Brennan 2000).

[10] On the Stoic definitions of knowledge or wisdom, see Aetius, *Placita*, Preface 2; Stob. *Ecl*. ii.73.16–74.3. Brouwer (2014) has a comprehensive treatment of the Stoic definitions of wisdom.

say that the wise man does all that he does equally in agreement with nature, including trivial activities such as walking (Stob. *Ecl.* ii.96.18–97.5). The goodness of all wise person's actions derives from the fact that all of these actions emerge from a sage's rational disposition. The rationality of nature, too, is equally operative regardless of what nature does or makes; whether it makes a human being or a fly, its workings are always supremely rational.

In contrast to Aristotle, not only the importance of what one does but also the importance of whether one is free from external impediments is diminished. Virtue is sufficient for happiness, and hence the Stoic sage remains happy in all kinds of circumstances.[11] Even in adverse circumstances, he has the necessary 'materials' (*hulê*) – the circumstances themselves and his own psychological responses to them – to work with.[12] In this respect, wisdom should be compared not so much to crafts such as navigation and medicine but rather to acting or dancing, 'so that its end is within itself and not to be sought outside' (Cicero, *Fin.* iii.24). But some Stoics took up the challenge of accommodating the self-contained character of wisdom even within the framework of productive crafts that seek to produce an external goal. The Stoic sage does pursue some objectives in the world, but whether he actually achieves them or not has no bearing on his happiness; what matters is only how he proceeds to achieve them; again, the *modus operandi* is decisive. Human agency is like archery.[13] The archer's 'objective' (*skopos*) is to hit the 'target' (*skopos*), but his 'end' (*telos*) is to exercise his skill impeccably. The notion of 'function' (*ergon*) plays an important role in this analogy. An archer's function is to shoot well, but not necessarily to hit the target. His arrow may be diverted by a gust of wind and miss the target, but we would still rightly call him an excellent archer if he did all he could to hit the target in the given circumstances. Like Aristotle and Plato, the Stoics tie happiness tightly to the exercise of the human function: the human function is to exercise reason well, and that is what happiness amounts to. But like a perfect archer who still fulfils his function even when he misses the target, the Stoic sage remains happy even if he is deprived of some of the things he tries to obtain.

---

[11] Unless he loses his virtue in some special circumstances (DL vii.127).

[12] On reason as the 'craftsman of impulse', see DL vii.86; on the notion of indifferents as the material of virtue, see e.g. Plutarch, *De com. not.* 1039e.

[13] This analogy was attributed to Antipater. The relevant sources are Plutarch, *De com. not.* 1070f–1071e and Cicero, *Fin.* iii.22. Striker (1996) provides an enlightening discussion of the archer analogy in its dialectical context.

The analogies between virtue and craft put us in a position to appreciate the central distinction of the Stoic theory of value. On the one hand, there are things that are good or bad in the strict sense, namely virtue and vice; these are the only things that matter for happiness or unhappiness, or living in agreement with or contrary to nature. These are concerned with *how we use* all other things: if well, we are happy; if badly, we are unhappy. All other things, that is, *what we use*, are, strictly considered, indifferent (*adiaphora*); they make no difference for happiness or unhappiness. To this category belong also the preferable things, such as health, wealth or reputation, and their opposites. This distinction goes back to Plato's notion of the right use from the *Euthydemus*: only wisdom is intrinsically good, because it always benefits; and only ignorance is intrinsically bad, because it always harms. The Stoics subscribe to this view (DL vii.103).

This sharp distinction between virtue as the only good and all other things as indifferent raises the question what legitimate motivation one could have to pursue one action rather than another. For whether the wise person counts how many hairs she has on her head or whether she saves another person's life, her action is equally virtuous. But this cannot possibly mean that she cannot have non-arbitrary reasons to choose the latter over the former. If these choices were arbitrary, it would be difficult to see how they could be instantiations of rational agency; for it is characteristic of rationality that it *compels* us to make certain specific choices rather than others. So it is necessary to draw some non-arbitrary, action-guiding distinctions of value even within the realm of indifferent things; otherwise, 'all life would be made completely undiscriminated, and no task for wisdom would be found' (Cicero, *Fin.* iii.50), just as there would be nothing for the archer to do if he were without a target to shoot at. To this end, the Stoics distinguish between different kinds of indifferent things, most importantly between those that 'activate neither impulse nor repulsion', such as 'having an odd or even number of hairs on one's head' (DL vii.104), and those that do activate impulse or repulsion, such as 'life, health, pleasure, beauty, strength, wealth, reputation, noble birth and their opposites, death, disease, pain, ugliness, weakness, poverty, low repute, ignoble birth and the like' (DL vii.101–102). Whereas we do not have any preferences as regards the former, and cannot give good reasons to justify our choices thereof, for the latter we typically do have preferences and can justify our choices. These things are neither good nor bad in the strict sense, but they have some genuine positive or negative 'value' (*axia*) (Stob. *Ecl.* ii. 83.10–84.2).

Now, some sources identify things which have this sort of selective value with 'things in accordance with nature' (*ta kata phusin; secundum naturam*) (*Ecl.* ii. 83.10–11; *Fin.* iii.20). This raises the question whether 'preferred indifferents' are to be identified with 'things in accordance with nature'. It has been suggested that the former might be understood as a subset of the latter (Barney 2003: 333), but this distinction is nowhere made explicit in the sources, and in fact some passages strongly imply the identity (e.g. *Fin.* iii.60). In the meantime, I shall treat the terms as synonyms and return to the rationale for this distinction in the next section.

The category of things in accordance with nature plays a crucial role in identifying certain actions as preferable to others. Once we know what things are in accordance with nature, we can recognise which actions are appropriate for us to take. In the Stoic theory, all our choices and actions ought to fall into the category of the so-called appropriate actions (*kathêkonta; officia*), that is, actions that possess or display 'consequentiality in life' and 'have a well-reasoned (*eulogos*) justification' (Stob. *Ecl.* ii. 85.13–14). The appropriate actions are those that accord with one's natural constitution, and all living things, including plants, have appropriate functions to perform (DL vii.107). The Stoics maintain that 'every animal, as soon as it is born (for this should be our starting point), has an affinity to itself and is inclined to preserve itself and its constitution' (Cicero, *Fin.* iii.16, transl. Inwood and Gerson). This appears to be a fairly uncontroversial descriptive claim that the Stoics support with empirical observations of newborn humans, but it also has a normative force: this is how all animals – including humans – are constituted by nature, and this is what they are supposed to do; all appropriate actions are 'activities appropriate to constitutions that accord with nature' (DL vii.107), and 'to preserve oneself in one's natural constitution' is the 'first' among appropriate actions (Cicero, *Fin.* iii.20; cf. DL vii.85), or the 'starting point' (*principium, archê*) (*Fin.* iii.16). Thus, actions aimed at self-preservation are usually appropriate because self-preservation is a naturally preferred (but indifferent) thing, or a thing in accordance with nature. Given that the natural constitutions of humans are more complex than those of plants, the actions appropriate for humans will also be more diverse and complex, ranging from the instinctive care for self-preservation to living up to one's social commitments, such as 'honouring country' or 'spending time with friends' (DL vii.108–9).

In the ideal case the human development towards rational perfection does not end at the stage of doing appropriate actions. When we reach the point that the selection of preferred indifferents comes to be 'consistent' (*constans*), it happens that the real good – virtue – 'comes to be present in man for the first time' (*Fin.* iii.20–21). Thus, the necessary corollary of this consistent conduct is a fundamental shift in the evaluative attitude: once someone 'has seen the regularity and, so to speak, the harmony of conduct, he comes to value this far higher than all those objects of his initial affection' (ibid.). As a good interpreter of god's works as they manifest themselves in his own conduct, this person from now on 'draws the conclusion' that it is the harmonious pattern of his own actions that is 'the only thing desirable through its intrinsic nature and value' (*solum vi sua et dignitate expetendum est*) (ibid.) But this evaluative shift does not entail that the preferred indifferents no longer have their value; even though the supreme value is now seen in the *way* one selects preferred indifferents, that is, in the ideal case, from a firm rational disposition, the value of preferred indifferents remains crucial for informing these selections. The point is well made by Seneca:

> The point might be made, 'If good health, rest, and freedom from pain are not going to thwart virtue, will you not pursue them?' Of course I will. Not because they are good, but because they are in accordance with nature, and because they will be taken on the basis of my good judgement. 'What then will be good in them?' Just this – being well selected (*bene eligi*). For when I put on the right sort of clothes, or walk as I should, or dine as I should, neither the dining nor the walking nor the clothes are good, but the intention (*propositum*) I display in them by preserving a measure, in each thing, which conforms to reason … So it is not elegant clothes which are a good in themselves, but the selection of elegant clothes, since the good is not in the thing but in the quality of the selection (*non in re bonum est sed in electione quali*). It is our actions that are right, not their results. (Seneca, *Ep.* 92.11–12)

In fact, it seems to be the Stoic position not only that preferred indifferents are important objects of our selections, but also that they are the *only* object. Virtue is the rational disposition *from* which one chooses, and hence it cannot ever become the content of choice; it is rather a purely 'formal' condition (Cooper 1989: 534). Since everything besides virtue and vice is indifferent, it is only the special status of preferred indifferents that can justify rational actions.

The idea that there are things indifferent for happiness and yet genuinely worth pursuing was a target of considerable criticism in antiquity.[14] Surely, if these things are not to be wholly indifferent, the Stoics must either make them components of happiness, or instrumental to happiness,

---

[14] Plutarch, *De com. not.* 1070f–1071e; Cicero, *Fin.* v.17–20.

or else concede that there are in fact two parallel ends of human life that correspond to happiness and worthwhileness as two different ways of doing well. What underscores the inescapability of this dilemma, it has been argued, is the sheer implausibility of the attempt to integrate the value of preferred indifferents by an inversion of the natural means–end relationship. To say that our happiness lies in doing everything in our power to secure things that are ultimately indifferent is like saying that a doctor does not prescribe drugs for the sake of making his patient healthy, but that he aims to make his patient healthy for the sake of prescribing drugs (Plutarch, *De com. not.* 1071d–e). 'Operation successful, patient dies' is the joke that comes to mind.

Recent commentators have been more sympathetic to the Stoic position. On the prevailing interpretation of the relationship between virtue and promoted indifferents, the Stoics posit a kind of axiological dualism, or two incommensurable realms of non-instrumental value.[15] Unlike Plato in the *Euthydemus*, then, the Stoics maintain that while the preferred indifferents are not unconditionally beneficial, they are to be selected for their own sake. Preferred indifferents are non-instrumentally valuable because they are in accordance with our natural constitution; virtue is non-instrumentally valuable because it is the perfection of our natural constitution. But the preferred indifferents are not on a par with virtue; they have a sub-ordinate axiological standing.[16] The majority view in the scholarship has been that the postulate of two different levels of non-instrumental value is not necessarily inconsistent. An attractive way to understand how these two levels hang together is the paradigm of games, which is prominent in some Stoic sources.[17] It is quite plausible to say that the end of playing a game of chess is to play well, or to have a good time playing the game, rather than to win. And yet winning, too, is also a non-instrumental objective;

---

[15] In the sense that they have a final value, i.e. are worth selecting for their own sake (*di'hauta*; DL vii.107). It has been common in the scholarship to refer to this value as 'intrinsic', or as interchangeable with 'non-instrumental' (cf. Klein 2015: 245–258). If we observe the distinction between non-instrumental and intrinsic value (cf. Section I.3), it seems more accurate to talk about 'non-instrumental' rather than 'intrinsic' value. For only virtue always benefits, and is thus intrinsically or unconditionally good, whereas preferred indifferents may in some circumstances be disadvantageous (DL vii.103; Sextus Empiricus, AP xi.64–7).

[16] Versions of this general interpretive outlook have been defended, for instance, by Inwood (1985: 208–210); Long and Sedley (1987: 357–359); Annas (1996: 241); or Vogt (2014). Other interpretations of the relationship between the two axiological realms, such as that preferred indifferents are commensurate with or are parts of happiness, or that they are instrumentally valuable for virtue (e.g. Frede 1999: 92; Lesses 1989), are suggested by some pieces of evidence but both face serious difficulties (cf. Klein 2015).

[17] Epictetus, *Diss.* ii.5; Seneca, *De beneficiis* ii.17.3–5; ii.32.

we do not say that we try to win merely for the sake of playing. In fact, we have to be seriously committed to the prospect of winning if we are to be serious players.[18]

While postulating two orders of non-instrumental value may in itself not necessarily lead to an incoherent ethical theory, there is a further important problem related to the role and scope of preferred indifferents. In accordance with their account of human development, in the course of which the perspective of what is beneficial for me as an individual comes to be extended to the larger perspective of the city and the cosmos, some Stoic sources imply that what is sometimes required from a fully developed humans is to fulfil certain social obligations, such as to sacrifice one's life to save another person. The question is whether such actions can be parsed and justified in terms of the maximisation of preferred indifferents. In what sense can a decision to die on behalf of a friend or one's country be cashed out in terms of pursuing what is conducive to preserving oneself in a natural constitution?

Broadly, there are two lines of response.[19] One is what has been called a 'dualist model' of rational deliberation (Barney 2003: 330 ff.), on which both the 'good' or 'virtue' and the preferred indifferents enter into deliberation. In Cicero's *On Duties* we read that, according to the Stoics, one is 'always to conform to virtue, and as for the other things which are according to nature, to select them if they do not conflict with virtue' (*Off.* iii.13). This suggests that good is on the line, certainly not as a competitor of preferred indifferents but as an overriding constraint on their pursuit: while we should do everything in our power to obtain the preferred indifferents, if this pursuit conflicts with virtue, we should forgo them.[20] On an alternative view, which we can call a 'monist model', different kinds of moral constraints can be exhaustively parsed in terms of certain 'arrangements of indifferents' (Brennan 2005: 210).[21] So, for instance, the reason I do not

---

[18] Cf. Barney (2003: 316–317); Striker (1996). But both these interpretations see other important problems in the Stoic theory.

[19] Not all scholars of Stoicism have thought that it is useful to frame the issue in terms of the monist vs. dualist model of deliberation. For one, Chris Gill has expressed his reservations to me in an e-mail communication, and frames the discussion differently in Gill (forthcoming).

[20] Inwood (2017); Annas (1993: 171); Bonhöffer (1996: 43).

[21] More precisely, Brennan (2005) presents his 'no-shoving' account of the Stoic deliberation as a better alternative to a radically monist 'indifferents-only' model and to the 'dualist' model: similarly to the latter, the 'no-shoving' model consists of a two-tier deliberation but, similarly to the latter, both tiers operate with a single axiological currency, that is, things in accordance with nature. (For a similar though unendorsed version of this account, cf. Barney 2003: 332–336.) So there are at least two slightly different versions of the 'monist' model.

snatch the property of others is not that such an action would be inherently unjust, and thus vicious, but that it would jeopardise social conventions and institutions that do not have the status of the good but that are still naturally preferred or, perhaps better, are in accordance with nature, because they are indispensable for the well-being of all citizens, including myself. This account rests on the view that even these other-regarding actions can be ultimately understood as extensions of the fundamental natural instinct for self-preservation.

The puzzle about the status of moral consideration within the Stoic ethics comes to the fore with urgency in Stoic discussions about the appropriateness of suicide. On the one hand, we have important evidence that construes the deliberation about departing from life very clearly in terms of the monist model; on the other, some accounts of Stoic self-sacrifice imply the dualist model. Should we conclude that each model is engaged to explain a different kind of suicide, one aimed at a prudential exit from an unsatisfactory life, and another one concerned with a morally motivated sacrifice? If so, is the Stoic theory of action consistent? In the following discussion, I shall support the monist model as a default theory; this is also able to accommodate the morally charged cases of self-sacrifice.

3.3   Life Worth Continuing

We have seen the Stoics denying that the virtue or vice of the person whose life is under consideration ought to play any role in deliberations about her suicide; rather, what is decisive is the quality of life understood in terms of the preferred indifferents and their opposites. This view can now be further explored and justified. The appropriate starting point is an important passage from the third book of Cicero's *On Ends*. The context of this passage is a discussion of the role of preferred indifferents in the determination of appropriate actions. The deliberation about when it is right to depart from life is a special case of deliberation about appropriate actions. Since appropriate actions are generally justified with regard to the preferred indifferents that they promote, it comes as no surprise that the deliberation about suicide will also 'proceed' from considerations pertaining to preferred indifferents and their opposites (iii.60). This claim is explicated as follows:

> It is the appropriate action to live (*officium est in vita manere*) when most of what one has is in accordance with nature (*plura sunt quae secundum natura sunt*). When the opposite is the case, or is envisaged to be so, then the appropriate action is to depart from life. This shows that it is sometimes the appropriate action for the wise person to depart from life though happy,

and the fool to remain in it though miserable. Stoic good and evil, which I have now often mentioned, is a subsequent development. But the primary objects of nature, whether they are in accordance with it or against, fall under the judgement of the wise person, and are as it were the subject and material of wisdom.

Thus the whole rationale for either remaining in or departing from life is to be measured by reference to those intermediates that I mentioned above (*omnis iis rebus metienda*). One who is endowed with virtue need not be detained in life, nor need those without virtue seek death. Often the appropriate action for a wise person will be to depart from life when utterly happy, if this can be done in a timely way (*si id oportune facere possit*). The Stoics hold that living happily – that is, living in harmony with nature – is a matter of timeliness. And so the wise person is instructed by wisdom to relinquish wisdom herself, if it is opportune. No vice, then, is potent enough to give a good reason for killing oneself. So evidently, even the foolish, despite being unhappy, will act appropriately by remaining alive, so long as they have a preponderance of what we call things in accordance with nature (*si sint in maiore parte rerum earum, quas secundum naturam esse dicimus*). The fool is equally unhappy dead or alive – prolongation does not make his life more undesirable. So there is good reason for the view that one who can enjoy a balance of natural advantages (*pluribus naturalibus frui possint*) should stay alive. (*Fin.* iii.60–61)

This account unequivocally testifies in favour of the monist model of moral deliberation. In establishing whether staying alive is an appropriate action, the balance of preferred and dispreferred indifferents, both present and expected, should be the sole criterion. For both sages and non-sages, there is a right time to depart, and this time comes when one's present and future life is (likely) not worth living. The threshold of life worth living is a 'preponderance' (*plura; in maiore parte*) of naturally preferred things over their opposites. On the one hand, this implies that, strictly considered, having an exactly equal balance of preferred and dispreferred things is not sufficient to clear the threshold; the preferred things should be in the majority. On the other hand, given the absence of any further qualification about the extent of this preponderance, it seems that life is at least barely worth living if the preferred things at least barely outweigh their opposites. Neither here nor elsewhere are we given a more detailed account of the principles of this weighing or measurement, including how much weight each of the preferred or dispreferred indifferents brings on balance. But some accounts of these deliberations, some of which we shall shortly consider, do indicate, quite common-sensically, that bodily health or freedom from pain are especially potent considerations and that their absence can possibly outweigh having other preferred indifferents, including wealth.

The argument for the view that virtue does not play any role in the determination of life worth living is that the sages will not be any less happy if they die earlier, and the non-sages will not be any more unhappy if they live longer. This follows from the thesis that goodness and badness generally do not allow for gradation or increase; and hence 'a happy life is no more desirable or worth seeking if long than if short' (*Fin.* iii.45–46). Life is neither virtue nor vice, and hence it must be an indifferent thing; indeed, it is a preferred indifferent, as we shall see in Section 3.5. Insofar as indifferents generally allow for increase, life can be accumulated, and that is why it is possible – and potentially meaningful – to choose to have more of it: health is the more preferred the longer it lasts (ibid. iii.47), and so is life. For this reason, worthwhileness of life is also subject to degrees: if worthwhileness depends on the balance of preferred and dispreferred indifferents that themselves come in degrees, then staying alive can be more or less worthwhile. The threshold is a barely positive balance of preferred indifferents over dispreferred indifferents. But, of course, it should be possible to clear the threshold with a greater or smaller margin, and in that sense we could say that life can be worth living to a greater or lesser degree.

Some ancient critics of Stoicism mocked this position: surely, it is wholly misguided to say that virtue and vice, which on the Stoic view are the only things that are truly beneficial and harmful, should not be taken into account in deciding the momentous question whether my continued existence is good for me. But the Stoic position is in fact compelling if we take into account their view about the value of the things that are being deliberated about, that is, life and death (see Cooper 1999: 534–6). Life and death are themselves indifferent, and hence neither beneficial nor harmful (DL vii.102–3); it stands to reason, then, that the question of choosing life or death should be decided on the basis of those other things that fall into the same category, namely preferred and dispreferred indifferents. Were one to insist that virtue should play a major role in this deliberation, virtue would either have to be degraded, as it would become a measure of indifferent things, or life *per se* would have to be accorded a higher order of value than it deserves. Either way, the sharp axiological divide between the good and indifferent things would be compromised. Also, the picture from Cicero accords with the Stoic view that the appropriate actions are defined by their capacity to promote preferred indifferents or avoid their opposites. So whether or not voluntary departure from life is timely, and hence an instance of appropriate action, should depend on the estimation of to what extent a continued existence will be filled by preferred indifferents or by their opposites.

What complicates this picture is other important evidence that gives the impression that the deliberation about suicide cannot be adequately captured by the accountancy balance sheet model of preferred and dispreferred indifferents. In his *Commentary on the Phaedo* (i.8.4), the Neoplatonist commentator Olympiodorus reports five legitimate Stoic reasons to commit suicide. As Miriam Griffin has correctly noted (1986: 73), only three of these – serious bodily incapacitation, poverty and 'madness' (as a psychological condition deriving from the body)[22] – can be neatly explained in terms of the standard list of preferred and dispreferred indifferents. Two remaining reasons for choosing death – being compelled to do or say shameful things, and being obliged to die for the sake of one's city – can be less straightforwardly explained in these terms. In a similar spirit, Diogenes Laertius (vii.130) reports that the wise man will depart from life for the sake of his country or friends if he has a good reason to do so. In general, cases of heroic death for the sake of noble ends, well attested by several sources and obviously favoured by the Stoics, might suggest that the account from *On Ends* does not give us the 'full picture' of Stoic deliberations about suicide (Long 2019: 199).[23] For the heroic decisions do not easily lend themselves to be parsed in terms of the balance sheet model. The deliberation about staying alive also has to take into account one's commitments and obligations towards other human beings: friends and family, as well as the larger community of fellow citizens. This raises the question whether the Stoics regarded these obligations as higher-order categorical constraints on the pursuit of preferred indifferents. On the basis of the preferred indifferents alone, it may seem appropriate to depart from life, or to carry on living; but some interfering, other-regarding commitments may override and reverse this decision. On this view, the worthwhileness of continued existence cannot be the sole criterion for decisions about staying alive.[24] This speaks in favour of the dualist model of deliberation.

Let me review more closely two pieces of evidence pointing in that direction, one from Cicero and one from Seneca, that exemplify well the role of social obligations in assessing whether life is worth continuing. In both these cases, a failure to live up (or to 'die up', as it were) to these

---

[22] Cf. Long (2019: 199), n. 52.

[23] A. G. Long also has a useful discussion of the political reasons that may have motivated Cicero to avoid discussing heroic cases of suicide (Long 2019: 198).

[24] Some commentators have suggested that in acknowledging the weight of these moral obligations, Stoics were deontologists and ancient predecessors of the Kantian ethics; for a recent account along these lines, see Visnjic (2021).

obligations is presented as a violation of virtues such as justice or courage. Given the balance of preferred and dispreferred indifferents, it might be beneficial for you to die (or to stay alive), but making that choice would be vicious, given your duties, and so you cannot but do the opposite. This recalls the idea of virtue as the overriding categorical constraint on the pursuit of preferred indifferents: you should pursue them as long as that pursuit does not compromise virtue.[25]

The first example is Seneca's explanation of his decision to move to the countryside in order to take care of his health. He justifies this decision by commitments to his wife, Paulina. Besides offering a helpful perspective on the role of virtue in his deliberations, this passage is a useful reminder that not only departing from life, but also staying alive, was in some circumstances regarded as an equally courageous deed. Under some circumstances, it may be 'thoroughly self-indulgent' to hasten one's exit:

> I told this to Paulina. She is very anxious about my health. In fact, realizing that her soul is completely bound up with mine (*sciam spiritum illius in meo verti*), I am beginning, in my concern for her, to be concerned about myself. ... One has to give in, you see, to honorable feelings. There are times when, to honor a family member (*in honorem suorum*), one has to summon back one's dying breath, however painfully, and actually hold it in one's mouth. A good man should live not as long as it pleases him but as long as he ought to. The person who does not think enough of his wife or his friend to prolong his life – who insists on dying – is thoroughly self-indulgent (*delicatus*). When the interest of loved ones demands it, the mind should require even this of itself: even if one not only wants to die but has actually begun to do so, one should interrupt the process and give oneself over to their needs. Returning to life for another's sake is the mark of a lofty spirit, as great men have often done. But, in addition, I think it is supremely kind to be especially careful of your old age if you are aware that such behavior is pleasing, useful, and desirable to any of your loved ones, highly enjoyable though it is at that time to be more relaxed about one's survival and more daring in one's manner of living. Besides, such self-care brings with it great joy and rewards, for what can be more delightful than being so dear to your wife that you consequently become dearer to yourself? And so my Paulina succeeds in burdening me not only with her fears but also with my own. (*Ep.* 104.2–5)

---

[25] We should note, though, that for the Stoics all actions done by non-sages are vicious and all actions done by sages are virtuous. It makes no sense for a Stoic to say 'you must fulfil your duty lest you act viciously'; for even if you make the right choice and fulfil your duty, your action will be appropriate but still vicious, if you are not a sage. So it is more precise to say that the price of making the wrong choice would be to commit to an inappropriate action, action that arises from rational flaws characteristic of vicious humans.

Here is one possible reading of this passage. Given the worthwhileness of Seneca's own continued existence, the balance envisaged may well seem to be in favour of choosing death. But there are considerations pertaining to Seneca's obligations to his loved ones, and these considerations prevail. In fact, it would be vicious – perhaps cowardly – not to live up to these obligations, whereas honouring them would be an act of courage.[26] So the duty takes the upper hand: one ought to carry on living even though continued existence is not worthwhile.

The second case I wish to consider is the story of Marcus Atilius Regulus, a Roman consul captured by the Carthaginians, discussed by Cicero in the third book of *On Duties*. Regulus was released, having sworn that he would return unless some Carthaginians captives were restored by the Romans. Upon his return to Rome, he persuaded the Senate that it was not advantageous for Romans to restore the captives, and yet he maintained that he should still keep his oath and therefore returned to Carthage, certain that he would meet a painful death. Thus, he gave up great benefits in order to keep his oath and therefore act justly. So, in this case, virtue seems to be, again, the overriding constraint on the pursuit of preferred indifferents. A continued existence back in Rome would be worthwhile, from the perspective of the naturally preferred things, but ultimately ought not to be chosen because it would compromise virtue:

> It was this: to remain in his own country, to be at home with his wife and children, to maintain his rank and standing as an ex-consul, counting the disaster that had befallen him in war as common to the fortune of warfare. Who can deny that such things are beneficial? Whom do you think? Greatness of spirit and courage can deny it. Surely you are not seeking authorities still more reliable? For it is characteristic of these virtues to fear nothing, to disdain everything human, and to think nothing that can happen to a man unendurable. (*Off.* iii.99–100)

In contrast to the passage from Seneca, what ought to be chosen now is death not life. But the deliberative set-up is similar: the prospect of a worthwhile continued existence is overridden by imperatives of virtue, specifically 'courage' and 'greatness of the spirit'. Insofar as Regulus actually embodies these virtues, he decides without hesitation to give up his life in order to act justly.

---

[26] This is also strongly implied in a similar passage where Seneca justifies staying alive by his commitments to his father: 'More than once I entertained an impulse to end my life; but my father was elderly, and that held me back. For although I thought that I could die bravely, I also thought that he, who was so kind to me, could not bravely bear the loss. So I commanded myself to live; for there are times when just continuing to live is a courageous action' (*Ep.* 78.1–2). For useful interpretations of these and other passages in the context of later Stoics views about the self, see Reydams-Schils (2005: 45–52).

How far these cases actually depart from the balance sheet model from the third book of *On Ends*? There are two considerations that make this shift less dramatic than it may seem. First, Cicero repeats over and over again in *On Duties*, reporting the Stoic theory of Panaitios and Hecaton, that the 'honourable' and the 'beneficial' must not be understood in terms of two competing axiological realms; rather, we learn that Hecaton 'in the end measures duty by what is beneficial, rather than by humanity' (*utilitate officium dirigit magis quam humanitate*) (*Off.* iii.89). This hardly comes as a surprise, given that appropriate actions have been defined in terms of promoting the acquisition of naturally preferred indifferents. Secondly, the Stoics were committed to the theory of the unity of the virtues, and even argued that different virtues are only different aspects or perspectives of a single virtue.[27] So, according to one source, all virtues, including courage, are different aspects of wisdom (Plutarch, *De st. rep.* 1034c–e); if that is so, and if wisdom is concerned with deliberation with regard to preferred and dispreferred indifferents (Stob. *Ecl.* ii.59.4–60. 2), it follows that Regulus' courage entails, and is informed by, an excellent deliberation about the consequences of his action.

Thus, with further qualifications, the balance sheet account actually does give us full picture. This account does not have to be transcended or supplemented by another model of deliberation. Rather, we have to appreciate that the preferred and dispreferred indifferents that determine the worth of my continued existence are not to be understood in the overtly narrow, utilitarian sense limited to my staying healthy or my being free from pain. The category of what is naturally preferred extends to the life and well-being of other persons that belong, as it were, to my extended self. It is in this context that the suggestion to regard 'preferred indifferents' as a subset of a broader notion of 'things in accordance with nature' has its appeal. While it is difficult to see how the value of self-sacrificing actions such as dying for one's country is comparable to the prudential value of health or wealth, it is easier to imagine how these heroic actions may count as actions 'in accordance with nature'. Humans are, in their nature, social animals, and thus bound to value highly their relationships to other humans or communities of which they are a part. That is not to say, of course, that the preservation of one's country is a good; it still remains an indifferent thing, but it has a selective value that exceeds, in Regulus' case, the cumulative selective disvalue of dispreferred indifferents, such as the loss of life or physical suffering due to torture.

---

[27] Stob. *Ecl.* ii.63.6–24; Plutarch, *De virt. mor.* 440e–441d.

The Stoics do not contrast the motivation for narrowly self-regarding action, such as caring for one's health, with the motivation for other-regarding actions such as dying for one's country. Other-regarding concerns are as instinctively natural to us as is the 'first impulse' (*hormê prôtê*) of humans and animals, that is, their 'self-preservation' (DL vii.85). These concerns manifest, typically, in the ingrained disposition to care for one's offspring: 'We have an appropriate disposition relative to ourselves as soon as we are born and to our parts (*merê*) and to our offspring.' (Plutarch, *De st. rep.* 1038b). The claim cannot be, of course, that babies actually feel concern for their offsprings, but rather that this concern is already a latent part of the self-preservation impulse which naturally extends to our 'parts', presumably the parts of the body, as well as to offsprings which are, as it were, extended parts of our minds and bodies. All other-regarding actions, including the heroic deeds of self-sacrifice, should be regarded as further extensions of this caretaking instinct (Cicero, *Fin.* iii.62), and thus, ultimately, of the impulse for self-preservation. Important supporting evidence for the view that other-regarding concerns are natural extensions of the primary impulse for self-preservation is the account of Hierocles (Stob. *Ecl.* iv.671.7–673.11), which envisages the human self in terms of concentric circles with one's mind at the centre. The achievement of fully developed humans is that they can 'reduce the distance' between the circles, so that, for instance, they care about their more distant relatives (cousins, aunts) as if they were their close relatives (brothers, mother). When a Stoic sacrifices the prospect of a worthwhile life for his country, he is not sacrificing his personal benefit for the sake of an impersonal good; rather, he extends the notion of his personal benefit, properly understood, to the benefit of his city, where this communal welfare is nonetheless still one among other preferred indifferents.[28]

The Stoic notion of 'roles' (*prosôpa*; *personae*) mentioned in the preceding section offers further support for this view. Stoics such as Panaitios or Epictetus often justify appropriate actions by reference to doing what befits one's roles. We have mentioned the peculiar 'role' of your individual character, as defined by a specific set of natural aptitudes. Cicero tells us that the reason why it was appropriate for Cato to commit suicide was that it befitted the 'seriousness' (*gravitas*) of his individual character but that the same course of action would not have been appropriate for some more

---

[28] Regulus justifies his decision not only by appeals to his duties but also on the grounds that 'it was not beneficial to restore the captives: for they were young men and good leaders while he was worn out by old age' (*Off.* iii.100).

'easy-going' (*mores faciliores*) natures (*Off.* i.112). There is an obvious agreement here between doing what is good for you, because it fits your nature, and doing what you ought to do from a moral point of view. But this agreement is also preserved when we move to other, explicitly social roles that imply moral obligations: a brother, a citizen, or, most importantly, a human being (Epictetus, *Diss.* ii.10). If you are a brother or a human, you have to honour these roles by acting like a good brother or a good human. If you fail to live up to these roles, you are not only doing something inappropriate by violating them: you are also harming yourself, insofar as you are a brother or a human being; you are not living up to who you are. So, just as it is at once morally appropriate and good for you to follow your individual nature, it is equally morally appropriate and good for you to do what your social roles require you to do.

The aspects of natural value that go beyond the value of one's own health or wealth, but are still sharply distinguished from the virtue or the good, lend themselves well to the concept of 'meaningfulness'. It is meaningful for Seneca to stay alive for the sake of his wife; it is meaningful for Regulus to sacrifice his life for the sake of his country. But if the value of these actions is axiologically commensurable with the value of health or wealth, then meaningfulness cannot ever conflict with life's worthwhileness but is rather one of its criteria. Staying alive out of his love for his wife is what makes Seneca's continued existence meaningful, but that is also what makes it worth living, all things considered. Dying for the sake of his country makes Regulus' death meaningful, but that is also what makes a continued existence not worthwhile. In both these cases, meaningfulness is the decisive factor for assessing life's worthwhileness; but the value of meaningfulness outweighs, rather than overrides, the value of other preferred and dispreferred indifferents that are on the line in this deliberation.

It might be instructive at this point to consider a thought experiment attributed by Cicero to Hecaton of two drowning sailors, both of them wise men, who decide that they will leave the plank to the one 'whose life most matters for his own or the republic's sake' (*cuius magis intersit vel sua vel rei publicae causa vivere*) (*Off.* iii.90). In this case, deliberation about whether I should stay alive will consider both the worthwhileness of my own continued existence as well as that of the other person. In fact, the worthwhileness of my own future life will depend on an assessment of its value in comparison to the value of other person's life, and meaningfulness is bound to play a decisive role. If my life is comparatively meaningless – for example, if I am childless and do not make any significant civic contribution – while the life of the other person is comparatively meaningful – for example, he has a family, supports a wide circle of friends and excels in his profession – his life will likely be more worthwhile than mine and I should cede him the plank. The situation will be even more clear-cut if I happen to be old and have a life-threatening illness, whereas the other person is young and healthy. In this situation, my own continued existence is clearly less worthwhile, all things considered. Note that all value considerations that enter into this deliberation fall into the category of what is beneficial in the sense of being naturally preferred but ultimately indifferent. But this also means that the differences between the value of any two lives can be cashed out as differences in the capacity of these lives to generate appropriate actions. Given that the other person has family and political office, and can be expected to live longer, he is bound to be in a position to accomplish in his remaining life more appropriate actions, or more significant appropriate actions, than me, and his death would entail the loss of a greater number or appropriate actions than mine. But if I were the one whose future life has a greater value, it would be legitimate – in fact, appropriate – to keep the plank for myself and let the other person drown.

Let us revisit, from the vantage point of this interpretation, the case of Seneca's deliberation discussed earlier. On this view, it is not the case that I stay alive for the sake of a higher-order moral duty, even though my life is not worthwhile, but rather because fulfilling that duty makes my life meaningful, and thus worthwhile, from my personal point of view. Given the close relationship between him and his wife, it is easy to see in Seneca's case why the commitments to his wife translate into the pursuit of his own benefit. Paulina's soul is 'completely bound up' with Seneca's, which entails a twofold predicament: on the one hand, the emotional load is doubled, since all emotions are shared; on the other, the bond with his wife strengthens Seneca's relationship with his own self – by being dear to his wife, as he says, he becomes dearer to himself. The close bond makes it impossible for Seneca not to consider the well-being of his wife along with his own; indeed, her own health becomes a matter of his own health, the interest of his loved ones becomes his own interest. In trying to make her life more worthwhile, his own life becomes more worthwhile. So what may appear as a purely moral demand to support Paulina's continued existence can be interpreted as a prudential demand to give due weight to those promoted indifferents that concern others.

The deliberation about the worth of continued existence can be extremely complex. Let me conclude this section with an experimental speculation about how a Stoic would deliberate in such more complex cases. Imagine that you have an incurable illness which has wholly incapacitated you physically, will soon incapacitate you mentally and will kill you in about two to three years. But you have a wife who is ready to give up her job so that she can take care of you full time. If you were a Stoic, should you choose to depart from life now? The answer depends on whether your continued existence would be worthwhile, all things considered. Things to be considered concern, first, your own person. These include not only the disvalue of living in pain, being ill or the resulting incapacity to do many appropriate actions, such as washing yourself. What you also need to take into account are considerations pertaining to your roles: first, whether your individual character is by nature tough enough so that it is befitting to choose suicide; secondly, whether departing from life will contribute positively to the way you enact your social role, in particular whether it will make you a better or a worse husband. By extension, you have to consider the implications of your decision for the life of your wife and her roles. Is she naturally such that she is well disposed to take care of someone seriously ill? Will your continued existence help her to enact appropriately her role of a wife? Finally, there are considerations having to do with the implications of your decisions for society at large. What are the economic costs of the healthcare that you will need? And what about the job that your wife will give up? What is the value of her professional contribution to the society and how easily can she be replaced?

I have argued that the positive and negative value inherent in all these very diverse considerations can, in principle at least, be cashed out and weighed in terms of a single axiological currency, namely the value of indifferent things that are in accordance with nature, and their opposites. By comparing the total positive with the total negative value, I can arrive at the net worth of my continued existence: if it is positive, life is worth continuing for me; if it is negative, life is not worth continuing for me. We are still in the territory of the balance sheet, but the items that enter the sheet are much more diverse than the suicide passage from the third book of *On Ends* might suggest. None of these considerations corresponds to a higher order of value that could override the value of any of the others, but some of them carry considerably more selective value than others. What we need – something that we do not really find in the extant sources – is a manual for how these different considerations should be weighed comparatively. Imagine that your wife would be firmly committed to the view that she cannot live up to her role of wife unless she devotedly takes care of you until you die, in which case you cannot do justice to your role of a husband if you do not let her enact this role. In this case, we would need to know how the amount of the natural disvalue inherent in living in pain compares with the amount of the natural value of being able to fulfil your role of the husband. A more detailed account along these lines is what we would require from a fully developed Stoic or neo-Stoic theory of the worth of continued existence.

3.4   Life Worth Beginning

While the Stoics were chiefly concerned with life worth living from the perspective of the worth of continued existence, there is one interesting passage among the extant texts that explicitly bears on the question of whether it is worth being born in the first place. It comes from Seneca's *Consolation to Marcia*, a text addressed to a daughter of a prominent Roman historian who is mourning the death of her son. Surely, losing a son is sad, but it is one of the many hardships that belong to the 'common lot of mortals'. We were born to 'lose others, to be lost, to fear ... and worst of all, never to know what our real position is' (*Ad Marciam* xvii). But we should not blame anyone for having to suffer these hardships, because they belong to the terms and conditions that we, or rather our parents, agreed to before they brought us into life. Seneca draws a parallel between choosing to enter life and choosing to visit a tourist destination. When you deliberate about whether to undertake a journey to Syracuse, you ought to take into account all the advantages and disadvantages, and on that basis make an informed decision. If you decide to go and later regret this decision, you can only blame yourself, for you knew, or ought to have known, the terms beforehand. This also applies to choosing life:

> Suppose that I am similarly advising you as you are about to be born. You are about to enter a city shared by gods and men, all-embracing, bound by definite and eternal laws, revolving with the tireless duties of the heavenly bodies. There you will see stars without number shining, you will see everything filled with the light of a single star, the sun which marks with its daily course the intervals of day and night and divides more evenly with its annual course summers and winters. You will see the nightly progress of the moon, borrowing from meetings with her brother a gentle and diminished light, alternately hidden and visible all around the world, changing as it waxes and wanes, constantly unlike its most recent self.
>
> ...
>
> You will see nothing untried by human courage and you will yourself be both spectator and a significant part of the endeavour: you will learn and teach the arts, some of which provide for life, others of which adorn it, others of which govern it.

But there will also be a thousand plagues for body and soul: wars, pillaging, poison, shipwrecks, bad weather, and the bitter longing for one's loved ones – and their deaths, perhaps easy deaths and perhaps bound up with pain and suffering. Think about it and ponder what you want: to get to your goal this is the path you must depart on.

You will answer that you want to live (*respondebis velle te vivere*). Of course you will. In fact, in my opinion, you will not go after anything that you would grieve about if part of it were taken away. So, live in accordance with the agreement. You say, 'nobody asked my opinion'. Well, our parents gave their opinion for us when, after learning the conditions of life, they accepted us into life. (*Ad Marciam* xviii, transl. Inwood 2005)

Seneca's view in the last paragraph implies that, given the balance of preferred and dispreferred things in human life, life is a reasonable object of choice. This view is not further explained or justified, but it can perhaps be received in the context of the more articulate Stoic views about the worth of continued existence. This approach is encouraged by the fact that here, too, the deliberations are portrayed in terms of weighing advantageous and disadvantageous things.

The choice of life would be reasonable, on those terms, because we can reasonably expect that in most human lives the preferred indifferents will at least to some extent outweigh the dispreferred indifferents. This expectation is justified by the Stoic view that the world is a creation of the rational and providential god who has made everything in the best possible way and for the sake of the good of the whole and its parts. It may happen, and we should take this into account, that a particular life may turn out to be not worth living. For it is possible, indeed unavoidable, that within the providentially organised whole there are some parts that sometimes have to suffer for the sake of the whole (Epictetus, *Diss.* ii.5.24–29). But insofar as we do not know what is fated to us or our children, the odds are, by default, in favour of life. We can expect, in the course of our lives, to have relatively more health, wealth, natural abilities and skills than their opposites. After all, it remains to a considerable extent within our power to control that balance, since we can, and indeed should, depart from life whenever the hardships are bound to prevail.

There is a further question whether life ought to be chosen even if we knew beforehand that it would be an unfortunate life. This question becomes especially relevant from the contemporary perspective since we can indeed tell, in some cases, that a life will be difficult even before it has started. Thanks to prenatal diagnostics, it is possible to forecast with a very high degree of confidence that some embryos will come into life with a serious and perhaps permanent disease or disablement. Would the Stoics say that these children ought to be brought into life nonetheless? We do not have any Stoic material that weigh on this issue, but there is some ground for plausible speculation on what the Stoics would think.

The first indication to consider is Seneca's view that parents can, and ought to, decide on their future children's behalf. In the absence of Stoic commitments to any overriding pro-life moral considerations, such as the sanctity of life, it would seem that the parents should decide in the interest of their children solely on the basis of the expected balance of preferred and dispreferred indifferents. If the expected disability is so serious that it is unlikely ever to be outweighed by any amount of naturally advantageous things, then this seems like a strong reason to choose death for the unborn child. But it might not be the only criterion. For, in making this decision, Stoic parents also ought to consider what the birth of a disabled child would possibly mean for the balance of preferred and dispreferred indifferents in *their* lives. Having to care for a disabled child seems something one would rather avoid, if possible; but there are also cases of parents who may have a natural aptitude for providing that kind of care, and indeed who could find their own flourishing in living up to that kind of commitment. In fact, we can easily imagine parents who find that such a committment is what has made, for the first time, their lives truly meaningful. Could this contribution to the life of a parent justify parents letting even disabled children be born? Perhaps so, especially in cases where the expected balance of the child's own preferred and dispreferred indifferents is not too unfavourable, and where the consideration of the parents' interest could make an overall difference. Again, the assumption is that all these different elements of value and disvalue – those related to the child's health, those related to the parents' well-being, and those related to the possible consequences of this decision for the broader social context – can be parsed as different sets of preferred and dispreferred indifferents that can all be thrown into a single set of scales and be weighed against each other to arrive at a single all-things-considered judgment.

The Stoic perspective on the theme of choosing life invites comparisons with Plato's perspective on this theme. Both Stoics and Plato believed that human beings come into life as a result of a choice or decision, and that procreation is generally a good thing. But we can identify two salient differences. In the myth of the *Republic*, souls embark on a new cycle of birth by necessity. Although it is up to them to choose a particular kind of life, the soul must enter a new body; birth cannot be avoided. In contrast, the Stoics did not regard the human soul as immortal and hence as existing prior to birth. In this sense, the decision of parents to bring children into life is more momentous, since without their choice a particular human being would not have been born.[29] Another difference concerns the motivation for procreation, that is, for choosing life on behalf of someone else. According to Plato's view in the *Symposium*, all mortal natures seek immortality, as far as possible, and the only way they can do it is by generation: 'since so they can always leave behind them a new creature in place of the old' (207d). So the desire for procreation is an expression of Love, a metaphysical desire for the approximation to the divine realm. The Stoics, too, believed that human desire for procreation belongs to human nature, and as such should be followed. But this desire does not have the transcendent, aspirational dimension it has in the *Symposium*. The Stoic sage will typically marry and beget children (DL vii.121).[30] By begetting children, he expresses his biological nature and makes his contribution to the city. In so doing, he embraces what belongs to his mortal nature, but does not seek to transcend it.

3.5 Mere Living As a Preferred Indifferent

So far, I have been discussing Stoic views about life worth living. What makes a life worth living, in their view, is a life's quality, which depends on the balance of naturally preferred and dispreferred things. But in that case the value of mere living itself also comes into the equation, since 'life' (*zôê*) appears in a list of preferred indifferents reported by Diogenes Laertius. It is useful to quote the passage in full:

> Preferred things are those which also have value; for example, among things of the soul, natural ability, skill, [moral] progress, and similar things; among bodily things life, health, strength, good condition, soundness, beauty, and the like; among external things wealth, reputation, noble birth, and similar things. Rejected are, among things of the soul, natural inability, lack of skill, and similar things; among bodily things death, disease, weakness, bad condition, being maimed, ugliness, and similar things; among external things poverty, lack of reputation, low birth, and the like. (DL vii.106, transl. Inwood and Gerson)

In the taxonomy of preferred indifferents, life is categorised among things pertaining to the body, along with health. Later, in DL vii.107, Diogenes reports the distinction between things preferred 'for their own

---

[29] Even though it is, of course, also necessary insofar as it is compelled by fate.
[30] But note that Stoic views about the value of marriage and family life were notoriously controversial (cf. Schofield 1991: 119–127; Reydams-Schils 2005: 145 ff.)

sake' (*di'hauta*), that is, things that have non-instrumental value; things pre-ferred 'for the sake of something else' (*dia hetera*), that is, things with instru-mental value; and things with both instrumental and non-instrumental value. To a large extent this classification maps onto the threefold clas-sification in the passage quoted earlier: the soul's natural ability or moral progress are chosen for their own sake; external wealth or noble birth are purely instrumental; and bodily strength, good condition and intact sense-organs have both instrumental and non-instrumental value. Health and life are not mentioned in this classification, but we would expect that they would fall, like other bodily goods, into the last category.

Thus, living in and of itself, or mere living, has some non-instrumental value. While the Stoics – like Plato – include life in the category of things that are only extrinsically valuable, insofar as they can both benefit and harm (DL vii.103), depending on how they are used, unlike Plato – and like Aristotle – they maintain that life belongs to things that deserve to be chosen for their own sake, or non-instrumentally. Other things being equal, it is reasonable for humans to strive to have as much life as possible, just as it is reasonable for them, say, to strive to be maximally healthy. But what it means to have 'more' life is not clear. Thinking of Aristotle, this could be understood either in quantitative terms, so that one stays alive longer, or in qualitative terms, in the sense that one's vital activities are free from impediments and are thus more articulated and abundant. But the Stoics cannot be committed to the view from the *Protrepticus* that 'living more' is 'living better'. Since living belongs to the category of indifferent things, living well, which is the good, cannot ever be understood as a maxi-misation of mere living. Moreover, living is assigned to the bodily realm, which further indicates that living more, in the Stoic sense, should be understood merely in the sense of being alive for a longer period of time.

There is an obvious rationale for the Stoics to include 'life' in their list of the preferred indifferents. The claim that the first impulse of humans is towards self-preservation just means that staying alive is what humans aim at from birth. The teleological framework provides additional normative weight to the animal and human drive for staying alive; we were made to do this. In fact, it is among the first impulses, and hence it stands to reason that life is the first item among the body-related preferred indifferents. As with other naturally selected things, however, the terms under which preferred indifferents are selected develop in the course of moral growth. This is why even a voluntary termination of one's own life can likewise be a natural thing to choose, and why the decision to depart from life does not violate the status of life as a naturally preferred thing (cf. Sellars 2006: 109).

In some cases, the value of one's own life can be outweighed by the negative value of its contents, that is, of the actual or expected dispreferred indifferents in it, or by the positive value of 'things in accordance with nature' that would be secured if a life were sacrificed.

In the absence of any evidence to the contrary, we would expect that life itself would be one among other indifferent items that enter into the deliberations about whether life is worth living or not. So, in deciding whether a life is worth living, we also have to take into account the value of life in and of itself. Whereas the worthwhileness of life depends on the preferred and dispreferred things and their ratio, the value of life, as one among these preferred indifferents, does not depend on these other things and their balance. One may object that if a life is fraught with too many hardships, its natural selective value evaporates, as Aristotle notes in the *Politics*. But the Stoic sources do not indicate that the value of life would be conditional in this sense; only life's worthwhileness is. This claim is psychologically plausible: it is quite common that people value life, or even cling to it, even though they are seriously ill and in great pain. Do they make a mistake? They do not, insofar they have a desire to stay alive, for this desire is natural; but they do if this desire overrides a due rational judgment that continued existence is not worthwile, given the present and expected preponderance of 'things contrary to nature'. That is why the Stoics are not preferentialists in the modern sense. Your desire to stay alive is natural and life always has some non-instrumental value, but this does not necessarily make continued existence worthwhile for you.

The value of mere living is related to but not simply contained in the value of health. I may be in poor health and expect to remain in that condition for the rest of my life, but this dispreferred condition will have to be weighed against the preferred status of the remaining years of life I would have if I were to stay alive. This complicates somewhat the idea reported by Olympiodorus that serious bodily incapacitation is a reason to depart from life. Of course, this incapacitation is a dispreffered condition that prevents us from performing some important appropriate actions. But if I stay alive, despite this condition, I shall remain in the preferred condition of being alive, which enables me to perform other appropriate actions, such as eating and drinking. For a Stoic to determine the right time of departing from life depends on a judgment about when the disvalue of incapacitation outweighs the value of staying alive.

The implication of this axiological status of life is that every life, whether worthwhile or not, has a grain of what makes it choiceworthy for me. But this also means that the balance of preferred and dispreferred indifferents is always tilted, by default, in favour of life rather than its absence, both in the sense of worth staying alive and in the sense of worth being born. If I live a life with exactly the same amount of health, wealth, and so on, and their opposites, the value of life would be the tie-breaker, and thus a conditional worthmaker.

3.6   The Necessary Meaningfulness of the Human Life

The Stoics characteristically argued that everything that happens is determined by the god to happen precisely the way it happens. This necessity is an expression of the divine providential design that arranges all things and events with view to crafting the best possible universe.[31] So everything happens from a particular cause and for a specific reason, and in so doing contributes, in its own specific way, to the divine plan, as different voices in a choir contribute to the harmony of the song (Plutarch, *De com. not.* 1065b). One consequence of this view is that *everything* that happens, including human lives and their contents, has some contributive value to the world. This applies also to evil in general, and vicious human lives in particular. Good and evil are interdependent like summer and winter and virtue cannot come into being without vice (Gelius, *Noc. att.* vii.1). Just as some medical treatments require snake venom, so the virtue of Socrates finds its particular use with regard to the vice of Meletus (Plutarch, *De com. not.* 1065b).

Thus, every life cannot but make its contribution to the cosmos regardless of whether it is virtuous or vicious; in other words, every life is meaningful, no matter how happy or unhappy it is from the internal perspective. But what if these lives are not worthwhile? Perhaps the thought is that vicious humans only make their contribution insofar as they ought to be alive, that is, insofar as there is a positive balance of preferred and dispreferred indifferents in their lives. But this does not seem right. Humans for whom life is not worth living ought, for their own sake, depart from life, but whether they do so or not makes no difference to the value of their cosmic contribution. From the cosmological point of view, everything that happens, and thus everything that humans do, plays an equally necessary and indispensable role in the delicate system of interconnections and counterbalances that constitutes the rational universe. On the whole, then, meaningfulness is insensitive to internal value

---

[31]   Plutarch, *De st. rep.* 1044d, 1050c–d; Cicero, DND ii.37–39; Epictetus, *Diss.* ii.5.

of any kind. If your life is happy or worthwhile, it is good for you (in one sense or another) *and* for the cosmos; but if it is not, it will be good for the cosmos anyway. In fact, the Stoics would even say that if your life is not worth living, it is good for the cosmos not *in spite of* it being not worth living, but *because* of it.

But could it possibly be the case that this cosmic meaningfulness can make my life worthwhile *for me*? There is an interesting problem here. I have argued above that the meaningfulness of other-regarding actions that are in accordance with one's social nature translates into a life's worthwhileness. Seneca's soul is so closely bound up with his wife's that his decision to stay alive for her sake makes his continued existence at once meaningful and worthwhile. Now, if (i) the souls of all humans are bound up with the soul of the world, so that what is beneficial for the world is also beneficial for them,[32] and if (ii) individual lives also make a positive contribution to the harmony of the world, no matter what, does it not follow that the cosmic meaningfulness of life translates to the worthwhileness of my life for me? If my life always matters for the world, does this not make it always worth living for me? Clearly, the Stoic answer is no. The sources are unambiguous that many human lives are not worth living. But is this answer consistent with the doctrine of necessary meaningfulness?

There are two arguments available to block the conclusion that cosmic meaningfulness of all lives implies that we should carry on living. First, if I decide to die, my death would be just as meaningful. It might make us feel better to know that what we do aligns with god. But then, everything we wind up doing will align with god, so it comes out even. The way your life matters for the universe is quite different from the way that Seneca's life matters for his wife. It makes no difference for the rational perfection of the world whether I stay or go; so the cosmic meaningfulness could make my life indifferent, at best. The world can easily do without you; Paulina cannot easily do without her husband. Secondly, some Stoic sources echo approvingly Plato's notion of a 'divine sign' for departure from life: "'What if god does not provide food?" "Well, in that case god has, like a good general, given a signal: the retreat'" (Epictetus, *Diss.* iii.26.29).[33] If a preponderance of dispreferred indifferents can be expected to mar the remaining part of his life, the sage, more confidently than non-sages, interprets this as a clear sign

---

[32] For a good recent discussion of the relationship between an individual soul and the world-soul in Stoicism, see Ademollo (2020).

[33] Cf. Long (2019: 202–203) for a discussion of the 'divine sign' in Plato and Stoicism.

that it is the god's will that he depart from life. If that is what the god wants, then stubbornly remaining in life can hardly be regarded as a meaningful contribution to the cosmic order.

3.7   Stoics and Aristotle on Life Worth Living

According to Aristotle, mere human living has a non-instrumental value. This value is virtue-independent: what makes life a good is not excellence but a natural finality. This is also the picture that emerges from the Stoic sources: mere living is a non-instrumental, virtue-independent value. But Aristotle does not categorically dissociate the value of mere living, and the abundance of life as its maximisation, from the value of good life; rather, he tends to regard it as an intermediate-level finality on a single axiological scale. That Aristotle makes this axiological distinction without mapping it onto a more robust axiological dichotomy leads to some potentially disturbing implications (see Section 2.4 above and Section 5.6 below). Now, the Stoics are ready to bite the bullet. Both mere living and good life are naturally valuable, but in two completely different and independent senses. Some of our natural objectives – preserving our life, maintaining bodily well-being or ensuring freedom from pain – are those that we to a significant extent share with other animals. But the *way* we pursue them, that is, rationally, whether in accordance with reason or contrary to it, is what sets us apart from other animals. This sharp distinction between *what* we pursue and *how* we do it corresponds to two different perspectives on the natural constitution of humans: from one perspective, we are animals; from another, we possess rationality and in that sense are god-like. We achieve rational perfection not by trying to transcend or escape our animal nature, but by attending to it.

On the Stoic view, the axiological level of life worth living is determined by the same order of value as the level of mere living, and both these are incommensurable with the axiological order of virtue and happiness. What makes life worthwhile is a preponderance of preferred indifferents over their opposites, and mere living itself is one of these preferred indifferents. All preferred indifferents, including life itself, are conditional worthmakers, since they make a life worth living on the condition that their cumulative value outweighs the disvalue of their opposites. An alternative and complementary perspective is that having a life worth living depends on our capacity to do appropriate actions or to play our social roles well. Insofar as we can keep doing appropriate actions, rather than omit them or do their opposites, our lives are worth living.

The central and controversial claim of the Stoic ethical theory is that virtue is a sufficient condition of happiness. In contrast to Aristotle, who acknowledged that happiness to some extent depends on external goods, or even to Plato, who suggested that serious bodily corruption could in some circumstances make life unfit to be lived, Stoics firmly maintained that the happiness of the virtuous person is impervious to misfortunes and impediments. This does not mean, however, that the life of virtuous person will always be worth living. In claiming that virtue is virtually irrelevant for passing the threshold test, Stoics likewise depart from Plato and Aristotle. But if the above interpretation is right, it implies not only that this view is compatible with the sufficiency thesis, but also that it is required by it. For the sufficiency thesis rests on a strict axiological dualism between goods and the indifferents, and the irrelevance of virtue for life worth living follows necessarily from this dualism.

The foundation stone of the Stoic account of life worth living is the explicitly defended view that staying alive or being born are, at base, matters of indifference. They must be, because only virtue is good and only vice is evil. This contrasts with Aristotle, who held that a life of too short a duration cannot be happy because it is 'incomplete' (*atelês*).[34] Of course, the mere fact of having a long life does not make you happy, but a premature death does make your life unhappy and in that sense is a bad thing. The Stoics do not grant this: while life has some non-instrumental value, premature death cannot ever be a bad for you – it is indifferent. If you are virtuous, early death does not detract from your happiness; if you are vicious, it does not make your life less unhappy. More years of a virtuous life are not necessarily better than fewer years. In fact, if a virtuous person is badly off in terms of the overall balance of preferred and dispreferred indifferents, a shorter virtuous life may be preferable for her to a longer. Given the Stoic insistence on the prominent axiological status of virtue as the only good, this is a hard lesson. But making any concession to this claim would ultimately ruin the sufficiency thesis.

The Stoic position on happiness and the life worth living is logically consistent, given the axiological premises of their theory. But does it convince? It does not if we insist that the question about the quality of life must be a unitary question to which there is a unitary answer. Consider a virtuous person who lives with a painful disease for many years and a virtuous person who is pain free. Which of these two persons is better off,

---

[34] E.g. EE ii.1, 1219a35–b8, though this does not necessarily mean that death before reaching one's prime would always have to make a life unhappy (cf. Lear 2015).

all things considered? Many would say that the second since he is *both* virtuous *and* free of pain: his well-being is greater by being pain free. For Aristotle, this rather intuitive answer would be quite unproblematic, but not so for the Stoics. They would insist that we cannot arrive at a single summative judgment about the quality of this life. Rather, we have to break the answer into two separate components: from the perspective of happiness, both lives are equal; from the perspective of life worth living, the second life is better. Insofar as these axiological perspectives are incommensurable, this judgment is final; there is no conceptual basis for an all-things-considered comparison of these two lives from the perspective of a single unitary notion of quality of life. Is this a weakness of the Stoic theory? Stoics, for their part, would say that it does not have to be. We should not require a unitary account of the quality of life precisely because our nature is irreducibly twofold: animal-like and god-like at once.

CHAPTER 4

Threshold Nears the Target:
Hellenistic Hedonists on the Life Worth Living

[The Cyrenaic] Hegesias whom I mentioned has a book called
Man Starving Himself to Death ... [and] believes that living is
advantageous for absolutely no one.

(Cicero, *Tusc.* i.84, transl. Lampe)

But as for the foolish man, neither will he gain a noteworthy good,
even if he should live for as long a time as Tithonus, nor is it too
unfitting for him [to die] in the quickest way when he is born, [rather
than] more slowly, even if we do [not] recommend it.

(Philodemus, *De Morte* xix.33–xx.1)[1]

4.1   Ancient Hedonists As Optimists?

From the modern perspective, the ancient philosophical theories of well-
being discussed so far could be regarded as the predecessors of objectivist theories. For Plato and Aristotle, both happiness and life worth living
depend on the presence of some good states in one's life – such as virtue
or health – whose value is largely constituted independently of any subjective feelings that these states typically bring about. It often feels good to be
virtuous or to be healthy, but the value of virtue or health is superior to and
independent of the good feelings that result from these conditions; it is constituted by the performance of the human function or, more broadly, by the
objective perfection of human nature. This objectivist picture also applies to
the Stoics, with the qualification that it is virtue that matters for happiness,
but other objective conditions – such as wealth or health – that matter for
having a life worth living. In this chapter, I turn to ancient philosophers
who, instead, identified the criterion of both happiness and life worth living
with a feeling (*pathos*), specifically the feeling of pleasure (*hêdonê*).

---

[1] The translations of Philodemus's *De Morte* follow the edition by Henry; Lucretius's DRN is rendered according to Latham and Godwin. All other translations of the Epicurean sources, unless
otherwise noted, follow the anthology by Long and Sedley. The Cyrenaic material from DL ii is
quoted according to Mensch and Miller.

Hellenistic hedonists were by no means the first philosophers in the Greek tradition who gave serious consideration to pleasure as a candidate for the highest good. Aristotle attributes the view that pleasure is the highest good to Eudoxus, who lived in the fourth century BCE; we find complex discussions of pleasure's claim to be the good in some dialogues of Plato, most notably the *Philebus*; and the atomist Democritus, a younger contemporary of Socrates, espoused a way of life aiming at 'cheerfulness' (*euthumia*), which arguably prefigured Epicurean notion of the *telos*.[2] But the Hellenistic hedonists were the first to work out the view that pleasure is the end as part of a systematic ethical theory. The first version of ancient hedonism was formulated by the Cyrenaics, and further developed, and in important ways corrected or modified, by the more famous Epicureans. While the Epicureans were, in the first place, hedonists, they can also be regarded as predecessors of the second predominant subjectivist approach to well-being today, namely the desire-fulfilment view. For one lives happily, that is pleasantly, precisely if and when all one's desires have been fulfilled.

The ancient philosophers' outlook on life worth living, which from the vantage point of contemporary theories appears rather pessimistic, seems to be the consequence of their measuring the worth of life by a standard of objective perfection. This aligns with Prodicus' description of the choice of Heracles (Xenophon, *Memorabilia* ii.1.21–34), where the path of virtue is portrayed as difficult and troublesome, whereas the path of pleasure is easy and short. If it is virtue that makes a life worth living, and it takes considerable education and training to become virtuous, then a life worth living is rather difficult to achieve. In contrast, if indeed it is pleasure that makes life worthwhile, then one might perhaps expect that the Cyrenaics and Epicureans would adopt a more optimistic outlook. If pleasure is the criterion of a worthwhile life, this promises at least a less elitist approach to defining the threshold. We have also read in the Introduction an upbeat passage from Epicurus' *Letter to Menoeceus* which castigates the tragic poets for their life-denying attitude. Finally, in contrast to the Stoics and Peripatetics, the Epicureans were more reserved in commending suicide. This, too, may be regarded as a sign that for them it takes less to clear the threshold of a life worth living.

And yet, as the opening quotations indicate, this expectation will be largely disappointed. As things are, in the view of the ancient hedonists

---

[2] A sustained case for the influence of Democritus on the Epicurean ethics has been made by Warren (2002).

most people end up having lives that are not worth living – not so much because these lives would be deprived of at least some pleasures, but because they are full of pain. The pleasures they have are not sufficient to make their lives worth living, while the pains they fail to avoid are sufficient to make their lives not worth living. This pessimism testifies to the fact that the ancient hedonists in general, and Epicureans in particular, do not depart from the ancient emphasis on objective perfection as much as one might expect in light of their hedonistic commitments.[3] It turns out that the psychological state that the Epicureans understand as pleasure proper is an objective health of mind associated with an attitude of confidence in the healthy state of the body and its likely continuity.

In fact, ancient hedonists can be regarded as even more pessimistic than Plato, Aristotle and the Stoics insofar as they have less to offer concerning the distinction between the target notion of happiness and the threshold notion of life worth living. For the peculiar brand of Cyrenaic philosophy that I consider, advocated by the so-called Hegesiacs, the target is assimilated to the threshold, so that a life just barely worth living is the best you can ever hope for. Inversely, the Epicureans assimilate, though with some important reservations, the threshold to the target. This means that if happiness turns out to be beyond our reach, or at least difficult to achieve, we shall also have difficulties achieving a life that is at least barely worth living. This is the consequence of Epicurean axiology, which has a monistic slant in comparison with the Stoic theory, in postulating freedom from disturbance (*ataraxia*) as the dominant good, one which does not allow for degrees. Either you have achieved *ataraxia*, and then your life is both happy and worth living; or you have failed, and then it is neither happy nor even worth living. Without any help from philosophy, our life is bound to be overwhelmingly painful. In contrast to some modern versions of the desire-fulfilment approach to a life worth living, the fact that you may desire to carry on living does not make your life any more worthwhile for you. In fact, this desire is a part of your misery, and the more you desire to live, the worse it is for you.

I start in Section 4.2 with a discussion of Cyrenaic ethical theory as represented by Hegesias. Hegesias' pessimism is not representative of the entire Cyrenaic school, though it has been argued that such a pessimistic outlook does follow from the consequent development of the Cyrenaic premises (Matson 1998). In any case, the focus on Hegesias here is motivated by the

---

[3] The differences between modern and ancient hedonist ethical theories have been noted in the scholarship on ancient hedonism (e.g. Annas 1993 and Mitsis 1988).

need to give due attention to what can be regarded as one extreme and exemplary case of approaching the question about life worth living in the Greek tradition. Section 4.3 turns to the Epicurean school and outlines the fundamentals of Epicurean ethics and value theory, including their engagement with the fear of death, an important theme in the vicinity of my agenda. In Section 4.4, I focus on the dominant status of *ataraxia* in Epicurean value theory, which prepares the ground for a discussion of Epicurean views about life worth living in Section 4.5. In Section 4.6, I attend briefly to Epicurean views about the value of life in and of itself, and conclude in Section 4.7 with a discussion of the Epicurean contention that only a life informed by philosophy can be worth living.

The extant evidence about the Cyrenaic school is thin; the doxography in the second book of Diogenes Laertius' *Lives* is the main source. We are fortunate to have some important Epicurean works. This includes three letters of Epicurus himself, the most salient of which is, for our purposes, the *Letter to Menoeceus*, which contains a synoptic outline of Epicurean ethics. We also have two collections of short maxims and sayings, compiled by Epicurus and his followers, *Key Doctrines* and *Vatican Sayings*. An informative and mostly reliable account of Epicurean ethics – though generally hostile – can be found in the first book of Cicero's *On Ends*. Besides Epicurus, there are two later Epicurean thinkers, both living in the first century BCE, whose views we shall consider more extensively: Lucretius, the author of the Latin philosophical poem *On the Nature of Things*; and Philodemus, an author of several philosophical treatises written in Greek, such as *On Death*, that are preserved in incomplete fragments.

4.2   Hegesias the Cyrenaic: Threshold as the Target

Cyrenaic ethical theory was appropriately characterised as a kind of 'hedonic presentism' (Sedley 2017).[4] According to the Cyrenaics, the end (*telos*) is 'bodily pleasure' (*hêdonê sômatos*) (DL ii.87), understood as a kind of 'smooth motion' (*kinêsis leia*) (ii.86). While they recognise the existence of mental pleasures and pains, the bodily pleasures are regarded as 'far superior' (*polu ameinous*) and the bodily pains as 'far worse' (*polu cheirous*) than the mental pleasures and pains (ii.90). In what appears to be a striking departure from the mainstream, Cyrenaics did not regard 'happiness'

---

[4] For a brief but substantive summary account of the Cyrenaic philosophy, see Warren (2014). For more detailed, comprehensive studies, see Zilioli (2012) and Lampe (2015).

(*eudaimonia*) as the 'end' (*telos*):[5] for happiness is 'the sum total of the particular pleasures' (*ek tôn merikôn hêdonôn sustêma*) in one's life, including both past and future pleasures, whereas the end is a singular pleasure experienced at a given time.

Hence the presentism: it is 'sufficient' (*arkei*) to 'enjoy, one by one (*kata mian*), the pleasures that come our way' (ii.91). The Cyrenaic motivation for dissociating the end from happiness is, presumably, that the focus on pursuing a eudamonistic 'master plan' may collide with the readiness to relax and enjoy piecemeal pleasures as they come (Sedley 2017: 93). If we worry too much about securing the best possible sum of pleasures over our lifetime, we unwisely sacrifice the innocence of present pleasures over unnecessary concerns about the uncertain future. As befits the focus on bodily pleasures, pleasure is generally not derived from memory or anticipation but from the perception of the present moment; in the Cyrenaic terminology, pleasure is 'unitemporal' or 'occupying one temporal unit' (Zilioli 2012) (*monochronos*), namely the present moment.[6] Even though happiness is not the end, the accumulation of present pleasures will, over one's lifetime, typically produce happiness in a wise person's life.

One branch of Cyrenaic hedonism, represented by so-called Hegesiacs, drew from these premises a pessimistic conclusion concerning the human condition. According to Cicero's testimony, Hegesias, the author of the book called *Man Starving Himself to Death*, was prohibited by Ptolemy from giving lectures due to the high suicide rate among his students (*Tusc.* i.83–84).[7] In contrast to other Cyrenaics, he maintained that 'happiness is wholly impossible' (*holôs adunaton*) because 'the body is infected by many sufferings and the soul shares the body's sufferings and is disturbed by them, and fortune disappoints many of the expectations' (DL ii.94). On the whole, then, the view that bodily pleasures and pains are more important than those of the soul, in combination with the inescapable frailty of the bodily condition, implies that one can typically expect in one's lifetime a negative hedonic balance. This implies not only that human life cannot be happy, but also a stronger claim that it is difficult, if not impossible, to clear the threshold of a life worth living. Indeed, Cicero attributes to Hegesias the view that 'living is advantageous for absolutely no one' (*omnino vivere expedire nemini*)

---

[5] The extent to which the Cyrenaics actually depart from the eudaimonist framework has been a matter of debate. Cf. Irwin (1991) versus Tsouna (2002).

[6] Athenaeus, *Deipnosophists* xii. 544a–b.

[7] This is corroborated by Plutarch, who says that Hegesias even 'persuaded' his listeners to commit suicide (*De amore prolis* 497d). Cf. DL ii.86, where Hegesias is said to have been nicknamed 'Death-Persuader'.

(*Tusc.* i.84). Nothing but the balance of bodily pleasure and pain matters, and hence virtue or other goods valued in the philosophical tradition cannot ever outweigh the amount of pain that every human life is unavoidably subject to. Hence, it would seem that life is generally not worth living. This outlook seems to favour the general recommendation of suicide as the appropriate response to the inherent disvalue of life.

And yet it might be too hasty to attribute this view to Hegesias. Strictly considered, the claim that living is advantageous to no one does not entail that life necessarily constitutes a net harm (cf. Lampe 2015: 126). For one may still aspire to a life which is neither to be chosen nor to be avoided, that is, what I have called an 'indifferent life'. This is suggested by remarks that 'both life and death may be equally desirable' (DL ii.94) or that to the wise man life is a 'matter of indifference' (*to zên tôi phronimôi adiaphoron*) (ii.95).[8] Presumably, death is in many cases preferable to life. But death *may* sometimes be *no more* desirable than life, namely when life does not have a net negative value but is indifferent. Once we achieve the state wherein death is no more desirable than life, then, since we are already alive, we have reason to remain in that state simply because we have no reasons to choose death either.

If this reading is along the right lines, it implies that Hegesias espouses answers to the question about the threshold of worthwhile life. But how precisely is the threshold of life barely worth living to be defined? Kurt Lampe has suggested that the threshold is reached once life 'breaks even in the balance of pleasures and pains' (Lampe 2015: 126). On this view, the procedure of defining the threshold is similar in form (but not in content) to Stoic deliberation: one needs to weigh value against disvalue, in this case pleasure against pain. It is unrealistic to expect that pleasures could exceed pains; but perhaps one can achieve a condition in which pains do not exceed pleasures. There is also a different interpretive option that Lampe does not consider: life is barely worth living when it is *not too* painful, regardless of how many pleasures it contains. This option is indicated by the Hegesiac definition of the end: 'the wise man will not have as great an advantage (*pleonasein*) in his choice of goods as he will in his ability to avoid evils, since he makes it his end (*telos tithemenon*) to live without pain

---

[8] In the same line, Diogenes also attributes to the Cyrenaics the view that 'for the fool (*tôi aphroni*) living is advantageous (*lusiteles*)'. This seems to clash with the claim from Cicero that living is advantageous to no one. For a discussion of how this apparent contradiction in the sources could be resolved, see Lampe (2015: 126–127). The most plausible solution is that the advantageousness of the fool's continued existence is strictly conditional upon an exposure to philosophy: fools have a chance to become somewhat less miserable if they learn philosophy.

and grief (*to mê epiponôs zên mêde lupêrôs*)' (DL ii.95). This implies that the prudence of the wise man will not help him so much to maximise pleasure as the worthmaker, but rather to minimise pain as the worthbreaker.[9]

It seems fair to acknowledge that, for all its gloominess, there is an aspirational dimension to Hegesiac pessimism. This aspiration is clearly defensive: it would be unrealistic to aspire to happiness, but it is appropriate to organise one's life around the goal to avoid pain, as far as possible. It is the peculiar feature of this branch of Cyrenaic hedonism that the threshold takes the place of the target. There is no happiness to be had; rather, the best we can aim at is to achieve a life that is worth living in the minimal, marginal sense of not being worse than death. The aspiration to minimise or eliminate pain is a central and familiar feature of the Epicurean theory, as we shall shortly see. But the Epicureans seem to have been more optimistic than Hegesias insofar as they allow, first, that it is possible to achieve a state of complete freedom from pain and, secondly, that this state is sufficient not only for a life worth living, but also for a happy life. This more optimistic outlook rests ultimately on a different understanding and valuation of the state of painlessness: it is not only an intermediate state between pleasure and pain, but it is *the* pleasure, and hence good, in the full and superior sense.

4.3 Epicureans on Happiness and Death

4.3.1 Pleasure

According to Epicurus and his followers, 'pleasure is the beginning and end of the blessed life (*archê kai telos tou makariôs zên*)' (*Ep. Men.* 129).[10] It is the beginning, or the 'starting-point', because all animals, including humans, pursue pleasure as soon as they are born (*Fin.* i.29). Like other schools of the Hellenistic period, specifically the Stoics and the Peripatetics, the Epicureans justified their account of the human end by appeal to nature. What is good for us must show in what we desire by virtue of our natural constitution, as manifested in our primal, pre-cultivated instincts.[11] In the Epicurean view, the object of this instinct is pleasure,

---

[9] This account of the *telos* raises the question – which we cannot pursue further – to what extent this stance is compatible with the Cyrenaic presentism. For the avoidance of pain does not align straightforwardly with the *carpe diem* attitude to enjoying pleasures 'as they come'.

[10] Epicurus uses 'blessedness' as synonymous with 'happiness' (e.g. DL x.128).

[11] See Brunschwig (1986) for a classic treatment of this so-called 'cradle-argument' in Stoicism and Epicureanism.

and hence pleasure is the 'good' (*agathon*) 'because it is naturally akin to us' (*dia to phusin echein oikeian*) (*Ep. Men.* 129). Along with being the beginning, pleasure is also the end, because all our decisions are ultimately justified by how they promote pleasure: pleasure is the 'greatest good', and its opposite, pain, is the 'greatest bad' (ibid.). But while every pleasure is good and every pain is bad, we ought not to choose every pleasure and avoid every pain. Rather, we should sometimes choose pain and forego pleasure if that would be conducive to a greater pleasure in the long run (*Ep. Men.* 129).[12]

The Epicureans distinguish between the pleasures of the body and the pleasures of the mind. While all pleasures of the mind have their roots in bodily processes (*Fin.* i.51, 55), and some evidence even gives a certain primacy to the bodily pleasures (e.g. *P. Herc.* 1232, 18.10–17), the Epicureans apparently maintain – and this is where they deliberately depart from the Cyrenaics – that mental pleasures are generally 'much greater' than bodily pleasures (*Fin.* i.55). This superiority of the mental pleasures is owed to the greater power of the soul's capacities in general (Diogenes of Oenoanda, fr. 49); these include, in particular, the capacity to experience pleasure and pain in all three temporal dimensions (*Fin.* i.55; DL x.137), so that in addition to present pleasures I can recollect past pleasures or anticipate future ones, as well as to override simultaneously occurring bodily feelings (DL x.22). This capacity provides the basis for a peculiar psychological power of the Epicurean sage, namely 'the art of locating and obtaining pleasure' (*Fin.* i.42), which takes full advantage of the three temporal dimensions of life, so that he is 'cheered by the prospect of future goods' and can 'enjoy the memory of the past ones' (*Fin.* i.57); he is also good at forgetting past misfortunes (ibid.).

The central contention of Epicurean ethics is that pleasure as the highest good, whether bodily or mental, is not so much an accumulation of a great quantity of pleasures obtained by the gratification of whatever desires one has, but rather the state of being free from all pain, both bodily and psychic: 'We do not simply pursue the sort of pleasure which stirs our nature with its sweetness and produces agreeable sensations in us: rather, the pleasure we deem greatest is that which is felt when all pain is removed (*maximam voluptatem habemus, quae percipitur omni dolore detracto*)' (*Fin.* i.37; cf. *Ep. Men.* 130). In adopting this view, the Epicureans distanced themselves from the Cyrenaics, who regarded the absence of pain not as pleasure but

---

[12] For a useful discussion of the Epicurean 'hedonistic calculus', see Warren (2014: 178–86) and Tsouna (2020).

as an intermediate state between pleasure and pain. So, Epicurean happiness amounts to a freedom from bodily pain (*aponia*) in conjunction with a freedom from mental disturbance (*ataraxia*). This freedom from pain is the best possible state: it is the 'limit' (*horos; finis*) of pleasure beyond which pleasure cannot be further increased (KD 3; *Fin* i.37).

The identification of blessedness with the freedom from bodily and mental pain rests on a central and innovative piece of the Epicurean theory, namely a distinction between two kinds of pleasure.[13] When Cicero mentions pleasures that 'stir our nature with sweetness' and thus 'produce agreeable sensation', this has been taken to refer to the so-called 'kinetic' pleasures. Some commentators understand the kinetic pleasures in the narrow sense of restorative pleasures, such as those that we experience when quenching thirst (e.g. Mitsis 1988: 45), but it is likely that the category of kinetic pleasures also includes a broad range of non-restorative pleasures, such as listening to music or anticipating pleasant future experiences (Tsouna 2020: 16). What all these pleasures have in common is that they are certain 'activations' (*energeiai*) and 'motions' (*kinêseis*) that involve pleasant stimulations of body or mind.[14] These pleasures are distinguished from the so-called 'katastematic' (from *katastêma*: 'state') or 'static' pleasures, which refer to the state of being free from pain. Once all pain has been removed, one comes to experience the static pleasure, no matter whether this state is accompanied by any pleasant stimulation. The Epicurean highest end is this condition of static pleasure.

This account of the end was ridiculed in antiquity as being akin to the condition of a corpse (DL ii.89); surely, a corpse is free from all pain. But there are effective rebuttals of this objection. One possibility espoused in the scholarship is that freedom from pain is experientially 'revealed' to us by different kinetic pleasures; the static pleasure amounts to a healthy condition of the bodily and mental capacities that is instrumental to experiencing pleasure, and the pleasant stimulation is how we come to be aware of this healthy condition (Wolfsdorf 2013). But other commentators have pointed out that if it is right to understand freedom from

---

[13] Some commentators have disputed the authenticity and/or saliency of the distinction (e.g. Gosling and Taylor 1982: 365–396; Nikolsky 2001), but the general scholarly consensus is in favour of authenticity. Cf. Tsouna (2020: 13–14) for references to further Epicurean sources in favour of the authenticity and importance of the distinction.

[14] 'The absence of disturbance and the absence of pain are static pleasures (*katastêmatikai hêdonai*), while joy and delight are seen to involve motion and activation' (DL x.136). This is the most explicit piece of evidence in favour of the distinction, though its reading, too, has been controversial (cf. Purinton 1993).

pain and disturbance in terms of bodily and psychic health, as many have
thought it is, then this state itself already has its peculiar felt quality: it
is a 'wonderful feeling of well-being that accompanies the unimpeded
functioning of our body and mind' (Tsouna 2020: 19) or 'a deeply felt
contentment permeating the conscious life of the agent' (Dimas 2015:
171).[15]

While the psychological and axiological relationship between kinetic
and static pleasures has been a matter of considerable controversy,[16] many
would agree with the following summary of Long and Sedley: 'Epicurus
firmly subordinates kinetic to static pleasure, treating the former either as a
stage on the way to the ultimate goal of absence of pain, or as a variation of
that condition when achieved' (1987: 123). Whereas the static pleasure is the
highest good, the *summum bonum* of Epicurean ethics, the kinetic pleasures
are lesser goods, and their value is, first and foremost, instrumental, namely
to conduce to the condition of freedom from pain (Dimas 2015: 172).[17]
So, when Epicurus says that a pleasant recollection of past conversations
with his friends enabled him to offset severe bodily pains (DL x.22), this
is an example of how kinetic pleasure can be instrumental to sustaining
ataraxia. Could kinetic pleasures also have non-instrumental value? The
answer depends on whether kinetic pleasures are purely instrumental or
whether they participate in, or are integrated in, the static pleasure as the
Epicurean *telos* proper. Two sources tell us that once the static pleasure is
achieved, kinetic pleasures cannot increase it but only 'vary' it (*poikillein*;
variare) (KD 18; *Fin.* i.38), that is, presumably, give to the static pleasure various 'textures' (Sedley 2017: 103). This might be taken to imply
that kinetic pleasures are included in the static pleasure as different guises
under which static pleasure comes to be experienced.[18] I shall return to
the question about the axiological status of kinetic pleasures in the next
section.

Another controversial question is whether happiness as static pleasure –
again in contrast with the kinetic pleasures – can be increased by duration.
A sequence from Epicurus' *Key Doctrines* bears precisely on this question;

---

[15] That static pleasure has its own experiential quality is also argued by Woolf (2009). Similarly,
Konstan (2009) talks about 'pleasure that accompanies well-being as such'. Cf. also Arenson (2019);
Rider (2020).
[16] See Rider (2020) for an up-to-date attempt to chart various positions in the debate.
[17] Dimas (2015: 173) notes, I think correctly, that the Epicurean claim that all pleasures are intrinsic
goods does not entail that kinetic pleasure must have some non-instrumental value. Static pleasure
is intrinsic and final, whereas kinetic pleasures may well be intrinsic and instrumental.
[18] This integrative view is proposed by Tsouna (2020: 161), but the matter is controversial; for one,
Dimas (2015: 174) denies the possibility that any kinetic pleasure can coexist with static pleasure.

this sequence is best read in terms of progressive explanations or qualifications. After KD 18, which states that the limit of pleasure is the removal
of pain, KD 19 makes a further claim, that 'infinite time and finite time
contain equal pleasure, if one measures the limits of pleasure by reasoning'.
This means that a life of limited duration – if pleasant – is not less happy
than a life of infinite duration. But does Epicurus mean *any* pleasant life of
limited duration? David Sedley (2017: 94–95) proposed, plausibly, that the
qualification is supplied in KD 20: '[in contrast to the unlimited desires of
the flesh,] the intellect, by making a rational calculation of the end and the
limit which governs the flesh, and by dispelling the fears about eternity,
brings about the complete (*pantelês*) life, so that we no longer need the
infinite time'. A finite pleasant life is equal in pleasure to an infinite pleasant life *if* it is, in some sense, complete.

But when does a life become complete? The sources are ambiguous.[19]
One possibility is that the life is complete *as soon as* one achieves *ataraxia*,
so that extended duration does not increase the value of a life once *ataraxia*
has been reached. This view is suggested by Cicero's report of Epicurus'
view that 'temporal duration adds nothing to the happiness of a life, and
that no less pleasure is enjoyed in a short space of time than in the whole
of time' (*Fin.* ii.87) and hence that 'pleasure does not increase with duration' (ii.88). But other evidence does add the qualification that life can be
considered complete only after one has been in the state of happiness for
a certain undefined period of time. Notably, Philodemus says that 'the
greatest good has been received by someone who has become wise and
lived on for a certain extent of time (*poson chronon*)' (*De Morte* xix.1–3).

4.3.2 Desires and Therapy

With this rudimentary outline of the Epicurean *telos* in place, we can
now turn to the Epicurean diagnosis of why most people fall short of this
end, as well as to Epicurean views about what is needed to achieve it. As
with Stoicism, the basic character of Epicurean ethics is therapeutic and
intellectualistic. The principal sources of pain and disturbance are what
Epicureans call 'empty' (*kenai*) beliefs, desires and emotions.[20] The empty
desires are contrasted with desires that are natural, that is, those in accordance with our natural constitution (*Ep. Men.* 126; KD 29). Both empty

---

[19] For a good discussion of different interpretive options, see Warren (2004), ch. 4.
[20] For the distinction between 'empty' and 'natural', see KD 29; *Ep. Men.* 127. Annas (1992: 193–99)
has a useful discussion of the 'emptiness' of beliefs.

beliefs and empty desires are, as it were, extra additions to what is naturally so: empty beliefs, such as the belief in the wrath of gods, adds to what gods actually are – indifferent beings that do not interfere in the human world; empty desires, such as the desire for luxury, are desires that go beyond what humans need by virtue of their natural constitution. 'What is insatiable is not the stomach, as people say, but the false opinion concerning its unlimited filling' (VS 59) – it takes little to be relieved from hunger; the desire for excessive gratifications adds to our actual natural needs.

In the long run, the empty desires are bound to promote pain, both bodily, by damaging health, and mental, by causing disturbance and insecurities about the fulfilment of desires that are, by their empty nature, rather difficult to fulfil. Therefore, the progress to wisdom consists chiefly in elimination of all empty desires and the satisfaction only of natural desires, and particularly those that are natural *and* necessary – the desires necessary for freedom from pain, the desires necessary for freedom from disturbance, as well as the desires necessary for life itself (*Ep. Men.* 127) – or generally those desires that bring relief from pain.[21] There are also natural but nonnecessary desires, such as the desire for sex, that do not bring relief from pain but can be pursued provided that their fulfilment does not harm.

The task of philosophy is to eliminate pains and disturbance, which comes down to the elimination of empty beliefs and desires. The words of philosophers who provide no therapy for human suffering are 'empty' (Porphyry, *To Marcella* 31); and this therapy should be delivered by means of 'arguments and discussions' (Sextus, AP i.169). So, for instance, once we appreciate that there is a limit of pleasure, we shall be in a good position to get rid of some empty desires that are enabled by the absence of this belief. But while the Epicureans were quite optimistic about the powers of human reason to relieve suffering, their intellectualism was rather rustic, with a lack of interest in those aspects of philosophical theorising, including logic, that, in the Epicurean view, are dispensable for the practical purpose of achieving freedom from pain (DL x.5). The Epicurean therapy can be characterised as a sort of intellectual habituation, as best exemplified by the injunction that we should 'accustom (*sunethizein*) [ourselves] to the belief (*Ep. Men.* 124) that death is nothing to us. The basic principles and injunctions of Epicurean ethics, as summarised, for instance, in the *Key Doctrines*, should be memorised and ingrained so that they exert a pervasive influence on one's thoughts and feelings.

---

[21] KD 29; Porphyry, *On abstinence* i.52.

Given their confidence in the powers of 'sober reasoning' to dispel confusion concerning the root of human suffering, it does not come as a surprise that the Epicureans regarded virtues, and most importantly 'prudence' (*phronêsis*), as indispensable for the blessed life. They understood virtues in intellectualist terms, as dispositions consisting of ingrained true beliefs, such as the belief that pleasure has its limits. There is an interdependence between virtue and happiness: 'it is not possible to live prudently and honorably and justly without living pleasurably, [and it is not possible to live prudently, honorably and justly] without living pleasurably' (*Ep. Men.* 132). While the pleasant life is therefore 'inseparable' from prudence and other virtues (*Ep. Men.* 132), ultimately the virtues are chosen 'because of pleasure and not for their own sakes' (DL x.138).[22]

In this regard, the value of virtues has a similar standing as the value of friendship (*philia*), another indispensable ingredient of the Epicurean life. While it is essential for friendship that we 'love our friends no less than we do ourselves' (*Fin.* i.67), we choose friendship because it is the 'most faithful sponsor' of pleasure (ibid.).[23] The main reason why friendship is conducive to pleasure is that it is an important source of protection against misfortunes and of psychological security. If times do turn rough, one can rely on a friend's support. A friendless life is beset by risks and fears (*Fin.* i.65–66; VS 34).

The therapeutic and intellectualistic orientation of Epicurean ethics can be best documented by the Epicurean treatment of the fear of death, which is regarded as perhaps the most pervasive source of disturbance. Once you get rid of this fear, you are close to achieving freedom from any kind of disturbance: 'For there is nothing fearful in living for one who genuinely grasps that there is nothing fearful in not living' (*Ep. Men.* 124). Since the Epicurean approach to death is also of special importance for the theme of life worth living, it deserves a brief presentation.

4.3.3 Death

As noted by the commentators, fear of death is a multi-faceted phenomenon. It is appropriate to distinguish at least four different kinds of this fear:[24] (1) fear of the condition of being dead, including the fear of what happens

---

[22] But see, e.g., Annas (1993) for a defence of the non-instrumental value of virtue in the Epicurean theory.
[23] Again, the axiological status of friendship has been controversial. Cf. Mitsis (1988) and O'Keefe (2001) on the non-instrumental versus the instrumental value of friendship.
[24] In distinguishing the different fears of death, I follow Warren (2004).

to one's dead body or the fear of suffering in a posthumous existence; (2) fear of the process of dying, that is, the transition from the state of life to the state of death; (3) fear of mortality in general, that is, the fear that one will die one day and will exist no more; and (4) fear of premature death, that is, the fear that one will die before one's life reaches a sort of completion. Epicureans espouse arguments against all these kinds of fears. Altogether, the arguments aim to show both that death is not a harm and that the desire for immortality, or temporally unlimited existence, is empty.[25]

There are two main Epicurean arguments against the fear of being dead: the argument from perception; and the argument from non-existence. The first is that, since pain is the only evil, we can only be harmed by what we perceive, but the dead have no capacity for perception, and hence they cannot be harmed: 'For all good and bad consists in sense-experience (*aisthêsis*), and death is the privation of sense-experience' (*Ep. Men.* 124, cf. KD 2). The second argument contends that there is no subject to which the badness of being dead – if any – could be assigned: 'When we exist, death is not yet present, and when death is present, then we do not exist. Therefore, it is relevant neither to the living nor to the dead, since it does not affect the former, and the latter do not exist' (*Ep. Men.* 125). The living person is a compound of body and soul, and ceases to exist once the soul separates from the body.

The non-perception argument and the non-identity argument are sometimes combined, as in the following passage from Lucretius, which presents the non-identity argument as more conclusive:

> Therefore death is nothing to us, of no concern whatsoever, once it is appreciated that the mind has a mortal nature. Just as in the past we had no sensation of discomfort when the Carthaginians were converging to attack, … so too, when we will no longer exist following the severing of the soul and body, from whose conjunction we are constituted, you can take it that nothing at all will be able to affect us and to stir our sensation – not if the earth collapses into sea, and sea into sky. Even if the nature of our mind and the power of our spirit do have sensation after they are torn from our bodies, that is still nothing to us, who are constituted by the conjunction of body and spirit. (DRN iii.832–44)

---

[25] The Epicurean arguments against the fear of death and against the view that death is a harm have received considerable attention in recent and contemporary philosophy (e.g. Nagel 1970; Feldman 1994; Raz 2001). Warren (2004) offers an excellent discussion of the Epicurean strategies for facing death, paying due attention to where the modern engagements with Epicurus's arguments misread ancient Epicureanism. The following overview is much indebted to this book, as well as to a chapter about the fear of death in Voula Tsouna's monograph on the ethics of Philodemus (Tsouna 2007: 239–311).

For the same reason, it is misguided to fear the prospect of one's dead body being buried or eaten by wild animals, or the fear of suffering the fate of Sisyphos or Tityos in the underworld (DRN iii.966–995) – for once someone dies, there is 'no other self left alive, able to mourn his passing' (DRN iii.886–7.).

The above passage also introduces what some commentators have regarded as an additional argument against the fear of being dead. The argument is based on the premise that our post-mortem non-existence matters to us no more than our pre-natal non-existence. Just as we had not perceived anything, and had not existed, before we were born, the same will be the case when we are dead: and hence post-mortem existence cannot harm us in any way. Commentators have had different views on whether the symmetry argument makes a substantive addition to the non-perception and non-identity arguments. One possible reading is that it does not. The reference to pre-natal non-existence merely restates that death as complete annihilation is nothing to us: just as the pre-natal non-existence was nothing to us, post-mortem non-existence will be nothing to us. On a different reading, the argument aims to show that post-mortem non-existence is – rather than just will be – nothing to us 'looking forward from within a lifetime' (Warren 2004: 60–62). This difference is quite significant insofar as, on the latter reading, the argument has a greater therapeutic effect: it addresses not only the fear of being dead but also the fear of mortality, that is, the distressing prospect of the inevitability of annihilation.

But an objector may press on: there is an important asymmetry between the pre-natal and post-mortem non-existence, in the sense that the former state is not a deprivation whereas the latter is; it robs us of the existence that we already have. This objection may seem to gain additional traction from the hedonistic premises of the Epicurean theory. Do not Epicureans have especially strong reasons to regret the finitude of the human existence because they hold that pleasure is the good, and, surely, pleasure can be increased by duration? According to Cicero, it is inconsistent for a hedonist to maintain that 'there is no greater pleasure to be had in an infinite period than in a brief and limited one' (ii.88). Epicurus does say that 'the wise man chooses the pleasantest food, not simply the greater quantity, so too he enjoys the pleasantest time, not the longest' (*Ep. Men.* 126). Fair enough: but is not a larger quantity of the finest food always preferable to a smaller quantity of the finest food? If this were right, it would easily follow that desire for immortality is unnecessary but still natural: the more overall pleasure we have, the better; and, if pleasure can be increased by duration, a longer life, if pleasant, is always more desirable than a shorter life. And hence death deprives us of some future goods that we may enjoy if only we were not to die.

We have cited some evidence that shows Epicurus' clear commitment to the view that pleasure – in the specific sense of static pleasure – cannot be increased beyond certain limits. Later Epicurean thinkers stick to this view and deploy new arguments against the desire for immortality. Invoking the image of the leaky jar familiar from Plato's *Gorgias*, Lucretius addresses those who complain about the inevitability of death in the personified voice of Nature:

> What is your grievance, mortal, that you give yourself up to this whining and repining? Why do you weep and wail over death? If the life you have lived till now has been a pleasant thing – if all its blessings have not leaked away like water poured into a cracked pot and run to waste unrelished – why then, you stupid man, do you not retire like a dinner guest who has eaten his fill of life, and take your carefree rest with a quiet mind? Or, if all your gains have been poured profitless away and life has grown distasteful, why do you seek to swell the total? The new can but turn out as badly as the old and perish as unprofitably. Why not rather make an end of life and trouble? Do you expect me to invent some new contrivance for your pleasure? I tell you, there is none. (DRN iii.934–946)

Here we find an implicit answer to the objection that the good life in a greater quantity – like fine food – is preferable to life in a smaller quantity. If life is like a dinner, there is an obvious limit to pleasure, namely satiety; there is only so much food we can truly enjoy at a single sitting. The wise man is satisfied with his share of life, has no unfulfilled desires and has stored the memories of past pleasant experiences firmly in his mind. With reference to the distinction between two kinds of pleasures, we could say that he has used the kinetic pleasures to securely achieve freedom from pain. In contrast, the fool who has lived in a state of permanent discontent – 'for ever feeding a malcontent mind, filling it with good things but never satisfying it' (DRN iii.1004) – has failed to achieve *ataraxia* even though he had a significant quantity of kinetic pleasures at his disposal. Rather than learning to be content with the past and present goods, these fools always look to the future in the hope of finding new sources of pleasure by fulfilling their 'empty' desires. Just like leaky jars that can never be filled, so too their lives will never be happy, or even any better, no matter how long they happen to live.

In order to counter the belief that goods are increased by duration, Philodemus cites the pointed case of Pythocles, an Epicurean prodigy, who died at eighteen (*De Morte*, xii.34–xiii.13). This argument bears not only on the fear of mortality in general, but on the fear of premature death in particular. Despite his early death, and thanks to his extraordinary talent and philosophical training, he 'achieved and enjoyed' the limit of pleasure that can be experienced in the human life and died with no desires unfulfilled. Therefore, he can be regarded as having lived a complete life. It is misguided to think that one has more of one's life if one lives longer. When Philodemus says that Pythocles has 'lived more of a life' (*pleon bebiôkenai*) than some old men, he infuses 'life' with a normative dimension.[26] We can think here of Aristotle of the *Protrepticus* who says that 'living more' means not so much living longer but living better. From the perspective of this redefinition, a desire for eternal life is absurd: you are not able to live more simply by living longer; rather, you have a greater share of life if you live well.

However, in contrast to his predecessors, Philodemus explicitly concedes that in some cases the prospect of death might bring about natural – rather than empty – distress. For our purposes, the particularly salient case here is the prospect of death as preventing one from completing one's philosophical progress. People who are progressing in wisdom but die before becoming truly wise can only achieve a less powerful happiness, in contrast to the 'most powerful' happiness (*De Morte* xviii.11–12), and on this ground 'being snatched away' by death is the cause of 'natural pain'. This is consistent with Epicurus' view that we have a natural and necessary desire for freedom from pain; death deprives us of the chance to achieve this state, and thus to achieve the complete life. This leads to pain – as the frustration of necessary desires generally does – all the more that we have already made some progress towards that goal.

4.4 The Axiological Dominance of *Ataraxia*

Given the Epicurean identification of pleasure with the good, different kinds of pleasure amount to different kinds of good. So, there are, as it were, goods of the body and goods of the soul, as well as static goods and kinetic goods. Every single pleasure will belong to one of the two categories within two axes. It is also possible for at least some of these goods to be achieved independently of others: for instance, you may experience lots of kinetic pleasures without achieving the condition of *ataraxia*. This

---

[26] Warren (2004: 248) attributes to Philodemus a distinction between a descriptive and a normative meaning of 'life'.

apparent axiological plurality raises questions whether the possession of some kinds of pleasures could be sufficient to make life worth living even when other kinds are missing. Two possibilities, in particular, come to mind. (1) Although one cannot be blessed without freedom from pain and disturbance, would not the abundance of kinetic pleasures throughout one's life alone make this life at least worth living? (2) Similarly, would not the condition of freedom from bodily pain (*aponia*) be a worthwhile condition that makes a life worth living even in the absence of freedom from disturbance (*ataraxia*)?

Interestingly, for our purposes, it has been suggested in the scholarship that the axiological structure of the Epicurean theory has some important similarities with the Stoic theory: allegedly, the status of the Epicurean kinetic pleasures is akin, in some respects at least, to the status of the Stoic preferred indifferents. In Stoicism, the distinction between two orders of value, the good and preferred indifferents, underlies the sharp distinction between happy life and life worth living. If indeed the parallel between Epicurean and Stoic theories of value has some substance, this may have important implications for answering the first of the above questions in the affirmative. This suggestion therefore deserves closer attention. I first discuss the axiological relationship between static and kinetic pleasures, which is relevant for the first question, and then turn to the relationship between *ataraxia* and *aponia*, which is relevant for the second.

Raphael Woolf has noted that the verb *poikillein*, which specifies the contribution of the kinetic pleasures once the freedom from pain has been achieved, would be better translated not as 'vary' but as 'embellish'. This translation should convey that kinetic pleasures in the painless state are something 'one can reasonably opt for but do perfectly well without' (Woolf 2009: 169), similarly to travelling business class instead of economy class. Once you are free from pain, kinetic pleasures are dispensable but worth choosing whenever they come your way, as long as they satisfy the natural desires. They are indifferent for your happiness, one could say, but nonetheless preferred. The category of kinetic pleasures has some further similarities with the Stoic category of preferred indifferents: in contrast to the Epicurean static pleasures, and to the Stoic good, they allow for accumulation and degrees. Moreover, both kinetic pleasures and preferred indifferents are natural objects of selection.

These parallels has been explicitly noted and developed in the interpretation of the Epicurean conception of *telos* by Jeffrey Purinton. The challenge is, Purinton argues, to understand how is it possible for Epicurus to firmly subordinate kinetic pleasures to static pleasure, on the one hand,

and, on the other, to claim that the good is 'inconceivable' without kinetic pleasures (Cicero, *Tusc.* iii.41). To offer a solution to this puzzle, he draws a parallel with the Stoics: 'just as the Stoic learns to make the acquisition of virtue the aim of his life as a whole, yet continues to pursue things in accordance with nature in his individual actions, so the Epicurean learns to make the attainment of undisturbed painlessness the aim of his life as a whole, yet continues to pursue kinetic pleasures in his individual actions', while still regarding success or failure of this pursuit as a matter of indifference (Purinton 1993: 312–313). So, similarly to the Stoic sage, the Epicurean sage pursues two independent kinds of non-instrumental goals. Moreover, kinetic pleasures have a role similar to the preferred indifferents insofar as they prevent the sage from falling into inertia once the freedom from pain has been achieved; without them, the Epicurean would 'lack a reason to go on living' (ibid., 313).

It is not my aim to assess the cogency of Purinton's interpretation; it is quite possible that the parallel he draws, in the respects in which he draws it, is pertinent and does help us to understand better the Epicurean theory. I note only that in one crucial respect the parallel between the axiological status of kinetic pleasures and preferred indifferents collapses.[27] For the Stoics, the non-instrumental value of preferred indifferents is independent of the value of virtue. When you happen to have a preponderance of preferred indifferents over their opposites, this makes your life worth living regardless of whether you are virtuous are not. Also, there is nothing wrong about the aim of maximising preferred indifferents even if you are not yet virtuous; it will not make you any less foolish, but it is still something you have valid reasons to do, given your natural constitution. But none of this seems to hold concerning the pursuit of kinetic pleasures in the Epicurean theory. It is one thing to aim at some extra kinetic pleasures when you have achieved *ataraxia*, and quite another thing to aim at maximising your kinetic pleasures when you are still a fool. Fools are like leaky jars, to recall the Lucretian appropriation of the Platonic image, so that no matter how much sensual gratification you happen to achieve, that will not make your life any better, nor indeed any more worth living. Whereas on the Stoic view it actually means something for your well-being to have an abundance of preferred indifferents, even if you are

---

[27] It is rather obvious that the parallel does not quite fit in other respects. For instance, for the Stoics, deliberation about how to best promote the preferred indifferents is *the* way of living happily; the pursuit of kinetic pleasure does not play this role in the Epicurean theory.

not virtuous, according to the Epicureans an accidental abundance of kinetic pleasures in the absence of freedom from disturbance does not make any real difference for your well-being.

Let me now turn to the second question that concerns the Epicurean end as the combination of *aponia* and *ataraxia*. Could freedom from bodily pain alone be enough to make your life worth living for you? It has been argued that 'painlessness of the body and tranquillity of the mind are interconnected and crucially depend upon each other' (Tsouna 2020: 17). A long-term freedom from bodily pain requires good management of one's desires as well as sound deliberation about which pleasures should be pursued and which not. This is the job of 'prudence' (*phronêsis*), which again is also the source of *ataraxia*. But even if it were possible to stay free of bodily pains without eliminating disturbances in the mind, Epicureans would be hardly impressed by such a life, for the pleasures and pains of the mind are generally much greater than those of the body. It is therefore rather unlikely, and the sources do not make any suggestion in this direction, that bodily painlessness would make a significant difference to your well-being in the absence of *ataraxia*.

Conversely, however, there are indications that the mind free from disturbance may be sufficient to sustain happy life even in the absence of bodily painlessness. So, the interdependence of *aponia* and *ataraxia* is somewhat asymmetrical. Freedom from bodily pain certainly is a fully fledged component of the Epicurean end. According to some sources, freedom from disturbance even primarily consists in a 'confident expectation' of bodily painlessness (Plutarch, *Non Posse* 1089d). Nonetheless, the Epicureans apparently maintained, like the Stoics, that the wise person is happy even on the rack (DL x.118). This is consistent with the claim that those who are virtuous necessarily also live happily (*Ep. Men.* 132). This may be explained by a wise person's psychological capacity to counterbalance, or even offset, present bodily pain by the recollection of past pleasures (DL x.22). More generally, Epicurus regarded bodily pains as manageable: acute pains are short, and chronic pains are even conducive to more pleasure than pain (KD 4).

So, the upshot of this discussion is that *ataraxia*, the freedom from mental disturbance, *is* the dominant Epicurean good. All non-ataraxic goods, that is, the kinetic pleasures, or the static pleasure of bodily painlessness, are by themselves relatively insignificant for overall well-being; in contrast, *ataraxia* is sufficient to warrant blessedness. As we shall see in the following section, this dominant status of *ataraxia* has implications for the Epicurean view about the worth of unhappy human life.

4.5 The Life Worth Continuing

In the passage from the *Letter to Menoeceus* quoted in the Introduction, Epicurus rebuts the tragic outlook of the poets. The poets were wrong both in claiming that never to be born is the best lot and that a swift departure from life is to be chosen if one is unfortunate enough to have been born. Among extant evidence, we do not find any further discussions of whether it is worth being born rather than not, but there is some scattered material bearing on the question of the worth of continued existence. As in Stoicism, some of this material can be extracted from the Epicurean discussions about the appropriateness of suicide. However, the Epicureans did not explicitly articulate the notion of a threshold. This has to do with the fact that – with one important qualification – the Epicureans did not distinguish between a happy life and a life worth living: life is worth living precisely when it is happy or – and this is the qualification – when it has a reasonable chance to achieve freedom from pain in the future.

In this section, I first explain why the Epicureans were not committed to a robust distinction between a happy life and a life worth living. Then I turn to a further question that is without parallel in other ancient schools, namely, whether continued existence is worthwhile, somewhat paradoxically, precisely once happiness has been achieved. One would expect that a happy life is worth continuing exactly when, and because, it becomes happy. But the question inevitably arises from the Epicurean commitment to the view that the good cannot be increased beyond a certain limit.

Epicureans had a rather reserved attitude to the practice of suicide.[28] While there are special cases in which suicide is endorsed as a legitimate option for the wise person, there are typically strong reasons not to commend it. As for the wise person, their life is free of disturbance and their mind is a secure storehouse of memories that provide reliable sources of pleasure; this alone gives them strong reasons to stay alive even in adverse circumstances, with possible qualifications that I shall discuss later. As for non-sages, Lucretius remarks that, ironically, their decision to commit suicide is often induced by their fear of death (DRN iii.79–82). What these unhappy persons should do instead is to make their lives worth living by removing the fear of death by means of the Epicurean teachings.

---

[28] For the Epicurean views about suicide, see Englert (1994); Cooper (1999: 536–37); Warren (2004: 205–12).

But this reserved attitude to suicide does not entail an optimism about what it takes to live a worthwhile life. In fact, the passage from Philodemus' *De Morte* quoted in the epigraph to this chapter suggests that the assessment of life's worthwhileness does not automatically translate into a recommendation for suicide: 'But as for the foolish man, neither will he gain a noteworthy good, even if he should live for as long a time as Tithonus, nor is it too unfitting for him [to die] in the quickest way when he is born, [rather than] more slowly, even if we do [not] recommend it'. (*De Morte* xix.33–xx.1). The 'fools' are all those who have neither assimilated the Epicurean teachings nor made any significant progress towards that goal. Philodemus does not explain why the Epicureans do not advise these persons to commit suicide, but the likely reason is precisely that their lives could be improved if only they would earnestly turn to philosophy. But unless this happens, these humans are such that they benefit no more from staying alive than from departing from life as soon as possible.

An even stronger statement can be found at the end of the passage in which Philodemus argues that a wise man who dies young is infinitely happier than many old fools: 'For I will not mention the fact that in many instances dying young would seem more advantageous (*lusitelesteron*) for many of the foolish, even when they are raised as children in thriving households' (*De Morte* xiii.14–17, transl. Warren 2004). For such people, it might indeed be better to 'make an end of life and trouble', as Lucretius puts it. Presumably, the reason why even those people who are privileged to experience significant amounts of kinetic pleasure would be better off dead is that they are bound to have overwhelmingly painful lives, unless they achieve *ataraxia*. As long as one lives with a chronically dissatisfied mind, the pervasive disturbance cannot be outweighed by any amount of pleasant stimulation.

So, are there no non-happy lives whatsoever that would be worth living? There does seem to be one important exception: the lives of those who are not yet wise, but who make progress towards or aspire to wisdom. We have seen that some Epicureans acknowledged that death is naturally fearsome if it deprives one of the opportunity to make progress in philosophy and thus to make one's life complete. It is never too late to begin with philosophy, 'for no one is under-age or over-age for health of the soul' (*Ep. Men.* 122). As long as there is some chance that one could make a progress towards wisdom, continued existence might be worthwhile even if one is not happy yet. In that case, the threshold of a life barely worth living would be defined by a promise of achieving the target in future. Thus, an unhappy life is worth living *on the condition* that it might turn happy one day. The value that defines the threshold is fully derivative upon the value of the target.

Having discussed the terms on which life is worth continuing for the non-sages, let me now address the condition of the sages. Can the continued existence ever become not worthwhile for them? The sources point at three conditions in which this could be the case. One is indicated by the claim that the sage 'will sometimes die for a friend (*huper philou*)' (DL x.121). This claim is repeated and further justified in a snippet from the *Vatican Sayings*: 'The wise man feels no more pain (*algei*) when he is tortured ‹than when his friend is tortured, and will die on his behalf (*huper autou*); for if he betrays› his friend, his entire life (*bios autou pas*) will be confounded and utterly upset because of a lack of confidence (*di'apistian sunchuthêsetai kai anakechaitismenos estai*)' (VS 56–57, transl. Inwood and Gerson). In the Epicurean view, friends are an important source of security and thus play an indispensable role in achieving and maintaining *ataraxia*. In that sense, the sage's *ataraxia* is generally vulnerable to the fate of his friends, all the more so since a wise person feels towards his friends exactly as he feels towards himself (Cicero, *Fin.* i.68). But the above passage seems to address a rather specific case of such a vulnerability that has to do with self-sacrifice on behalf of a friend. Just how this altruistic sentiment sits with the hedonist commitments has been a matter of debate.[29] Presumably, the wise person's self-sacrifice will be motivated by a projection of the disastrous consequences that the omission of such an act would have for his long-term hedonic balance, both on account of losing a friend, an important source of security, and on account of the feelings of self-blame for breaking the principle of loyalty important to friendship. The wise person recognises that such a life would be not happy or worth living, and therefore regards the sacrifice of their own life as the only rational response to the predicament.

The second condition that may make a continued existence not worthwhile for a sage is bodily pain. The picture that emerges from the fragmentary evidence is somewhat inconclusive. The remarks about the relationship between *aponia* and *ataraxia* from the preceding sections suggest that a wise person's life is worth continuing despite severe bodily pains. Epicurus on his deathbed lost his freedom from bodily pain, but still managed to maintain his *ataraxia*, buttressing it by the mental kinetic pleasures derived from pleasant recollections of past conversations with

---

[29] Cf. O'Keefe's view of this claim as 'extravagant' (2001: 302–3) though ultimately compatible with the egoistic premises. Mitsis (1988: 104), however, takes these passages as an indication that Epicurus recognises 'an end other than pleasure'.

friends (DL x.22). This is consistent with the controversial view that the wise person will be able to find pleasure – and thus to counteract or offset pain – thanks to his art of 'locating and obtaining' pleasure.

At the same time, some sources indicate that bodily pains may be a sufficient reason, possibly even for the sage, to depart from life: 'Thus if pain is tolerable, we can endure it, and if not, if life no longer pleases us, we can leave the stage with equanimity' (*Fin.* i.49). This claim sits uneasily with the view from KD 4 that pains are generally endurable, all the more so for the sage who has mastered the art of locating pleasure. But it is possible that in some cases the sages might lose this art, namely when their intellectual capacities and memory are failing.[30] This impairment might in itself be sufficient to choose death, and even more so if it is associated with bodily pains that are severe and chronic. Once the sage's life has achieved completion, there will be little reason to cling to a life burdened with chronic physical pain.

Finally, the third possible reason against sage's continued existence is simply the achievement of life's 'completion'. There is a worry that the Epicurean arguments against the fear of death are so effective that they undermine the value of continued existence: if the limit of pleasure to be had in this life cannot be increased, why should I carry on living once I achieve it? Hence the conclusion looms that 'the Epicureans appear to offer no significant positive reason for wishing to continue to live, beyond a mere inertia' (Warren 2004: 210). On the one hand, there is no reason to commit suicide; on the other, there is no positive reason to carry on living. This conclusion is rather unattractive: do we aspire to happiness only to find out that we have no compelling reasons to stay alive once we have achieved it?

In contrast to the preceding two conditions, those related to friends and bodily pains, this third worry seems neither to reflect an actual Epicurean position nor to necessarily follow from the premises of the Epicurean theory. There are three reasons for this view. First, in a fragment from *On Choices and Avoidances*, Philodemus claims that the wise man takes good care of his health, and 'spares no effort in all those opportunities which can bring something better, in the expectation of living longer' (xxiii.1–5; transl. Indelli and Tsouna-McKirahan); these opportunities include, in particular, opportunities for making friends. This implies that a longer life may bring more pleasures, and these have to be the kinetic pleasures, such as joy in the new friendships. These pleasures do not increase the static pleasure, but

---

[30] Warren (2004: 208) According to Lucretius, Democritus chose death due to the decline of his memory (DRN iii.1039–41).

they are – if we follow Woolf's reading – welcome 'embellishments'; they do not make a big difference to the quality of life but they are nice to have. Secondly, a life could be worth continuing even without these additional kinetic pleasures. For while the static pleasure does not increase once the limit has been reached, it does not decrease either. A wish to remain in such a pleasant state seems to be a sufficiently positive reason for staying alive. Thirdly, as pointed out by Alex Long (2019: 142), the wise person's necessary desires for freedom from pain, freedom from disturbance, and life itself do not just disappear once the best state has been achieved; they remain in place and the wise person has good reasons to continue to fulfil them.[31]

4.6 Epicureans and the Value of Mere Living

In the *Letter to Menoeceus*, Epicurus contends that it is 'naive' to advise an old man to die because 'life is something to be welcomed' or, on an alternative translation, 'because of the pleasing aspects of life'. The phrase *dia to tês zôês aspaston* is ambiguous: life is inherently pleasant, but it is not clear whether this pleasure derives from the vital activities that constitute the mere fact of being alive, or only from certain pleasant experiences that fill a life. The same ambiguity can be detected in Lucretius' talk about 'love of life' (*amor vitae*). The way Lucretius puts this suggests that all those who have been born have 'tasted' this love (DRN v.179), which implies that life is pleasant also to the many who live painfully. So, perhaps, what is pleasant is the life itself, whereas what is painful refers to the bad contents of life. He also says that because of the inherent pleasantness of life, 'man must will to remain alive so long as beguiling pleasure holds him' (DRN v.178). Could the view that every human life has some pleasure in it be a reason for the Epicureans not to commend suicide to the fools? A further potential indication for the view that even mere living has some non-instrumental value is that there are natural desires that are necessary not only for *ataraxia* and freedom from bodily pain but also for 'life itself' (*auto to zên*) (*Ep. Men.* 127). These include desires for food, drink and sleep. Could this possibly imply that we need to pursue the satisfaction of these desires because life in itself has a non-instrumental value, and in that sense is on par with freedom from pain and freedom from disturbance?

Overall, this evidence seems insufficient to attribute to the Epicureans the view that even mere living has a non-instrumental value. To take the

---

[31] *Pace* Rosenbaum (1990: 24) and Dimas (2015: 178), who maintain that those experiencing katastematic pleasures have no desires at all.

last bit first, the desires that are necessary for life itself can be purely instrumental for the fulfilment of the desire for freedom from pain and disturbance. It is natural to desire *ataraxia* and the freedom from bodily pain, but in order to fulfil these desires, one needs to be alive in the first place. If the desire for life itself is necessary as instrumental to fulfilling the desire for freedom from pain, then it may well be the case that the value of mere living is itself only instrumental as well: the state of being alive is valuable only as a necessary condition for living pleasantly. In fact, since the fools, or at least those among them who have no real chance of ever benefiting from philosophy, will never achieve happiness, the fulfilment of the desire for life is bad for them. Their desire for staying alive turns out to be nothing but what Lucretius calls 'lust for life' (*cupido vitai*; DRN iii.1077) or 'thirst for life' (*sitis vitai*) (ibid. 1084). In contrast to the natural and necessary desires, the lust for life is an empty desire because it assumes that the prospect of living longer, quite on its own, will make a life better.[32]

There is also a deeper conceptual reason against the non-instrumental valuation of the mere living, namely that it may not be possible for the Epicureans to evaluate mere living as separate from its contents at all. For if to be alive means to have perceptions, as the arguments against the fear of death presuppose, then these perceptions will always be either painful or pleasant, since there is no intermediate state between pleasure and pain, and in that sense, we are already talking about pleasant or painful contents of life, rather than about life itself as independent from its contents. The Stoics or Peripatetics also held that life is constituted by perception but maintained that its value does not derive from any pleasure it may contain but from instantiating a certain level of finality. The finality inherent in living a recognisably human life can be distinguished from the value of different contents of that life, such as health, virtue or pleasure. But such a separation is not available to the Epicureans. Since pleasure is the only end, there is no reason to value mere living non-instrumentally on the basis of pleasure-unrelated teleological grounds.

4.7 No Life Worth Living without Philosophy

We began by noting that the ancient hedonists departed from the mainstream tradition by proclaiming pleasure, rather than virtue, to be the end of human life. In this respect their outlook may appear to have some

---

[32] See also Lucretius' description of people who are so terrified by the prospect of death that they are willing to suffer from terrible and unnecessary pains (DRN vi. 1208 ff).

affinity with the modern approaches to a life worth living, which define a worthwhile life by reference to subjective well-being, rather than to objective perfection, and thus promise a comparatively low-threshold account of life worth living. We are now in a position to confirm, focusing on the Epicureans, that all aspects of this expectation remain largely unfulfilled.

The view that the criterion of life worth living is a feeling should not eclipse the fact that the specific feeling that makes life worth living – the freedom from disturbance – strictly supervenes on the objective state of a healthy or, if you like, well-functioning mind. This state is achieved through eradication of empty beliefs and desires. In this sense, the Epicurean ethical outlook is not too far from the Platonic view that a life worth living depends on a healthy soul which has been rid of unreflectively held misconceptions about what is good.[33] Returning to the choice of Heracles, we could say that the Epicureans indeed did not regard the path of pleasure to be easier that than the path of virtue; this is simply because, for them, the path of virtue is necessary for the path of pleasure. In two respects, the Epicurean approach puts an even greater emphasis on the objective and specifically intellectual perfection than Plato did, taking the *Republic* as the point of reference. First, remember that there is some evidence for Plato's concession that a life with a corrupted body may not be worth living. We would expect that philosophers who value freedom from bodily pain, or at least the expectation of a pain-free life in the future, as part of the highest good would emphatically endorse such a view. But we have seen that bodily well-being is not a dominant consideration either in favour of or against life worth living. Secondly, in contrast to the Plato of the *Republic*, the Epicureans are uncompromising in their view that there is no happiness – and indeed no life worth living – to be had for those who do not practise philosophy. Plato granted that even non-philosophers can achieve a life worth living – if not necessarily the happy or supremely happy life – provided that they are good citizens who exercise their function as appropriate. For the Epicureans, there is only one way – not only to happiness but also to a life worth living – and that is the way of philosophy.

In maintaining unequivocally that the absence of philosophical practice is an unconditional worthbreaker, Epicureans were in the minority. There is, of course, the Socratic dictum that an unexamined life is not

---

[33] Cf. the recent study by Kelly Arenson (2019) that systematically pursues the parallels between Plato's notion of psychic health and the Epicurean account of happiness.

worth living, but on the interpretation I have defended this means only that your life must be informed by philosophical expertise. There is also a less famous dictum, 'reason (*logos*) or noose' (DL vi.24), attributed to the Cynics, specifically Diogenes, but the broader context in which this dictum is embedded makes clear that the rationality deemed necessary for a life worth living is conceived more broadly here than the philosophical life, as it is enacted by the work of 'physicians, philosophers and pilots' (ibid.). This leaves Epicureans in the company of philosophers with Platonic or Pythagorean leanings, perhaps including early Aristotle, who would be inclined to endorse the statement from the *Protrepticus* cited earlier (Section 2.5) that life without philosophy is all 'trash and non-sense'.

This insistence raises the worry that many humans will be denied a realistic aspiration to a life worth living. Overall, the available Epicurean sources that reflect on the accessibility of philosophy give rise to a somewhat ambivalent picture. On the one hand, there is a strong insistence in the Epicurean vision of a utopian society that everybody can practise philosophy and therefore live a good life (Diogenes of Oenoanda, fr. 97 and 119). Lucretius contends, optimistically, that thanks to philosophy there is 'nothing to prevent men leading a life worthy of gods' (DRN iii.221-2). He acknowledges an objection that some individual inborn aptitudes may be a handicap in philosophical pursuits. But after discussing how the multiplicity of atomic shapes and their possible combinations gives rise to different kinds of temperaments, he dismisses the role of natural aptitudes as insignificant: 'The lingering traces of inborn temperament that cannot be eliminated by philosophy are so slight that there is nothing to prevent man leading a life worthy of gods' (DRN iii.319-20).

At the same time, this optimism clashes with a rather disturbing claim that 'not every physical constitution would permit a man to become wise, nor every nationality' (DL x.117). These sound like rather significant restrictions. For the Epicureans, the importance of bodily constitution derives from their view that all mental processes are fundamentally embodied, and that the physical constitution is bound to influence the robustness of the mind. If even some kinds of bodily constitution can make one unfit for wisdom, this should apply – contrary to Lucretius' assessment – all the more to some mental constitutions, especially since they are influenced by the underlying bodily constitutions. This suspicion is reinforced by some attributes of the Epicurean conception of wisdom mentioned earlier that have to do with the control of one's feelings: for instance, if the mind should be capable of counterbalancing severe bodily pain by a pleasant recollection of past experiences, one needs, at least, a very good memory to make these recollections sufficiently vivid. One may doubt that this is the kind of psychological attribute that can be acquired by philosophical training alone.

In sum, we can say that the Epicureans had a rather demanding account of life worth living. This is a result of the combination of two views. First, it takes as much to achieve the life worth living as it takes to achieve the blessed life. One important exception concerns those who are not yet blessed but who are making progress in philosophy. Second, there is a single path to a life worth living – philosophy – which may nonetheless not be accessible to all humans, as the Epicureans would like to have it.

CHAPTER 5

Peripatetics on Vicious Humans and Caged Animals

For good men should flee life among great misfortunes, bad men even among very good fortunes; for they go wrong more. That is why bad people are not properly speaking fortunate.

(Stobaeus, *Ecl.* ii. 134.3–6)

The [inborn human] desire for activity (*cupiditas agendi*) continues to grow as children do. And so none of us would choose the sleep of Endymion, even if we were given the sweetest dreams to go with. We would consider this a fate as bad as death. Even the laziest people, as extravagantly idle as they may be, can none the less be seen in constant activity, both physical and mental. … Even the animals that we keep caged for our amusement find captivity difficult. Despite the fact that they are better fed than they would be in the wild, they miss being able to move about and roam freely as nature allows. Thus the more able and accomplished one is, the less one would even want to live at all (*esse omnino nolit in vita*) if prevented from going about one's business, however well provided one may be with pleasures to graze on.

(Cicero, *Fin.* v. 55–57)[1]

5.1 Introducing Later Peripatetics

Besides the Epicureans and Stoics, the Greek and Roman philosophical debates of the Hellenistic and post-Hellenistic periods were also shaped by philosophers of other allegiances. Most influential among them were the followers of Plato and Aristotle, known as the Academics or Platonists, and the Peripatetics, respectively. In philosophical debates about happiness and the good, Peripatetic thinkers in particular played a major role, and in many contexts were the main interlocutors and opponents of Stoicism, the most influential school of the post-Classical world.

---

[1] Translations of the epitome of the Peripatetic ethics from Stobaeus follow Tsouni (2017); Piso's account from *Fin.* v is rendered according to Annas and Woolf (2001); and translations of other Peripatetic material follow Sharples (2010), unless otherwise noted.

While the ancient neo-Aristotelians have not enjoyed as much attention from modern commentators as have other schools of the Hellenistic
period, some important recent studies have done a great deal to help us
understand and appreciate their contributions to philosophy in general,
and ethics in particular.[2] These contributions generally consist in recast-
ing or revising some elements of Aristotle's ethical theory to provide
relevant answers to burning questions as they emerged in the new terrain
of Hellenistic philosophy. But in so doing they also qualify or develop
Aristotle's theory in an independent-minded manner, and often make
original points that go significantly beyond what Aristotle himself had
to say. The Peripatetic contribution to the themes of life worth living
and the value of life is a case in point. Not only do the Peripatetics
address these themes with considerable focus, they also undertake sustained attempts, not found in Aristotle, to explicitly define the threshold
notion of life worth living as different from the target notion of happiness. They explicitly articulate this distinction and endow it with a
conceptual robustness matched only by the Stoics.

Let me start with several observations about the epigraphs in order to
introduce the general approach and to draw attention to some remarkable
pieces of philosophical theory to be discussed and explained in the following sections. The first citation brings out that, in contrast to Aristotle, the
Peripatetics approached the theme of life worth living from the vantage
point of Hellenistic and early Imperial debates about the appropriateness
of suicide. The characteristically Aristotelian concern with good and bad
fortune is brought into the picture to make a counter-statement to the
Stoic view that even vicious humans may have good reasons to remain
alive if only they have a preponderance of naturally preferred indifferents,
such as health or wealth, over their opposites. The Peripatetics flatly deny
this: not only should vicious humans generally 'flee life', which is a clear
reference to suicide, they should do so even in the most favourable circumstances when they are optimally supplied with these goods. What is
more, the good fortune does not diminish, but exacerbate, the inherent
harmfulness of vicious living. Whereas in the case of normal, non-vicious

---

[2] This includes, in particular, Robert Sharples's annotated anthology of Peripatetic texts from 2010;
Brad Inwood's 2014 study of the development of Peripatetic thought, with particular emphasis on
its programmatic naturalism; William Fortenbaugh's studies on the Didymus epitome and a 2017
volume edited by him dedicated to this work; and Georgia Tsouni's 2019 monograph along with
David Sedley's 2012 volume, both dedicated to the thought of Antiochus. All of these works are
indebted, in different ways, to the monumental work of Paul Moraux, published in the 1970s, on
the Aristotelian tradition.

lives, good fortune has positive value, vice inverts this value into the negative. That is why bad humans cannot ever be fortunate, in the strict sense
of the word, and why their life is the worse for them the more favourable
their life circumstances are.

This idea of inverted positive value is without a clear parallel in Aristotle's
original theory; instead, it reminds us of the idea of the good and bad use
of extrinsic goods from Plato's *Euthydemus*. But there is an Aristotelian
motivation here for adopting this idea that has to do with the characteristically Aristotelian interest in the notion of 'activity' (*energeia*). According to
Aristotle, favourable external circumstances are good insofar as they provide the necessary context in which the distinctive human capacities can
be optimally actualised; adverse circumstances are bad because they thwart
or impede these actualisations. If, therefore, some external goods enable
one to maximise one's activities, but these activities happen to be such
that they harm the person who exercises them, it follows that the external
goods are in fact harmful.

The notion of activity as the good is the dominant theme of the second
citation. This passage exemplifies the Peripatetic ambition to espouse,
similarly to the Epicureans and the Stoics, a naturalistic account of the
human good, where the process of development towards virtue is regarded
as proceeding from certain 'starting points' (*archai*) found in the inborn
inclinations of all humans (compare Sections 3.2 and 4.3). The Peripatetic
starting point, as presented in this passage, is neither pleasure nor the
instinct for self-preservation; instead, it is a 'desire for activity'. All humans
have an inborn desire to be active rather than idle, and it is the freedom to
satisfy this desire, that is, to be active without impediments, that appears
to be the necessary condition of having a life worth living. The view that
a life of perpetual sleep is not worth living goes back to Aristotle, but
here it is restated with new sets of emphases owed to the postulate of the
inborn human desire for activity. One is that a life of inactivity, besides
being worthless in an objective sense, also necessarily frustrates the desire
of those who live it. Thus, we find here an element of the desire-fulfilment
view: activity is good not only because of its objective ontological status of
realisation or fulfilment, but also because it satisfies the natural desire for
activity. Another emphasis worth mentioning concerns the notion of pleasure. Insofar as pleasures supervene on activities, according to Aristotle's
theory (NE x.4-5), the claim of the inborn desire for activity could easily
integrate the Epicurean view that humans also have an inborn desire for
pleasure. But in this passage and elsewhere the text stresses that it is the
activity – *not* pleasure – that is the object of primary impulse; sleep may

be more pleasant than some painful activities, and yet humans consistently choose the latter over the former. This contrast between pleasure and activity is motivated by pervasive anti-Epicurean agenda.

The second passage takes a position on life worth living that likewise deploys the notion of inverted positive value. But here, unlike in the first epigraph, the inversion does not concern cases where bad capacities can be freely exercised but rather cases where good capacities are impeded. In general, it is good to have well-developed natural capacities, and the better they are, the better it is for you. But what ultimately matters is whether, or to what extent, you can actualise them. The idea that one would rather be dead than idle, and that even trivial activities are better than none, shows a more explicit and committed valuation of freedom from impediments than what we know from Aristotle. In fact, in cases of deep and chronic inhibition of these capacities, their goodness becomes a burden that makes life all the worse for you. 'The more able and accomplished one is', the more life is *not* worth living if one is 'prevented from going about one's business'. This is a striking claim without antecedent in the tradition. In effect, it means that the psychic goods are, for all their indisputable value, also liabilities that put you at risk. If this idea sounds familiar it is because it was mentioned in the Introduction in the review of some modern approaches to life worth living. McMahan's person with dementia will be the worse off the more intellectually active and accomplished she was in her pre-dementia life. It is in these Peripatetic sources, then, that we find a neglected ancient predecessor of this argument.

The aim of this chapter is to present and explain these and related neo-Aristotelian views on life worth living in the philosophical context of Hellenistic and early Imperial thought. I shall focus, in particular, on the two texts that are the sources of the epigraphs. Both these texts likely originate from the first century BCE and both were written by authors who themselves were not Peripatetics. Still, given the fragmentary state of the evidence, they are the most intact and most informative sources about Peripatetic thought up to the early Imperial period. The first text is the fifth book of Cicero's *On Ends*, where the Roman consul Marcus Piso presents the ethical theory of Antiochus, the Academic philosopher who combined Stoic and Peripatetic teachings. Despite its syncretist orientation, Piso's account, arguably, reliably presents distinctly Peripatetic doctrines;[3] these are, particularly in the final part of the book, explicitly

---

[3] Tsouni (2019) is a sustained study that qualifies Antiochus 'syncretism' and emphasizes the decisely Peripatetic orientation of Piso's account.

contrasted with the Stoics. The second text is an epitome of the Peripatetic ethics included in the anthology of Joannes Stobaeus and attributed to a person called Didymus, possibly referring to Arius Didymus, a Stoic philosopher at the court of Caesar Augustus. Terminologically, the text is heavily influenced by Stoicism, but this may simply testify to the pervasive influence of this school in the Hellenistic and post-Hellenistic periods; in terms of content, the text presents recognisably Peripatatic views. There are other relevant Peripatetic sources from both earlier and later periods, and I shall refer to some of them as appropriate. These include, in particular, fragments from Aristotle's followers at the head of the Lyceum, the Peripatetic school in Athens, as well as the oeuvres of great commentators on Aristotle's works from the second and third century CE, Aspasius and Alexander of Aphrodisias.

I start with an overview of the major shifts away from Aristotle's account of happiness in later Peripatetic thought (Section 5.2). Next I discuss the Peripatetic engagements with the value of life (Section 5.3). The following two sections are dedicated to the theme of life worth living. Similarly to the procedure from the chapter on Aristotle (Chapter 2), I first establish under what conditions the Peripatetics regarded a life as *not* worth living (Section 5.4) and then discuss what this implies, in combination with the conclusions of Section 5.2, for the possibility of unhappy lives worth living (Section 5.5). The concluding section will reflect on the value of freedom as a characteristically Peripatetic criterion of a life worth living.

5.2   Peripatetic Happiness After Aristotle

In the chapter of this book dedicated to Aristotle, I characterised his account of happiness in terms of the fulfilment of three conditions. To be happy, one must: (1) exercise certain types of activities (the 'what' condition), namely contemplative or political activities; (2) exercise these activities with 'excellence' (*aretê*) of the soul (the 'how' condition); and (3) remain free in this exercise from misfortunes that would impede the exercise of these activities (the 'whether' condition). The later Peripatetics adopt this general account, but they subtly depart from Aristotle in how they understand both the content and relative weight of these conditions. I shall first outline these shifts, and then suggest how were they motivated by the generally Hellenistic orientation towards naturalistic approaches in ethics.

As for the first condition – the required types of preoccupations or activities – the sources retain the privileged standing for the contemplative and political life, but broaden the scope of the political life somewhat, while also enhancing its relative standing. Consider the following account of 'important' (*maiora*) activities from Piso's account from *On Ends*:

> There are many forms of activity, however: so much so that one may lose sight of the trivial amidst the more important ones. As to the most important (*maximae*), it is my view and that of the thinkers whose system I am discussing, that these are: the contemplation and study of the heavenly bodies, and of the mysterious secrets of nature that rational thought has the power to uncover; administration of public affairs, or perhaps knowledge of its theory; and a way of thinking that displays practical reason, temperance, bravery and justice, and which manifests the other virtues too and the actions that flow from them. We may sum up this latter category under the single heading of 'morality' (*honestum*). (*Fin.* v.58)

Two subtle departures from Aristotle's theory can be identified in this passage. First, there is not a clear hierarchy among these activities, so that the contemplative life does not necessarily have a higher status than the political life. Secondly, the political life seems to be understood both in narrow terms (the life of politician or administrator proper) and in broader terms (as engagement in activities consisting in a certain way of thinking and acting, namely 'morally' or, perhaps less controversially, 'honourably').[4] A possible influence of the Stoics comes to mind: virtue is equally realised in all sorts of activities, including the most trivial and ordinary ones.

Turning now to the relevant passage from the Didymus epitome, we can confirm that these shifts constitute a more general tendency:

> The virtuous person will choose a life that exhibits virtue whether as a ruler himself, if the circumstances promote him to that status, or if he has to live in the service of a king or legislate or in any other way be involved in politics. Obtaining none of the above (*toutôn mê tunchanonta*), he will turn to the way of life of an ordinary citizen (*pros to dêmotikon*) or the contemplative life (*to theôrêtikon*) or that of an educator, which lies in the middle (*meson to paideutikon*). For he will choose both to accomplish and to contemplate noble things (*kai prattein kai theôrein ta kala*). In case he is hindered by circumstances (*kôluomenon*) from occupying himself with both, he will become engaged in one of the two, assigning on the one hand a greater value to the contemplative life, but on the other hand, because of his social

---

[4] The relevant Latin word is *honestum*, a key term of Cicero's ethics, which he uses as the equivalent of the Greek *kalon*. Though the semantic connotations of *honestum* do not neatly overlap with those of *kalon*, both terms refer to praiseworthy character and actions. For a good discussion of *honestum* in *De Finibus*, see Graver (2015).

nature inclining toward political actions. That is why he will get married and will have children and will take part in government and will experience temperate love and will enjoy heavy drinking in accordance with social gatherings, albeit not as a primary activity. (Stob. *Ecl.* ii. 143.24–144.5)

Here, the political life in the narrow sense is even regarded as the first choice, whereas the contemplative life is considered as a respectable alternative whenever an appropriate political office is out of reach. In that case, the virtuous person will choose, as the second-best choice, a combination of 'accomplishing and contemplating' noble things – what is later referred to as a 'combined life' (*bios sunthetos*) of practical and contemplative pursuits (144.16). If it turns out to be impossible to unify or integrate practical and contemplative pursuits, the third choice is to choose the contemplative life on the condition that the political nature will still receive adequate expression through participation in established social practices. Again, the life of ordinary morality outside of the political arena proper is affirmed as a way of life that may be sufficient to achieve happiness.[5]

It has been noted by the commentators that the valorisation of political engagement and practical life more broadly considered reflects the general trends of Hellenistic philosophy, and the influence of Stoicism in particular.[6] I would add that the above passages also imply an inspiration by the Stoic theory of different social 'roles' (*personae*), and specifically the third role from Panaetius' account reported by Cicero in the first book of *On Duties*, namely the role imposed on us by fate or fortune (*Off.* i.116–117). The Didymus text is more concerned than Aristotle with the fact that our social position, and hence the type of our lifetime preoccupation, is largely determined by good or bad fortune. Many are not fortunate enough to become a king or high official. But even the less preferable or prestigious social roles, such as the life of an ordinary, decent citizen, are still compatible with life worth living.

Turning to the requirement of *how* one must live, namely virtuously, we again find that virtues are regarded as necessary for the excellent exercise of contemplative and practical activities, and thus for happiness, but also that the set of excellences necessary for the best life has been broadened. Besides the virtues of the soul, both intellectual and moral, texts also affirm the importance of the 'virtues of the body' (*aretai sômatos*) – excellences such as health, bodily power, beauty, swiftness of foot and soundness of

---

[5] The notion of 'demotic' life reminds us Plato's notion of 'ordinary' or 'demotic' virtues from the *Republic*, i.e. those that are ingrained by the philosophers into non-philosophers and that are sufficient for a life worth living (see Section 1.4).

[6] Inwood (2014a: 22–24; 31–32); Fortenbaugh (2018a); see also *Magna Moralia* 1198b4–8 on the primary role of *phronêsis* in contrast with that of *sophia*.

the senses (Stob. *Ecl.* ii.122.20–24). Remarkably, the Didymus epitome draws an analogy between virtues of the soul and virtues of the body, claiming that each bodily virtue has its definite counterpart among the psychic virtues: so, for instance, the counterpart of bodily health is psychic temperance, and the counterpart of the acuity of senses is practical wisdom (124.19–125.8). The virtues of the soul are 'much more valuable' (*polu timiôteras*) than the bodily virtues (123.28–29), but still the bodily virtues are both the necessary ingredients of the best human life and have non-instrumental value, as Piso's account from *On Ends* explicitly states:

> Health, strength and freedom from pain we shall seek not just for their utility but for their own sake (*non propter utilitatem solum, sed etiam ipsas propter*). Our nature wants all of its parts to be fully realized (*omnibus expleri partibus vult*), and therefore seeks on its own account a bodily condition that maximally accords with nature. If our body is ill or in pain or weak, then our whole nature suffers (*tota perturbatur*). (*Fin.* v. 47)

The text stresses that the body is as much a part of our nature as the mind, which is why bodily deficiencies and ailments affect the flourishing of our nature as a whole. Interestingly, the inclusion of the body is stressed by the idea that some bodily flaws, such as languid posture, are expressions of a 'mental flaw' (*animi vitium*) (*Fin.* v. 35). So bodily evils cannot be easily dismissed, both because they are bad in their own right, and because they are often symptoms of an underlying psychic corruption.

We have seen that Aristotle does make some room for acknowledging the importance of bodily goods, or rather for conceding that their absence may diminish happiness. But here we find a claim that cannot be traced back to Aristotle, namely that 'the ultimate good is realized in the category of mind and body' (*Fin.* v. 68). It is in the realm of bodily well-being where a part of our overall flourishing is to be achieved. Aristotle's definition of the *telos* as *ergon* in the first book of the *Nicomachean Ethics* mentions only the activity of the soul, not of the body. There is a remarkable Peripatetic argument for why Aristotle *could* have in fact included the body. He was looking in his function argument for some natural capacities that are 'unique' (*idia*) for the human species. Clearly, what comes to mind first are certain psychological capacities, but Piso notes that even the human body also contributes to what is distinctive for humans, since 'the human body has a configuration superior to that of all other creatures' (*Fin.* v.34). This is a controversial claim; one may quibble that in some respects the bodily capacities of other animals far exceed those of humans, and that all animals in a healthy state have an equally superior constitution insofar as it is ideally suited to the exercise of their specific function. But perhaps the thought is that the human body as a whole is superior to bodies of all other plants and animals because it exceeds them in complexity, as befits the fact that the human body is artfully constituted so as to both house complex psychic functions and provide adequate means for their expression.

The Peripatetic tendency to attribute a greater weight to bodily perfection than Aristotle did can be regarded as an expression of a more general shift in Peripatetic ethics after Aristotle. This shift concerns the question whether virtue is sufficient for happiness; and that brings us to the third condition of happiness in Aristotle's theory, that of unimpeded activation. Whereas Aristotle wavers in the first book of the *Nicomachean Ethics* between the view that the value of virtue is so great that it is sufficient for a happy life, and the concession that great and repeated misfortunes can make even the virtuous person unhappy, what we see in the later Peripatetic thought is a resounding tendency to concede that not only psychic virtues, or goods of the soul, but also the bodily goods and the so-called external goods, things such as wealth, good family and reputation, are indispensable for happiness.[7] We find a clear affirmation of this view in Diogenes Laertius' doxography, which attributes this view to Aristotle himself but couches it in terminology that clearly points to a later, Hellenistic context:

> He said that happiness was a completion (*sumplêrôma*) made up of three [types of] goods: those concerning the soul, which indeed he calls first in power; secondly those concerning the body, health and strength and beauty and the like; thirdly external [goods], wealth and good family and reputation and things like these. Virtue is not sufficient for happiness; for there is also need of bodily and external goods, since the wise man will be unhappy in pains, poverty and the like. But vice is sufficient for unhappiness, even if it possesses external and bodily goods to the greatest extent possible. (DL v.30)

The precise status of bodily and external goods was articulated along two different, competing lines. This duality goes back to Aristotle's original distinction between 'living well' and 'things without which' (*ha aneu ouk*) living well is impossible (EE i.2, 1214b12–27). Are bodily and external goods also *parts* or *ingredients* of the good life, or rather only *necessary conditions* of such a life? Both these possibilities can be traced back to Aristotle's account from *Nicomachean Ethics* i. On the one hand, he says

---

[7] This threefold division of goods goes back to Aristotle and even Plato, but in later Peripatetic thought it becomes the standard default scheme in the categorisation of goods. For discussions of the significance of the Peripatetic tripartition in the context of Hellenistic debates, see Inwood (2014b) and Hatzimichali (2018).

that happiness must be something 'complete' to which no additional good can be added (NE i.7, 1097b12–22); this could be taken to mean that all goods are necessary parts of happiness. On the other hand, the explicit reason given to explain why hardships could undermine the virtuous person's happiness is that they impede his activities (NE i.10; 1100b30); this suggests, again, that they are needed as necessary conditions.

The previous quotation from Diogenes Laertius articulates the role of the bodily and external goods as that of ingredients: happiness is a life that is jointly *filled* by all three kinds of goods. Whenever your life is deficient in any of these goods, it is incomplete. The extant fragments attribute this view to Critolaus, an influential head of the Peripatetic school from the second century BCE.[8] Among later texts, this view is adopted, with regard to bodily goods, in Piso's account, where the goods of the body are regarded as the necessary parts of the highest good. But in Piso's account, this status is explicitly denied to the external (i.e. non-bodily and non-psychic) goods – if these were to be 'included' in the supreme good, the supreme good could hardly ever be attained (*Fin.* v.68).[9] Even though the external goods are still valuable 'in their own right', their relationship to the highest good must be different from that of the parts to the whole; rather, they are instrumental for discharging virtuous actions (Tsouni 2019: 177–78).[10]

Several later Peripatetic sources express a clear preference for the 'necessary-conditions-view' over the 'parts-view'. Thus the Didymus epitome criticises the 'parts-view' on ontological grounds: a happy life is an activity, but bodily and external goods are not activities, and hence cannot be parts of happiness. So we should not say that happy life is 'completed' by these goods but rather 'surrounded' (*en*) by them, insofar as these goods are 'productive' (*poiêtika*) of happiness by 'contributing something by their presence' (Stob. *Ecl.* ii.126.14–127.2). The Peripatetics argued, in a debate against the Stoics, that unfavourable external circumstances that impede the exercise of virtue can be sufficient for unhappiness. According to the Stoics, virtue is sufficient for happiness, and hence the adverse circumstances cannot be evil. Seneca reports the following Stoic argument (*Ep.* 85.30–32): (1) What is evil causes harm; (2) what causes harm to someone makes him worse; (3) pain and poverty do not make someone worse;

---

[8] For reconstructions and discussions of Critolaus' thought, see White (2002); Hahm (2007); and Inwood (2014a), ch. 3.
[9] Irwin (2012: 153–55) makes plausible suggestions to explain why Piso (or Antiochus) thought that this was the case.
[10] I shall discuss the apparently odd view that something can be valuable both intrinsically and instrumentally in the next section.

(4) therefore they are not evils. We have seen how the Stoics use analogies with skills to make precisely this point: an expert archer will not be made worse in his skill if an unpredictable gust of wind happens to divert his arrow, for he has exercised his skill impeccably. The Peripatetics grant that the archer will not be worse in his skill, but they do not grant (2): 'for what causes some harm to someone does not also make him worse'. So a storm and squall will not diminish a good navigator's skill, but will impede its 'execution'. Under heavy wind, even the best navigator will lose control of his ship altogether, so that the exercise of his skill will be partly or wholly inhibited. Similarly, a flute-player will not be able to play at all if he does not have a flute.[11]

No matter whether the contribution of external goods to happiness is understood in terms of parts or necessary conditions, the explicit recognition of this contribution as indispensable for happiness goes beyond what we find in the extant works of Aristotle. Cicero recorded that Theophrastus, Aristotle's immediate successor as the head of the Peripatetic school, conceded that 'floggings, the rack, overthrow of one's country, exile and bereavement had great power to make life evil and pitiful' and that if 'fortune is opposed in everything and body is overwhelmed and worn out by all sorts of pains, one will lack a little a happy life (*paulumne ad beatam vitam deesse*), let alone the happiest (*non modo ad beatissimam*)' (*Tusc.* v.23–25). This suggests that the unfortunate virtuous life may not even make it to the level of a life worth living. Whereas some later Peripatetics, as we shall shortly see, criticised Theophrastus for conceding too much to the role of external goods, and thus diminishing the goodness of virtue, there is a consensus – against the Stoics – that an adequate supply of bodily and external goods is indispensable for the best human life. This is clearly brought out by a distinction in the Didymus epitome between a life which is 'happy' (*eudaimôn*) and a life which is merely 'fine' (*kalos*):

> The activity of virtue is (in the definition called) 'primary', as it is altogether necessary (*pantôs anankaion*) for it to be surrounded by goods which are in accordance with nature (*en tois kata phusin agathois huparchein*); for the morally good person could make a fine use of virtue even among evils but will not be blessed, and even the tormented could show a high-born character, but will fail to attain happiness. (Stob. *Ecl.* ii. 132.8–14)

---

[11] Aspasius, *On Aristotle's Ethics* 24.3–9: 'Happiness needs external goods not as parts or as things that complete it but as instruments, just as pipe-playing needs instruments for its own end, in order to achieve its particular end'; cf. also ibid., 24.24–25.2 for an explanation of how even such circumstances such as 'exceedingly humble birth' can be 'an impediment to noble activities'.

This account refers to the definition of happiness as 'activity in accordance with virtue expressed in primary actions as one would wish (*en praxesi proêgoumenais kath' euchên*)' (126.18–19). 'Primary actions' are precisely those that enable one to be active 'as one would wish', that is, in a manner that is optimally supported by the adequate supply of bodily and external goods. In this context, the notion of primary actions serves to differentiate happiness from a life which is noble but not happy or blessed: just like an expert flute-player who cannot perform in the best possible manner if he has an inferior instrument, so a virtuous person who does not have the opportunity to perform primary actions will live finely but not happily.[12] Remarkably, the text even allows for the possibility that bad fortune may deprive the virtuous person not only of happiness, but also of his virtue and thus, by implication, of the fine life: 'for the virtue of morally good men is still not altogether secure, since they can be deprived of it by many and big evils' (132.20–23). The text does not elaborate on this claim nor provide an explanation of how this loss could come about; presumably, extreme hardships could irreversibly alter the psychic constitution – for example, by inducing madness.

The distinction between fine and happy life in the Didymus epitome finds its counterpart in a distinction between 'happy' and 'happiest' life in Piso's account (*Fin.* v.81). But these two distinctions between different degrees of happiness are not wholly equivalent. Whereas the former further articulates the Theophrastan view, the motivation for the latter is to show, in the spirit of Antiochean synthesis, that the Peripatetic position is not all that far from the Stoic one, because virtue is, after all, sufficient for happiness. In comparison to the overwhelming weight of virtue, which will 'outweigh the earth and the sea' (*Fin.* v.92), the weight of bodily goods is 'slight and insignificant'; they are 'lost in the glow of virtue, like starlight in the rays of the sun' (*Fin.* v.71). Given its weight, virtue is sufficient for a happy life; nonetheless, if that life is bogged down by many bodily evils, it will be marginally but still genuinely incomplete, and thus fall short of the 'happiest' life.[13]

Crucially, the imagery of weighing presupposes that virtue and bodily goods, as two components of the highest good, are, despite their unequal

---

[12] For an informative discussion of the Peripatetic notion of 'primary actions' and its different uses, see Szaif (2018).

[13] The distinction between the 'happy' and the 'happiest' life recalls Aristotle's suggested (but not consequentially implemented) distinction between the 'happy' and the 'blessed' life. Irwin (2012) has an excellent discussion of how these two pairs of distinctions overlap, and concludes that the Antiochean distinction is in significant respects different from Aristotle's.

weight, commensurable. This contrasts sharply with the Stoic axiological dualism, in which the value of virtue and the value of bodily health correspond to two radically incommensurable domains of value, so that it is in principle impossible to weigh one against another. Ultimately, in Cicero's words, in the Peripatetic view, 'these things differ from each other in magnitude and, as it were, in degree, not in kind (*magnitudine et quasi gradibus non genere different*)' (DND i.16). They both contribute to a single, unitary notion of well-being. It is a further question whether we agree with Cicero's charge that this amounts to 'mixing what is honourable with what is advantageous' (ibid.). For, given that both virtue and bodily goods are equally parts of the highest end, *each* of them should be regarded as being both honourable and advantageous from the start; after all, some bodily goods are called 'virtues'.

We can conclude this section by discussing how these shifts in the Peripatetic ethics after Aristotle reflect, and are motivated by, the generally naturalistic approach of Peripatetic thought, which derives and justifies the account of the good life using a theory of human nature. Some elements of the naturalistic approach were common to all major Hellenistic schools – Epicureans, Stoics and Peripatetics. Here belongs the view that there is an 'alignment' between the biological 'starting-points' (*archai*), that is, instinctual impulses that we have from birth, and the 'end' (*telos*), happiness, so that our nature orients us towards the good from the start.[14] What the Peripatetics share with the Stoics – but not with the Epicureans – is the teleological perspective on human nature and its development: all our inborn natural capacities are wired to develop, unless impeded by unfavourable circumstances or bad education, towards perfection; this view is suggestively captured by the notion of 'seeds' of virtue, which appears in both the Peripatetic and Stoic sources.[15] But there are also some features of Peripatetic naturalism that are without parallel in competing schools. Unsurprisingly, these features draw on Aristotle's emphasis on the notion of activity, but cast this emphasis in a developmentalist framework heavily influenced by the Stoic theory of *oikeiôsis*.

Like the Stoics, Peripatetic accounts start from the observation that all living things 'love themselves' and 'strive to preserve themselves' as soon as they are born (*Fin.* v.24). But the precise understanding of what this self-love amounts to shows unmistakable traces of Aristotle's legacy: the

---

[14] Inwood (2014a: 118) talks about the 'alignment condition' that the naturalistic accounts of the end must meet.

[15] *Fin.* v.18; Seneca *Ep.* 94.29; 108.8.

expression of the natural affinity to oneself is the 'desire for activity' or, as the Didymus epitome puts it, the 'desire for existence' (*orexis tou einai*) (Stob. *Ecl.* ii.118.13). It is this fundamental desire for existence that motivates all humans to seek 'things according to nature', most importantly health, not the other way round. If the desire for existence is the beginning, how does it lead us to the end, which consists in 'fulfilling one's nature' (*Fin.* v.25)? The answer is that the development of certain human capacities will be conducive to the full satisfaction of this desire for existence. This is possible if this development is understood as a maximisation of one's existence. It suffices to recall some passages from Aristotle's *Protrepticus* to see how this can be the case. This maximisation has two aspects. In one sense, we desire to maximise our being by perfecting the set of psychic and bodily capacities that define who we are. By achieving higher degrees of perfection, we make steps towards our full self-realisation or self-fulfilment. In another sense, we desire that these capacities are active rather than idle. All humans desire 'constant activity' – 'continual rest is unendurable'. Moreover, insofar as activities are typically sources of pleasure, this account can integrate pleasure, as befits an Aristotelian account of pleasure as a naturally desirable object of choice, while maintaining that pleasure itself is not the end; for it often happens that humans are able to endure considerable discomfort in order to carry on with their activities (*Fin.* v.57).

While Peripatetic naturalism is clearly Aristotelian in its emphasis on species-specific capacities and their actualisation, it is also more programmatically naturalistic than Aristotle's own theory. This means, first, that nature and its workings are regarded as explanatorily sufficient to undergird and justify the theory of good life; in particular, no reference to god or the divine activity of intellection enters the picture (cf. Inwood 2014a: 81). Secondly, human nature, even more strongly than in Aristotle, is regarded as analogous to the natures of other living things, including plants (*Fin.* v.39–40). Consider the argument that the life of inactivity is unbearable for humans, as it is for other animals, and that humans who are seriously impeded in their activities are like animals in captivity (*Fin.* v.57).

Altogether, then, humans are more like plants than like gods, and this has obvious consequences for the account of the human good. One such consequence is a somewhat less privileged standing of the godlike or contemplative life, or, perhaps more precisely, of a comparatively higher standing of the practical life in a broad sense. Another consequence is a higher valuation of the bodily aspect of human nature. While Aristotle puts emphasis on what is distinct for humans in comparison to other species, Peripatetic texts tend to give due consideration to embodied existence as the common predicament of all ensouled things. Finally, the naturalistic perspective calls for an acknowledgement of the inherent vulnerability and frailty of the human condition. Just like plants, which cannot flourish without sun and water, so humans, no matter how excellent, need sufficient external resources.

5.3 Life as an Intrinsic Conditional Good

Given the shared view among the Hellenistic schools that the 'end' of the human life should be aligned with natural 'starting-points', we would expect that the Peripatetics would have a rather strong notion of life as a good. For if the end of the human life is to exist, or live, to the greatest possible extent, so that one's natural capacities are perfected and fully actualised, then even the unperfected life that we are attached to once we are born should be a kind of good. Alexander of Aphrodisias sums up this expectation as follows: 'How is it not inconsistent to say that [life] is something to which we are endeared by nature, and that we do everything with a view to our own preservation, and simultaneously to deny that nature endears us to it as a good?' (*Eth. Quest.* 119.23–26). As Alexander himself puts it, life cannot be merely one of 'indifferent' (*ta adiaphora*) or 'intermediate' (*ta metaxu*) things. These terms refer in Stoicism and in Plato to things that exhibit a double potential of use, so that they can be used well or badly, in contrast to those other things, typically virtue, that are 'naturally good in themselves' (*kath'hauta pephuken agatha*) (Plato, *Euthyd.* 281d), and hence can only be used well.

Obviously, the Platonic view of life as purely instrumental is not an attractive option for the Peripatetics: if living *per se* were no more valuable than non-living, the desire for existence as the driving force of natural development would be misguided or, at best, arbitrary. The Stoics reconciled the indifferent status of life with their naturalism by classifying life as a 'preferred indifferent', so that they were able to attribute to life a non-instrumental value while maintaining that this value is incommensurable with the value of virtue. It is clear that the Peripatetic defence of the value of life must adopt a different approach, one which regards – following Aristotle – life as a genuine good, rather than as an indifferent thing. The following reconstruction will show that this is precisely what the Peripatetics did, and yet the account they offer, again, is not quite what we know from Aristotle.

The goodness of life is clearly affirmed in the opening section of the Didymus epitome by appeal to its being among 'things according to nature': 'For [humans] take care to preserve their health and they desire pleasure and strive for life, because these things are according to nature and choiceworthy and good for their own sake (*kata phusin kai di' auth' haireta kai agatha*)' (Stob. *Ecl.* ii.118.15–18). The phrase 'good for their own sake' indicates that the value of life goes beyond purely instrumental value, so that life has either final or intrinsic value. But both these possibilities are complicated by the axiological theory developed in the course of the epitome. Later on in the text, we find the following division of 'things choiceworthy for their own sake': 'some are final (*telika*), some productive (*poiêtika*); final are the primary actions in accordance with virtue, whereas productive are the material of virtues' (134.15–19). This division makes clear that the category of things that are 'good for their own sake' (*di'auth'agatha*) is broader than the category of things which have final value; for it also includes goods that are 'productive' of happiness, such as health or wealth, insofar as these are the necessary conditions for the exercise of the primary acts of virtue.[16] While life is not mentioned on this occasion, we would expect that it falls into the latter category, since living is a necessary condition for living well. This is corroborated by classifying 'life' among the goods that are 'necessary' (*anankaia*), in contrast to those that are 'fine' (*kala*) (129.9–18), which suggests that, in contrast to Aristotle, who attributed to mere living a portion of the 'fine', some Peripatetics denied that life had this non-instrumental value and regarded it in more instrumental terms. 'Necessary' goods are assimilated to the 'productive' goods (129.13–15).

So perhaps life is choiceworthy for its own sake not in the sense of final but rather intrinsic value: it is not an end, but it has some essential properties that make it unconditionally good. The Didymus text does not explicitly distinguish between final and intrinsic value, but there is one passage that clearly bears on intrinsic, rather than final, goodness. We are offered here yet another division of goods:

> Some of the ends are good for everyone and others not good for everyone. Virtue and practical wisdom are good for everyone, as they benefit (*ôphelein*) whomever has them; wealth and offices and powers, on the other hand, are not unconditionally good for everybody (*ou panti hopôsoun agatha*), in so far as we have determined that they are good by the way the good man uses them; for [such people] appear to seek for them and are benefitted by their use. The things that the good person uses in a good way are used by the

---

[16] Cf. also 135.12–13 for a distinction between intrinsically choiceworthy things that are not ends and those that are.

bad person in a bad way, just as the things that the musician uses in a good way are used in a bad way by the non-musical person. At the same time, [someone] is harmed by the bad use of things, just as a good horse benefits the one who is skilled in riding but damages a lot the one who is not. (Stob. *Ecl.* ii.135.18–136.9)

The distinction between goods that are good for everyone and those that are not good for everyone is articulated in terms of the distinction between intrinsic and extrinsic goods. Whatever is good must benefit, and whatever always – or unconditionally – benefits is an intrinsic good, in contrast to things that sometimes benefit and sometimes harm, depending on how well or badly they are used. This argument is familiar from Plato's *Euthydemus* and, in the specific version that includes 'life' among the extrinsic goods, from the *Clitophon*. This passage does not make an explicit reference to life but it is clear that on these terms life cannot be regarded as an intrinsic good because – as we shall see in the next section – for many humans life is not worth living, and thus is not a benefit.

So we are faced with a puzzle: on the one hand, life is included among the things that are 'choiceworthy for their own sake'; on the other, it has neither final value nor intrinsic value, at least not in the sense of what is unconditionally beneficial. Is there perhaps yet another way to construe the value of life? Alexander's discussion about the value of life in the first chapter of his *Ethical Questions* can be regarded as making precisely that contribution. The core of his proposal lies in assigning 'life' to the category of 'powers' or 'potentialities' (*dunameis*). Originally this was a metaphysical notion, but in the Peripatetic texts it appears as a technical term within the theory of value. The last passage from the cited Didymus epitome mentions 'wealth and offices and powers' as things that are only extrinsically valuable. Earlier in the same text, 'powers' are mentioned as a special axiological category including things such as 'wealth, office and authority' (Stob. *Ecl.* ii. 134.20–25). Powers are 'good in themselves' (*kath'hauta agatha*), 'being things that the good man could use and seek for', and those that 'he could use well' (135.3–8). The powers are distinguished both from 'honourable' things, such as the god and from (merely) 'beneficial' things, such as gymnastic exercises, whose value derives wholly from their contribution to producing and preserving the powers (135.4–11).

Now, in regarding life as a 'power' Alexander underscores its instrumentality: since potentialities are generally instrumental to actualities, so 'life', too, is a potentiality that is instrumental to 'living well' (*Eth. Quest.* 119.17). Like other instrumental or productive goods, such as health or wealth, life, too, 'will be a thing to be valued with a view to the *best* of the things that can come about in us' (119.22–23) and that is the good life. And yet this instrumental status of health does not disqualify it (and other powers) from being something valuable 'in itself' (*kath'hauto*).[17] The reason is that 'life' in the primary sense is a potentiality for living well rather than living badly. For it belongs to the nature of powers that they are for the sake of their actualisations, and actualisations in the full sense are *good* actualisations.

The familiar analogy between crafts (*technai*) and nature (*phusis*) is deployed to make the point. Craft consists in the exercise of certain characteristic activities – for example, sailing consists in the exercise of navigation. These activities are instrumental for the full actualisations of crafts, for it is impossible to navigate well if one actually does not sail. By themselves, these powers allow for contrary actualisations, good or bad, so that, for instance, sailing can bring the ship right to its destination or to a place far away from it. But the value of powers is not entirely neutral. The reason is that a power always 'has as its goal the better of the things for which it is a potentiality' (*Eth. Quest.* 118.27–28); sailing has come to be for the sake of navigation and its proper goal – to navigate well. Sailing can be actualised to yield a wrong outcome but this bad actualisation is not, as it were, in the essential nature of sailing. If the powers have the better outcome as their proper goal, and things are defined in their essence by what they aim at, then it follows that the powers are, in some sense at least, good in themselves. They are 'biased for the good' (Inwood 2014a: 111), which is why it is the good person who can use them to their full potential. The same bias towards the good is characteristic for powers in the realm of nature, as follows from the Peripatetic view that crafts and nature share the same teleological *modus operandi*. So, life has been 'given to us by nature with a view to [our] living well' (*Eth. Quest.* 119.18), rather than our living badly. It is this intrinsic orientation towards goodness that makes life itself a good.

Javier Echeñique has usefully linked Alexander's account of the value of life from the *Ethical Problems* with a distinction from his *Commentary on Aristotle's Topics* between things that are valuable 'in themselves' or 'intrinsically' (*kath'hauto*), defined as things valuable 'because of their proper nature' (*dia tên oikeian phusin*) (*Ar. Top.* 229.20–21), and things that are good 'incidentally' or 'accidentally' (*kata sumbebêkos*). Whereas life would

---

[17] Echeñique (2021) offers an excellent analysis of Alexander's argument for life's goodness and discusses it in the broader context of Peripatetic and Stoic thought.

fall into the former category, death, similarly to other privative notions, would fall into the latter. It is possible that death may be incidentally good for us, for there are cases when life constitutes a net harm. But it is in the natural order of things that life is good, insofar as it is in its nature to be conducive to living well; in contrast, death is bad, since it deprives us of the possibility of achieving that goal.

Alexander's case could be further strengthened by the idea of inverted positive value (mentioned in the introductory section of this chapter). Recall that the reason why vicious persons cannot ever be fortunate in the proper sense of the word is that good fortune is not really good for them. Technically, good fortune is a 'power' that has a double potential of use: by allowing for the maximisation of one's activity, it can be beneficial if the activities are good, but harmful if they are bad. But it is in the natural essence of good fortune that it is beneficial for those who have it, which is why we need a special explanation of how it can be harmful in some abnormal cases. We can think about 'life' along similar lines. The power called 'life', like other 'powers', has a natural bias for the good, which is why only the good can fully exhaust its potential. As for bad living, it is of course an actualisation of this power, but one that goes, as it were, against the grain of life. And so it would not be inappropriate to ask whether vicious humans can be, strictly speaking, considered alive at all.

Thus, on Alexander's view, it is possible to say that 'life' qua 'power' is good not only instrumentally but also intrinsically. This account usefully explains how it is in the Didymus epitome that some goods are classified as good 'in themselves' (kath'hauta), even while it maintains that they do not have a final or non-instrumental value. But we should be cautious in talking about life as an intrinsic good without qualification. For life can be harmful, too, and hence it does not seem to be an unconditional good; it is not good in the same sense that wisdom in Euthydemus is. Thus, if we should count life among the intrinsic goods, according to Alexander's account, then it is an intrinsic good in a special, limited sense of intrinsic, but only conditionally good.[18]

Finally, we can reflect on how Alexander's account of the value of life, and that of the Peripatetics more broadly considered, differs from Aristotle's. Later Peripatetics seem less inclined than Aristotle himself to consider human life itself, no matter whether good or bad, as being non-instrumentally valuable qua certain kind of activity, namely activity that fulfils the human

---

[18] The possibility of intrinsic conditional value has been debated in the recent and contemporary philosophical scholarship. Some have argued for it (e.g. Kagan 1998), others against it (e.g. Bradley 2002).

essence. At the same time, Alexander's idea of the good as intrinsically valuable is constructed from axiological and metaphysical premises drawn from Aristotle's own theory. Aristotle himself says that living is 'good in itself' (NE ix.9, 1170a), or intrinsically, and Alexander's account can be regarded as a further articulation and justification of that claim. Moreover, Aristotle's view that every human life is non-instrumentally (and not only intrinsically) valuable by having a definite degree of intermediate finality is clearly compatible with Alexander's proposal that life is intrinsically valuable because it belongs to its nature to be for the sake of good life. For what, in Aristotle's eyes, makes mere human living non-instrumentally good – the exercise of rationality and reason-related capacities – is arguably also a kind of power that has a double potential of use: one can exercise reason well, in the case of virtue, or badly, in the case of vice. But it is in the essential nature of reason to be used well, for it is for the sake of the good use that this natural capacity has come about. So what makes mere living non-instrumentally good (for Aristotle) coincides with what makes it intrinsically good (for Alexander).

5.4 Lives Not Worth Living

The claim of the intrinsic goodness of life in the later Peripatetic tradition does not imply that this value would be sufficient to make life worth living. It is one thing to grant that any human life has some intrinsic goodness, and quite another to say what it takes for a human life to pass the threshold test of life worth living. The aim of this section is to reconstruct how the Peripatetics conceived of this threshold. Both Piso's account from *On Ends* and the Didymus epitome contain relevant material. I start from the passage about the fundamental undesirability of inactive life from the former, and then connect it with discussions in the latter about remaining in or departing from life. The passage about the human desire for activity is worth quoting in full:

> Here are some even clearer cases from nature – in fact absolutely obvious and indubitable ones – of the desire, most evident in humans but also present in animals, for constant activity. Continual rest is unendurable under any circumstances. This is readily seen in children of even the most tender age. I hope I am not concentrating too much on this group, but all the ancient theories, especially the one I espouse, visit the cradle, in the belief that the easiest way of understanding nature's intentions is to look at early childhood. We note, therefore, that not even infants are capable of keeping still. When not much older, they start to enjoy even quite boisterous games, and are hardly deterred by punishment. This desire for activity (*cupiditas agendi*) continues to grow (*adolescit*) as they do. And so none of us would

choose the sleep of Endymion, even if we were given the sweetest dreams to go with it. We would consider this a fate as bad as death.

Even the laziest people, as extravagantly idle as they may be, can none the less be seen in constant activity, both physical and mental. Once they have any unavoidable business out of the way, they still call for the dice-board or look for a game to play or someone to gossip with. Lacking the nobler delights of intellectual pursuit, they seek out any kind of company or social gathering instead. Even the animals that we keep caged for our amusement find captivity difficult. Despite the fact that they are better fed than they would be in the wild, they miss being able to move about and roam freely as nature allows (*facile patiuntur sese contineri motusque solutos et vagos a natura sibi tributos requirunt*).

Thus the more able and accomplished one is, the less one would even want to live at all if prevented from going about one's business (*esse omnino nolit in vita, si gerendis negotiis orbatus*), however well provided one may be with pleasures to graze on. One chooses either a life of private pursuits, or, if more ambitious, aspires to a public career and the authority of office. Alternatively, one devotes oneself entirely to intellectual study, a life far removed from that of the pleasure-seeker. Indeed those who take this course endure worry, anxiety and sleeplessness as they exercise the cutting-edge of their talent and intellect, the finest element of a human being, and one that should be considered divine. (Cicero, *Fin.* v.55–57)

This important passage should be received in the broader context of the developmental and ethical account in *Fin.* v. At base, this account is couched in the framework of what we would today call a desire-fulfilment theory: happiness comes as a result of satisfying a set of natural desires that collectively drive us towards a condition in which our human nature is fully realized or 'fulfilled' (*expleatur*; *Fin.* v. 37, 25). One specific kind of desire that belongs to this set, which we mentioned earlier in Section 5.2, is the desire for self-perfection: 'we want every aspect of mind and body to be perfect (*perfecta*)' (*Fin.* v. 37, 26). We desire a higher degree of self-actualisation by desiring to actualise a degree of excellence that is potentially present in our capacities. The desire for activity, too, belongs to the desire for self-fulfilment broadly considered, but *prima facie* at least it seems to be a different kind of desire than the desire for self-perfection. For instance, lazy humans without aspirations, as mentioned in the above passage, would seem to have the desire for activity but not necessarily the desire for self-perfection. This example also suggests that the desire for activity is more universal, and for that sake more fundamental, than the desire for self-perfection. This is confirmed by the fact that it is the desire for activity, rather than the desire for self-perfection, that is espoused as the Peripatetic version of the primary impulse in the cradle argument.

It is conceivable that these two kinds of the ovearching desire for self-fulfilment, that is, the desire for perfection and the desire for activity, could be closely interdependent, in one way or another, or could even be two different aspects of a single desire. In fact, Piso makes an implicit case for such an interdependence when he says in the above passage that it is the most talented intellectuals who tend to be most active, that is, most focused on their activities and least susceptible to interruptions: their perfection promotes their activity, and hence the desire for former helps to fulfil the desire for latter. But the interconnections between these desires do not get fully worked out in the text. We can easily imagine cases where the relationship between two kinds of desire would be inimical: for instance, a child's desire for activity as manifest in their reluctance to go to bed early might be detrimental to fulfiling their desire for self-perfection, since sleep deprivation is bad for study.

The twofold character of the desire for self-fulfilment raises the question whether it is complemented by two different goods that different types of this desire are directed at. The desire for perfection aims at securing the good in the sense of excellence, whereas the desire for activity aims at securing the good in the sense of abundant activity, that is, activity that is long-lasting and free from impediments. In the present context, it is the absence of the latter good that is a worthbreaker, but not necessarily the absence of the former. Not only is the happy life a life of activity, but life would not even be worth living if deprived of activity, or if activity were seriously inhibited. To have a life worth living, one must not be 'prevented from going about one's business'. This may happen, we may presume, due to social or political but also bodily inhibitions.

The desire for activity is so ingrained in human nature that any kind of active preoccupation, including trivial activities such as games or gossip, is better than idleness. But would just *any* kind of unimpeded activity be sufficient to make life worth living? We have mentioned the distinction between 'important' and 'trivial' activities (*Fin.* v.58), where the former includes political and theoretical pursuits, while the latter includes things such as games and gossip, but also the category of 'private pursuits' more broadly considered, which would perhaps include the leisured life of a private hobby gardener.[19] These private pursuits are different from both political and theoretical activity. But we are actually not told that uninhibited

---

[19] 'There is no kind of gainful employment that is better, more fruitful, more pleasant and more worthy of a free man than agriculture' (Cicero, *Off.* i.151). Cicero does not attribute this view specifically to the Peripatetics, but it reflects how *salonfähig* this activity was among the Roman elite.

lives spent on trivial activities – in contrast to severely inhibited lives of serious pursuits – would not be worth living. This may well be a sign of the relatively greater weight given to the freedom from impediments (the 'whether' aspect of *eudaimonia*), in comparison with the status of the activity (the 'what' aspect), as something desirable for its own sake, and perhaps even with the degree of perfection in its exercise (the 'how' aspect). The valuation of freedom from impediments is also reflected in the definition of the end as 'the unimpeded use of virtue among things in accordance with nature' (Stob. *Ecl.* ii. 130.20–21). From this perspective, the most distinguished or 'important' activities, such as high-profile political activities, are not necessarily always the most choiceworthy. For high-level political pursuits, for instance, make one especially vulnerable to impediments arising from external contingencies; a lower-status activity, such as private gardening, may not be the typical first choice, but it may well be more safely conducive to a life worth living under certain circumstances. A serious and excellent but impeded life is not worth living, whereas an ordinary, mediocre but unimpeded life may well be.

But that does not necessarily mean that just any kind of activity, or one done in whatever manner, would be sufficient to make a life worth living. In the Didymus epitome, we read that the good man, 'generally practicing virtue (*katholou tên aretên askounta*), will remain alive or again, if it ever becomes necessary (*ei deoi di'anankas*), will depart (from life) having taken forethought for his burial' (Stob. *Ecl.* ii.144.10–13). This implies that the necessary circumstances that make suicide appropriate may be those that impede or inhibit the practice (*askêsis*) of virtue. This practice consists in engaging in certain activities and accomplishing certain kinds of actions, such as marrying, having children and taking part in the government (144.8–10). These items remind us of the Stoic category of 'appropriate actions' (*kathêkonta*), and indeed this is the term that the Didymus epitome uses, defining them, again in the Stoic manner, as actions that have their origin in the 'selection of things according to nature and the rejection of things contrary to nature' (119.14–20). If accomplishing these actions is the reason, and condition, for staying alive, it seems that a life is worth living when, and insofar as, one can appropriately function in one's social context as befits the natural inclinations to obtain things in accordance with nature. This view is confirmed in the following passage:

> Both remaining in life is measured (*parametreisthai*) by the social, political and contemplative actions (*tais koinônikais kai politikais kai theôrêtikais praxesi*), and the departure from it by the opposites. Therefore, both for wise individuals it is reasonable (*kai tois sophois eulogon*) to consider

departing from life, and for base individuals (*kai tois phaulois eulogon*) it is reasonable [to consider] remaining in life. For those – good and bad (*kai tôn spoudaiôn kai tôn phaulôn*) – who are able to accomplish (*ektelein dunamenois*) social, political and contemplative actions, remaining in life is reasonable (*eulogon*), while for those not able to accomplish such actions departure from life is reasonable. (Stob. *Ecl.* ii.126.2–12)[20]

Again, this passage bears unmistakable traces of the Stoic influence on the terminological level. The idea that the deliberation about departing from life should be 'measured' – compare the use of the verb *metior* ('measure') used by Cicero in his account of the Stoic theory[21] – by appropriate actions is characteristically Stoic, as is the notion of the 'reasonable' (*eulogon*). But there is also a distinctly Peripatetic feature to be found here, namely the emphasis on 'accomplishing actions' (*praxeis ektelein*). The necessary condition for having a life worth living is to be able to do things corresponding to social, political and contemplative pursuits, but also to get them done. Your life is not worth living if you fail to be an all-things-considered successful practitioner of (at least) some kinds of naturally worthwhile human activities. This implies, again, that unimpeded activity *per se* may not be sufficient to make life worthwhile: your activities should be of the sort that befits your human nature, and they should also bear fruit.

There are two puzzling elements in this passage that deserve closer discussion. One is the phrase 'the social, political and contemplative actions ... and ... [their] opposites'. The wording follows the standard Stoic distinction between appropriate actions and their opposites, actions that are not appropriate – those that lack sufficient rational justification. But the appropriate actions are defined in this passage by reference to their specific content, namely that they are contemplative or political, rather than merely by the fact that they are *eulogon*. For the Stoics, all actions, including very trivial ones, can count as appropriate. In contrast, for the Peripatetics the status or type of activity (the 'what'), such as contemplation, does seem to

---

[20] As it stands, the view expressed in this passage sits uneasily with other passages from the epitome (see below in this section). Hence Wachsmuth's change of *kai* to *kakôs* at 126.6, followed by Sharples (but not by Tsouni) who translates: 'So it is wrong to consider that departure from life can be reasonable for the wise and remaining in life reasonable for the bad' (Sharples 2010: 116). This aligns better with the official Peripatetic position, but it does not help with *kai tôn spoudaiôn kai tôn phaulôn* at 126.9–10. One possibility to circumvent this was suggested by Simpson (2017: 91), who takes this phrase to refer to 'studies of things virtuous and base', that is, not to virtuous or vicious persons but virtue and vice as object of studies. Grammatically, this is possible but strained. It is also difficult to see how vicious things could be a proper object of 'theoretical' studies.

[21] 'Thus, the whole rationale for either remaining in or departing from life is to be measured by reference to those intermediates that I mentioned above' (*Fin.* iii.61).

matter for the assessment of their appropriateness. But then it is difficult to see what the 'opposite' (*enantion*) of contemplative or political actions could possibly be. One option is that the 'opposite' are actions that lack any serious status, that is, those that are neither contemplative, nor social, nor political. But that would leave out some respectable 'private pursuits', leisured agriculture perhaps, that do not fall into any of these categories. So the second option is preferable, namely that these actions and 'their opposites' refer rather to the accomplishment of these actions or a failure to accomplish them, respectively. Thus, to make the text more intelligible, we could perhaps read the phrase as follows: remaining in or departing from life should be measured by doing and accomplishing appropriate actions in the domain of social, political and contemplative pursuits, and the opposite of this, that is, the failure to do and accomplish these actions. You must both do certain types of actions and be successful in accomplishing them.

The second puzzling element is more difficult to resolve. A claim is made that both good and bad individuals may have equally strong reasons to remain in life or to depart, depending on whether or not they are able to do appropriate actions. Thus stated, this sounds very much like the Stoic view, not just in terminology but in content. Both virtuous and vicious humans can successfully exercise and accomplish some worthwhile social or intellectual activities. It is this success – and not virtue or vice – that is the criterion for whether a continued existence is worthwhile for them. Moreover, there is a rather unnerving concession that even bad humans can be decent accomplishers. This brings to mind, again, Haybron's Gengis Khan: a vicious human who despite, or perhaps even because of his vice was able to make significant accomplishments and to be well-respected in his community. But if someone like Genghis Khan should carry on living, then this view clashes with twofold evidence from the Didymus epitome that vicious humans cannot, ever, have lives worth living. One is the following passage that presents a ranking of kinds of lives, where two are worth living and one is to be fled:

> The best life is the virtuous one surrounded by the things which are according to nature; second best is the one which is according to the intermediate disposition in possession of the majority and the most important of the things which are according to nature; these [forms of life] are worth choosing (*hairetous*), whereas the vicious one should be fled. (Stob. *Ecl.* ii.144.22–145.2)

Vice disqualifies anyone from having a life worth living, no matter how free, accomplished or fortunate their life may be. The second piece of evidence is the first passage quoted in the epigraph to this chapter: 'For good men should flee life among great misfortunes (*en tais agan atuchiais*), bad men even among very good fortunes (*kai en tais agan eutuchiais*); for they go wrong more' (134.3–6). The 'great misfortunes' are, presumably, extremely adverse circumstances that prevent the virtuous person from practising his virtue, such as a debilitating bodily condition. As for the vicious person, good fortune, even very good fortune, will not be of any help; on the contrary, it will only make his life worse.

How can it therefore ever be reasonable for bad humans, on the Peripatetic view, to remain alive? It is difficult to avoid conclusion that the Didymus epitome contains two different, and in fact incompatible, perspectives on the significance of badness for life worth living: (1) even bad humans can have a worthwhile live, if they are unimpeded accomplishers of human actions; and (2) badness is an unconditional worthbreaker. Is (2) the orthodox Peripatatic position that follows in the footsteps of Aristotle, whereas (1) is an aberation prompted by Stoic influence, so much so that we should doubt that it is a proper Peripatetic position at all?

Not necessarily. Rather, what (1) may reflect is the characteristically Peripatatic tendency to value an abundance of activities in the sense of their duration and freedom from impediments. Consider the desire for activity from *Fin.* v. If this desire cannot be adequately sastisfied, no matter what degree of perfection one has achieved, life won't be worth living. Could the above problematic passage perhaps be interpreted as saying that life could be worth living, if only one's human nature, regardless of its perfection, can be freely exercised?

This tendency to value activity *per se* goes back to Aristotle himself. Take some of his arguments for the superiority of contemplative activities: these activities are best because they are most 'continuous' (*sunechês*; NE x.7, 1177a22), 'free from weariness' (*atrutos*; ibid. 1177b22) and immune to external impediments (NE x.8, 1178b1–4). Contemplative activities are superior not only because they engage the god-like element of our soul, but also because they approximate us, as far as possible, to the pure, unimpeded activity of the god; they enable us to be more active. Now, it takes several additional steps from the view that activity's freedom from impediments increases activity's overall value to the more controversial view that this freedom could be a good independently of activity's degree of excellence, or even in spite of its badness. But if my interpretation from Chapter 2 is right, then we can indeed attribute at least some version of the latter view to Aristotle: if even mere human living has some non-instrumental value, independently of virtue and vice, then obviously the value of the freedom to exercise human function, albeit barely, is independent of the goodness or badness of this exercise. What we do not find in Aristotle is the further possibility that the positive value of freedom from impediments could in principle compete with, or even outweigh, the negative value of vice. But if this is an idea that some later Peripatetic entertained, if not explicitly endorsed, it can be regarded as a further exploration of the logical space opened by Aristotle's nod to the notion of an excellence-independent natural goodness. I shall return to this problem in the concluding section of this chapter.

5.5   Unhappy Life Worth Living, or the Decent Life

According to the Peripatetic position in the Didymus epitome, happiness is a fairly tall order: in addition to virtue, one also needs to be adequately supplied with bodily and external goods, so that virtue can be brought to its optimal expression. Among the unhappy lives, some are not even worth living, namely those that are overwhelmingly inhibited in activities or those that are vicious. It remains to be seen whether there are also lives that, though unhappy, are worth continuing. We can find in the sources a special technical term, the 'middle' or 'intermediate life', to designate the state into which unhappy lives worth living fall. These are lives that are not great, but still decent and worthy of choice. After an emphatic endorsement of the Solonic view that we should not call anybody happy until they are dead, the text affirms that not all those who fall short of living happily are automatically wretched:

> The one who is deprived of happiness is not wretched (*kakodaimona*) like the one who does not possess it at all, but is sometimes found between the two. For sometimes both the sage and the one who is not a sage (*kai sophon kai mê sophon*) live the so-called middle life (*ton meson legomenon bion*) which is neither happy nor wretched. (Stob. *Ecl.* ii.133.6–10)

Again, we find the view that non-sages can have a life that is not wretched. Does this category include even vicious humans? An answer is implied in the following passage, which specifies that 'intermediate life' is a broader category that includes two more specific forms of intermediate life: a noble life (the life of unhappy sages); and the intermediate life in a narrow sense (the life of non-vicious non-sages):

> Now, the happy life differs from the fine one (*diapherein de ton eudaimona bion tou kalou*) in that the former is meant to be surrounded constantly by things which are according to nature, whereas the latter one includes also things which are contrary to nature. And for the former virtue is not

sufficient, whereas for the latter it is. An intermediate way of life is the one which is according to the intermediate disposition in which appropriate actions (*kathêkonta*) are exhibited; for right actions (*katorthômata*) are found in the life which is according to virtue, wrong actions (*hamartêmata*) in the vicious life and appropriate actions in the so-called intermediate life. (Stob. *Ecl.* ii. 145.2–10)

The fine life is the life of the virtuous person in adverse or suboptimal conditions that are 'contrary to nature', such as bodily illness or poverty, which inhibit the unimpeded exercise of virtue. On the one hand, this person can 'make a fine use of virtue even among evils' but 'will fail to attain happiness', for happiness does not merely 'want to endure terrible things' but also 'to enjoy good things' without deprivations (Stob. *Ecl.* ii. 132.14–15). The intermediate life in the narrow sense is the life of humans who are in the 'intermediate disposition' and actually perform 'appropriate actions' that flow from this disposition. The 'intermediate disposition' (*mesê hexis*) is not further specified in this text, but I find it a plausible suggestion that it is the disposition of those who have received proper moral education, have good manners and are reasonably well integrated in their social context, but lack practical wisdom and thus do not have a properly philosophical understanding of what they should be doing and why (Fortenbaugh 2018b: 249). They are decent people but, thinking back to Socrates, do not live an examined life. Given their lack of practical wisdom, their actions are not 'right' – that is, done with the proper understanding and motivation that is characteristic of the fully virtuous – but are appropriate nonetheless. Into this category might also fall the actions of self-controlled persons who do the right thing but not from the wholly virtuous disposition, since they have to fight some residual vicious appetites of their souls.

This strict assignment of appropriate actions to 'intermediate disposition', a notion incompatible with the Stoic view that virtue and vice are contradictories, pushes against the Stoic contention that all humans, both virtuous and vicious, can perform appropriate actions. By affirming that the virtuous act rightly, the non-virtuous and non-vicious appropriately, and the vicious badly, the text uses the Stoic terminology to espouse a distinctly Peripatetic account of the relationship between dispositions and actions, where each disposition has its own corresponding type of action. We can also note the claim that vicious humans cannot perform appropriate actions, and in that sense – contrary to the controversial passage quoted in the preceding section – cannot accomplish anything which would make their lives worth living.

This notion of intermediate life agrees with the notion of the 'second-best life' (*deuteros bios*) mentioned in the preceding section. The second-best life is distinguished, on the one hand, from the best life of virtuous persons in optimal circumstances, and, on the other, from the life of vicious persons. It is a life 'which is according to the intermediate disposition in possession of the majority and the most important of the things which are according to nature' (Stob. *Ecl.* ii. 144.24–145.1). One may be puzzled why this life is defined as a combination of having *both* the intermediate disposition between virtue and vice *and* the intermediate condition with regard to the external goods (i.e. not all goods are present, but a majority). However, the broader context suggests that we can plausibly understand the second-best life as comprising lives that are intermediate in at least one of these two senses, that is, are *either* between virtue or vice, *or* intermediately supplied by external goods, *or* both. On this reading, this passage aligns well with the above account of intermediate lives.

Finally, it remains to ask whether all intermediate lives are worth living. The answer, it seems, is that there is one kind of intermediate life that might possibly not be worth living, namely the noble life which is extremely inhibited, similarly to the life of a caged eagle. On the one hand, the noble life is sharply distinguished from the wretched life, and there is no suggestion that a virtuous person could ever become properly wretched. On the other hand, the sources insist strongly on the satisfaction of the desire for activity as the necessary condition of worthwhile life. So we cannot exclude the possibility that on the Peripatetic position even some fully virtuous lives might not be worth continuing. To the extent that the Peripatetics would be inclined to commit to this view, they would again adopt a position which is without a clear parallel in Aristotle. For while Aristotle concedes that extreme impediments to the exercise of virtue may deprive the virtuous person of happiness, he does not suggest that they might deprive them even of a life worth living.

In sum, then, Peripatetics make a substantive distinction between happiness and life worth living. Whereas happiness is difficult to achieve, life is still worth living unless it is wholly corrupted, unfortunate or inhibited. But while leaving room for this distinction, their axiology does not make a distinction between incommensurable orders of value. And hence life worth living is distinguished but not radically dissociated from the axiological order of happiness, as it is Stoicism. There is an overlap: any life worth living must have a portion of the overall sum of goods that are necessary for the happy life. The threshold is located on the single continuum between happy and wretched life, but the axiological theory is pluralistic enough to distinguish life barely worth living from the happy life.

This plurality is warranted, firstly, by the distinction between psychic and non-psychic goods, where the former have greater weight but the latter are not insignificant. In contrast to the Epicurean sage, who can offset bodily pain by his art of locating mental pleasures, the virtue of the Peripatetic good person is seriously limited in making up for, or counterbalancing, bodily evils. So the possibility of having psychic goods in combination with having bodily evils is more real, as is the resulting condition of having a life which is worth living but not happy. Secondly, in contrast to the Epicurean *ataraxia* – the unconditional Epicurean worthmaker – which does not allow for degrees, the Peripatatic notion of virtue – the conditional Peripatetic worthmaker – allows for the intermediate state between virtue and vice. This opens additional space for lives that are not virtuous and therefore not happy, but still not vicious, and hence worth living.

5.6 No Life Worth Living without Freedom

Let me conclude by highlighting what is perhaps the most original and distinctive aspect of the Peripatetic views after Aristotle about life worth living, namely a high valuation of the unimpeded and successful exercise of psychological capacities. Just as it is in the nature of animal to desire that they can freely exercise movements and accomplish activities that define their natural kind, so it is in the nature of humans to desire that they enact their human nature without major inhibitions caused by their bodies or adverse social environment. This uninhibited functioning seems to be valued – to some extent at least – independently of its standing in terms of virtue or vice. This is the philosophical intuition behind Haybron's Genghis Khan case. He was able to thrive in his place and time. Maybe he was a cruel and greedy human being but a human being he was, and an unimpeded accomplisher too. His life was bad insofar as it was a vicious life but it was good because it was an abundant life – a life which achieved a high degree of accomplishment and actualisation of human capacities. The reason why even such a vicious life has some value goes back to the view, which I attributed to Aristotle, that even mere human living, that is, living that fulfils the human essence, is a non-instrumental good.

Inspired by the image of captive animals from *Fin.* v, let us call this value of unimpeded actualisation of natural capacities 'freedom'. Consider now three kinds of lives: the life of a virtuous but unfree human, such as a life of a talented politician who was unjustly sentenced to life imprisonment without any future chance of communication with the external world; the life of a vicious but free human, someone such as Genghis Khan; and the life of the caged eagle, well-fed but prevented from the exercise of the characteristic activities of eagles. All of these lives are defective, in some sense. But is any of them nonetheless worth living, from the Peripatetic point of view? We can confidently exclude, I think, the two unfree lives, insofar as serious and permanent impediments are an unconditional worthbreaker. In fact, unless the imprisoned politician manages to turn to a life of contemplation, which can perhaps be pursued even in prison, his life would be the least worth living of all three, insofar as his capabilities, on account of their inhibitions, make his life in prison all the worse for him. Whether or not the life of a vicious but free human being can be better than these lives, or even reach the threshold of a life worth living, depends on the status of vice as an unconditional worthbreaker. There is strong Peripatetic evidence that affirms this status, but there is also a nod to the possibility that the vicious might have lives worth continuing if they can accomplish activities in accordance with human nature. The more confident the latter concession is, the more the Peripatatic position would depart from Plato and Aristotle, and the more would it approximate to the Stoics, for whom vice is not a worthbreaker.

This wavering reflects, I think, a deeper axiological predicament of later Peripatetic thought. The valuation of unimpeded actualisation, or what I call freedom, has a foothold in Aristotle's theory, but this valuation seems to go further than it does in Aristotle. The impediments are regarded as a more serious obstacle for a life worth living than they are by Aristotle, and the freedom from them might, correspondingly, be regarded as something good *per se*. This shift should be understood against the background of the decisively naturalistic commitments of later Peripatetic ethics, which allows for a greater weight of virtue-independent value. Genghis Khan is vicious, and hence his life is bad, but in a sense he is like an uncaged eagle, capable of unimpeded functioning in accordance with its nature. And yet, while the Peripatetics regard the excellence-independent value of life as significant, they do not go the Stoic way – that is, they do not assign this value to an axiological realm that is strictly incommensurable with the axiological realm of virtue or excellence. That is why, in principle at least, a comparison, or even competition, between the value of virtue and the value of freedom becomes possible.

CHAPTER 6

Plotinus on the Worth of Embodied Existence

But if life is good, how will death not be an evil? ... In fact, life is good for those for whom it is good, not insofar as there is a joining with the body, but because evil is avoided through virtue. But death is more of a good.

(*Enn.* i.7.3.16–19)

It is just as on stage when one of the actors who has been murdered changes his costume for a new one and enters again as a different character. But this person has really died. If his death, too, then is a change of body like the change of costume ... what would be so terrible for animals to be changing into each other, which is much better than their never existing in the first place (*polu beltion tou mêde tên archên auta genesthai*)?

(*Enn.* iii.2.15.19–20)[1]

6.1 Competing Perspectives on the Value of Embodied Life

In the first chapter of this book, I focused on the *Republic*, a Plato text which is notable for envisaging the good life, and the life worth living, as something that is to be achieved within, and is heavily dependent on, the political context and social structures in which one lives. That means that the happiness under discussion is the happiness of citizens and, more broadly, the happiness of embodied human souls. But there are also voices in Plato's works, most notably in the *Phaedo*, which espouse the view that the truly worthwhile life is exclusively the life of pure intellection, in which the soul, while still embodied, is dissociated from the body as far as possible, and identifies itself with the divine life of the intellect. This vision is not necessarily incompatible with the *Republic*, but there is certainly a difference in emphasis: true happiness is not to be sought in this world, but in a higher, transcendent world of thought concerned with true, immaterial beings.

---

[1] All translations of Plotinus follow Gerson et al. (2019), unless otherwise noted.

This otherworldly strand in Plato's thought was vigorously reaffirmed, and further developed, in the Platonic philosophy of late antiquity, widely referred to as Neoplatonism.[2] Insofar as the ideal of otherworldly life became dominant among the Neoplatonists, their approach can be regarded as a counter-statement to the Peripatetics. Whereas the Peripatetics adopted a perspective that was more radically naturalistic than Aristotle's, consequentially explaining the human good as emerging, in a bottom-up manner, from psychological capacities that humans share with animals and even plants, the later Platonists espoused a vision of reality in which all existing things, and indeed all value, derives, in a top-down manner, from a single source, the transcendent One, which itself is beyond being and even thought. Since the One is also the Good, which is what all living beings desire, all human aspirations are directed towards transcending the material world and approximating, by means of contemplative activity, the One. We humans are 'denizens of a higher realm, exiled for a space in the physical, sublunary sphere' (Dillon 1996: 316).

Given this otherworldly outlook, it is hardly surprising that the Neoplatonists leaned, by default, towards a fairly dismissive, even hostile view of the value of embodied existence. This pessimistic stance is brought out by the first epigraph: life is not necessarily bad for you, if you are good; but death is better anyway. The reason is that embodied life necessarily contains evil, since it contaminates the purity of the soul with evil matter. Hence becoming virtuous, in the first instance at least, is not so much a victorious ascent to the good but rather an attempt to avoid or minimise, as far as possible, the evil. Death is good because it is a separation of soul from body, and hence it is, in a way, even more effective in fending off evil than virtue. Also, the body is an impediment to the soul, since 'the soul actualizes more what belongs to it without the body' (*Enn.* i.7.3.7–8). Now, if even the goodness of good lives does not trump the goodness of death, the outlook must be all the bleaker when it comes to bad lives. Indeed, Plotinus says about bad humans that their life 'is not a life for them, but a sentence' (iii.4.6.17), or that 'death is not an evil for them, but life' (i.7.3.12–13).

So, on the face of it at least, it would seem that there are no human lives – in the sense of embodied existence – that would be robustly worth living. Even virtuous life, though not harmful to those who live it, is *faute de mieux*. Thus it is with some surprise that we read the second

---

[2] Cooper (2012: 305–17) has a useful, crisp account of the otherworldly turn of Neoplatonist thought in the broader context of the Greek tradition.

epigraph. The context of this passage is Plotinus' defence of cosmic providence. Like the Stoics, he is committed to the view that the world is an ordered and unified multiplicity, where individual entities are arranged by the cosmic soul so as to contribute to the harmony of the whole. But, Plotinus objects, if that is so, how is it possible 'that animals eat each other and human beings attack each other, that war goes on forever and never takes a respite or pause' (iii.2.15.4–5)? The answer is that war is a 'necessary' corollary of the harmonious arrangement of the world, and that being killed and eaten is, after all, not as bad as it may seem. This suffering belongs simply to the process of the soul changing bodies, similarly to actors who change costumes. Moreover, and more controversially, Plotinus contends that it is better to continue living in another body than not to exist at all. As we shall see, this claim does not apply only to animals but to humans as well.

This more optimistic view raises the question whether it is consistent for Plotinus to claim, on the one hand, that death is superior to even good lives, and, on the other, that embodied existence, miserable as it is, is better than non-existence. For if death is good by virtue of dissociating the soul from the body, then it is not clear why the continued existence of the soul in another body should be preferable. The new embodiments may be necessary from the metaphysical point of view, but does this also make them good, or even good *for* those who undergo them? Would it not be better for an individual soul to escape the necessity for any bodily attachments, if at all possible?

These questions point to a more fundamental tension in Plotinus' philosophy between the clear tendency to deprecate embodied existence *tout court*, and a generally optimistic, life-affirming stance that also pertains to the embodied life. On the one hand, the body, insofar as it is involved with matter, is the source of evil; on the other hand, life in all its various forms is non-instrumentally valuable, insofar as all these forms are derivations of the Good. Plotinus inherits this ambivalent perspective on the value of embodied life from Plato, whose ascetic view of the body as the prison of the soul from the *Phaedo* contrasts with his account from the *Timaeus*, where body appears to be, to use a suggestive metaphor, more 'like a comfortable hotel' (Johansen 2004: 157) designed to promote the actualisation of the soul's capacities. However, Plotinus further exacerbates this ambivalence. This exacerbation betrays the influence of Plotinus' engagement with various Gnostic schools and their wholesale hostility towards the material world: on the one hand, he adopts some Gnostic views, such as the myth of individual souls' fall into matter; on the other, it is this and other Gnostic sentiments that motivate him, all the more, to vigorously defend the goodness of sensible world – and of a life in this world – as a manifestation of the intelligible world.[3] This leaves us with the question whether these tensions can be reconciled so as to yield a clear and coherent account of life worth living – both in the sense of coming into existence and in the sense of remaining alive – for different kinds of embodied human life: the happy or fully virtuous life, the vicious or bad life, and the life that falls short of happiness but is not outright bad.

Plotinus was the most influential among the Neoplatonists, his philosophy is broadly representative of the Neoplatonist movement, and he also had more to say about life worth living and the value of life than other Neoplatonist philosophers. While his philosophy does not exhaust the entire scope of the Neoplatonic contribution to these themes, he is the obvious choice of focus. Before we turn to a closer exposition of his views, some preliminary remarks are in order that justify the overall approach adopted in this chapter as well as chapter's structure.

Plotinus understands his philosophical role primarily as that of an interpreter of Plato. He therefore remains true to Plato; yet his interpretation of Plato's core doctrines is original and constructively integrates the views and concepts of competing philosophical schools, particularly of the Stoic and the Peripatetic traditions. In one important respect, however, Plotinus' general approach to ethics and value theory differs from that of other schools. It should be uncontroversial to say that Plotinus' ethical views are deeply embedded in his metaphysical theory. The level of dependence of his ethical views on metaphysics exceeds what we find in Plato, some of whose dialogues on ethical themes do not make any reference to metaphysics, not to mention in Aristotle, for whom ethics is an independent discipline within philosophical theory, albeit one informed by metaphysics. Although Plotinus' philosophical aspirations are first and foremost metaphysical, as is brought out by the proportion of his corpus, the *Enneads*, dedicated to metaphysical themes, that does not mean that he did not have anything to say about what it takes to live a good human life. Rather, it seems more appropriate to say that his metaphysics is 'permeated by ethics' (Remes 2008: 178). In postulating that the One, the ultimate source of reality, is identical with the Good, the ultimate source of value, Plotinus' metaphysical theory cannot but have immediate axiological implications.

[3] I am grateful to Filip Karfík for helping me to understand the broader historical context of Plotinus' engagement with the value of embodied existence.

But it has been a matter of controversy whether Plotinus' ethical thought goes beyond the rather abstract axiological implications of his metaphysical theory. Do these implications translate into a compelling account of virtue? Are they developed into a consistent ethical theory of action? Does Plotinus offer any practical guidance on how to progress towards the good life? As a matter of fact, several treatises in the first *Ennead* are explicitly dedicated to ethical themes, such as the virtues (i.2), happiness (i.4; i.5) or the morality of suicide (i.9). Some commentators have expressed their doubts about the real practical import of these theories (Dillon 1996: 323) or about their consistency (Rist 1967: 167), while others – and this appears to be the more recent tendency – have pointed out that we can glean from Plotinus' treatises fairly rewarding contributions to major ethical questions, and even to political theory (Schniewind 2003, O'Meara 2003, Remes and Slaveva-Griffin 2014).

This controversy bears directly on the question of the extent of Plotinus' otherworldliness. Insofar as the issue of the worth of embodied existence has implications for this fundamental question, our discussion can be regarded as an indirect contribution to this debate. I shall argue that we can glean from Plotinus an account of life worth living – one which is not quite identical with his account of happy life – that goes some way towards reconciling the tension between the positive and negative evaluations of being embodied, though a degree of ambivalence remains. This ambivalence can be explained in terms of the relationship of Plotinus' theory to Plato. Whereas Plotinus, following the Plato of the *Phaedo*, regards the life of intellect as the only respectable way of life, he also departs from Plato, and follows Aristotle and the Stoics, in assigning a degree of non-instrumental value to mere living alone.

In the previous chapters of this book, it was possible to outline the essentials of ethical theories without sustained excursion into physics or metaphysics. In the case of Plotinus, the metaphysical background is truly indispensable for even a basic grasp of his ethical views, and hence I start from a rudimentary sketch of his metaphysics (Section 6.2). This is followed by an outline of his views about happy human life, which is inextricably linked to his view about the value of life (*zôê*) in general (Section 6.3). The next two sections offer a reconstruction of Plotinus' views about the worth of embodied existence, both in the sense of the worth of being born (Section 6.4) and in the sense of the worth of staying alive (Section 6.5). I conclude with a comparative discussion of Plotinus' account of the value of life, contrasting this account with those of other philosophers in the tradition, including Plato, Aristotle and the Stoics (Section 6.6).

6.2 Metaphysical Fundamentals

Plotinus envisaged the totality of all existing things as a hierarchically structured whole.[4] This hierarchy consists of different metaphysical levels, where the lower levels logically and causally depend on the higher levels. At the top of the hierarchy there is a single, ultimate principle that is the source of all lower levels. Plotinus' original contribution does not lie so much in espousing a hierarchical model of reality, since with some modifications the model just described could be attributed to Plato and Aristotle; rather, the most characteristic and distinctive feature of Plotinus' metaphysical vision is perhaps that he defines the single source of reality as a wholly transcendent and independent principle. Plotinus calls it the One (*Hen*) or god (*theos*). As the One is the cause of all being, or the 'origin of everything' (*archê pantôn*) (vi.9.5.24), it is 'not "something" among all things, it having itself no designation' (v.3.13). It cannot even amount to *all* beings, for beings are many, 'and hence it would no longer be one' (vi.9.2.45). Rather, it is itself 'beyond being' (i.1.8.9).

Plotinus assigns to the One several value attributes, such as being self-caused, self-sufficient and perfect, that derive from the One's paradigmatic unity and simplicity. This unity is the necessary logical condition of all being: 'All beings are beings due to unity … For what could be, if it were not a unity? For if you take away the unity which they are said to be, then they are not those things' (vi.9.1.1–4). As the perfect unity, the One is without shape, form and limits, since these would give rise to differentiation and multiplicity. Being without limits, the One is everywhere (v.2.2.24–29), and for that reason it is also self-sufficient and hence without desires, and perfect, that is, completely fulfilled and actualised. This supreme perfection of the One explains why the One generates all other things: 'Since it is perfect, due to its neither seeking anything, nor having anything, nor needing anything, it in a way overflows and its superabundance has made something else' (v.2.1.7–10).

Plotinus relies on some suggestive images to account for the generation of all things from the One: this generation is like fire producing heat, snow coldness or perfumes fragrance (v.1.6.34–37). This process has come to be known as the process of 'emanation', but one should be aware that this is merely a metaphorical manner of speaking. Most importantly, the process of metaphysical generation, in contrast to the physical process of emanation, does not take place at a specific place and particular time; it

---

[4] The following account is heavily indebted to O'Meara (1993) and Remes (2008).

is a purely logical relationship between what is metaphysically prior and what is metaphysically posterior, and hence the term 'derivation' may be more appropriate. Having said that, we can note that in two respects the imagery of physical emanation is quite helpful. First, it brings out that the process of derivation is necessary, just in the sense that fire, as long as it is fire, necessarily produces heat. This necessity of production is also entailed in the notion of the perfection of the One, which *cannot but* generate – and indeed Plotinus envisaged the derivation as proceeding 'necessarily' (*hupo anangkês*) (vi.8.10.15–20; vi.8.13.36) – and in this sense is importantly unlike the Christian creation. This raises difficult questions about the compatibility of this view with the idea that the One is the supremely autonomous free will and the principle of self-determination (vi.8.20–21). The gist of Plotinus' solution to this problem is that self-determination should be understood as an absence of coercion by anything external; after all, there is nothing external to the One.

Another aspect of the Plotinian derivation that is well captured by the imagery of physical emanation is the nature of the ontological dependence relation between the One and its products. This is a peculiar combination of transcendence and immanence within a single account of reality (O'Meara 1993: 48), which is summed up in the following sentence: 'These things [produced by the One] are and are not the One; they are the One, because they are from it; they are not the One, because it endowed them with what they have while remaining in itself' (v.2.2.25–27). This statement expresses a principle that is common to derivations between any two levels of reality. On the one hand, the producer (i.e. a higher level) transcends what it produces (i.e. a lower level), in a way that fire transcends heat. It follows from this transcendent status that the producer remains independent of its product, and is not diminished in its power by generating it. On the other hand, the producer is immanent in the product, in a way that fire is immanent in the particles of hot air, without being dependent on it. For this reason, the One can at once transcend and be essentially different from all beings, and yet be immanently present in all of them. To express this relationship of 'non-reciprocal dependence' (Remes 2008: 43–44), Plotinus repeatedly uses the image of father and child (e.g. v.1.1): the father is the cause of the child and imprints itself into the child, while remaining separate from it; the child causally depends on the father and carries in itself a share of its father's powers.

The image of father and child (but less so the image of fire and heat) points to the dynamics inherent in this peculiar combination of separation and unity. These dynamics are constituted by two antithetical but complementary metaphysical pulls: that of 'procession' (*proshodos*) and that of 'reversion' (*epistrophê*). All beings in their relationship to the One are like children who, on the one hand, are driven to separation from their father and to affirmation of their own independent existence (iv.8.4.13–18). Plotinus describes this drive to 'procession' from the One towards increasing multiplicity and differentiation at once as compelled by the One (iv.8.6.15–17) and as caused by the 'audacity' (*tolma*) of individual souls and their 'willing that they belong to themselves' (v.1.1.4–5). On the other hand, though, all beings long for a reversion to the higher levels of reality from which they emerged, and ultimately for reconnection with the One as the ultimate object of desire (vi.8.7.4–5).

The unfolding of the One proceeds at three distinct levels, each of which corresponds to a metaphysical 'reality' (*hupostasis*) or 'principle' (*archê*).[5] The second highest level, or the immediate expression of the One, is the Intellect (*nous*). Intellect consists of Beings in the strict sense, that is of Forms (*eidê*) – immaterial, unchanging essences that are the paradigms of existing entities for all lower degrees of reality. It belongs essentially to these Forms that they are actually intelligible, and hence they necessarily presuppose that there is something that thinks them. The Intellect therefore includes both Forms as the objects of thought and the activity of thinking them itself (v.4; v.6). Intellect is thus the object of its own thought, which gives it a high degree of unity. Still, its unity falls short of the unity of the One: Intellect is composite both because of the multiplicity of Forms that it contains and because of the division between the act and the object of thought.

The Intellect expresses itself in Soul (*psuchê*) (v.1.3), which stands both for the soul of the world as well as for the individual souls that it includes, including the human souls. Very roughly, the role of Soul is to mediate between Intellect and the material world by expressing the Forms in bodies, or in the realm of Nature (*phusis*). The bodies are created, organised and operated by Soul as changing, temporal images of the Forms. As the source and principle of material things that are always situated in time and space, Soul transcends them in its immateriality and eternality; at the same time, it is present in them as their intelligible structure. In the Greek tradition, soul was regarded as the source of life. For Plotinus, this is not quite

---

[5] I cannot embark on explaining how precisely the derivation of individual levels is supposed to work. Plotinus' account of this process is complex, even abstruse, and the details have been much discussed in the secondary scholarship. See Gerson (1994), ch. 2 and 3, or Emilsson (2017), for accessible treatments.

true insofar as Soul is the pure actuality of Intellect that is the principle of Life (*zôê*) (i.4.3; iii.8.10; vi.7); it merely extends this Life to the bodies from the Intellect.

In contrast to the three metaphysical realities, the One, the Intellect and Soul, the realm of Nature contains 'evil' (*kakon*). This is the consequence of the existence of matter, which is the 'primary' evil, understood as 'a sort of absence of measure as opposed to measure, or absence of limit as opposed to limit ... or what is always in need as opposed to what is self-sufficient; always indefinite, in no way stable, absolutely passive, insatiable, and completely impoverished' (i.8.6.13–17). Matter is evil due to its absolute distance from the One. In other words, it is understood privatively: it is not a corruption or perversion of the Good, but rather an absence or lack of goodness.[6] The moral evil, or 'vice' (*kakia*), is understood as the consequence of the metaphysical evil of matter: it arises in mismanaged cases of the prolonged preoccupation of the soul with the body and its attachment to it (i.8.4.13–17). As befits the privative notion of evil, vice too is understood as general 'weakness' (*astheneia*) of the soul, since it prevents the soul from properly exercising its capacities (i.8.14).

With these rudiments of Plotinus' metaphysics in place, we can attend to how he envisaged the position of humans within this hierarchy. Rather than being confined to one particular level of reality, human beings span several different levels: by having ensouled bodies, they belong to the realm of Nature but also to that of Soul. In addition, they also participate, in some sense, in the activity of Intellect; this highest dimension of human lives is of paramount importance for Plotinus' aspirational vision. The human soul has a threefold structure (ii.3.9): the lowest level comprises the capacities for growth and perception that it shares with animals; the middle level consists in the capacity for discursive reasoning or rational argumentation (*logismos*); the highest level is what Plotinus calls the 'separated soul' (i.1.10) or undescended intellect (iii.4.3.24; iii.8.5.10–15), since 'even our own soul does not descend in its entirety, but there is something of it always in the intelligible world' (iv.8.8.1–3). We have this element not only 'collectively' but also 'individually' (i.1.8). By virtue of having this undescended intellect, we have a share in the pure noetic activity of the Intellect that thinks itself, that is, the multiplicity of Forms. This

---

[6] Given Plotinus' monistic metaphysics, the existence of evil is bound to become a sensitive philosophical problem. The details of how Plotinus tackles this problem have been the subject of considerable debate and controversy. O'Meara (2005) and Narbonne (2014) usefully state the main problems and discuss the different positions taken in the scholarship.

means, paradoxically, that the transcendent intellect exists, somehow, in the sensible world. But no matter how difficult the metaphysical questions that this postulate raises, it follows from the general principle that higher levels of reality are, despite their transcendence, immanent in the lower levels that they produce. So the soul is deeply divided between the embodied and the 'separate' element, and thus necessarily 'amphibious', living in two radically different metaphysical realms: 'Souls, then, come to be, in a way, amphibious, as of necessity they live part of their life in the intelligible world and part of their life in the sensible world' (iv.8.4.32–34).

Plotinus sometimes refers to the separate, transcendent element of the soul as our 'true self', or as who 'we' (*hêmeis*) really are (ii.3.9.15–16; i.1.10), as distinct from the embodied or 'composite' (*sunthetos*) soul: 'For each of us is double; one is a sort of complex, and the other is the self' (ii.3.9.31–2). But besides using the notion of self in the sense of the highest element of the human soul, he also uses 'we' to refer to a 'power of identification' (Aubry 2014: 310) with either the lower or the higher element of the self (i.1.10.6–7). Some passages tend to attribute this power of identification to the 'middle' level of the soul, the one of discursive reasoning: 'We are this … in the middle between two powers, a worse and a better one, the worse being that of sense-perception and the better being Intellect' (v.3.3). In contrast to the discursive reasoning, the intellective activity of the separated soul is inarticulate and non-propositional: it consists in the pure, intuitive seeing of Forms unmediated by language (iv.4.1.21–25). But the discursive reasoning, while distinct from pure intellection, has the power to bring us into the vicinity of intellection since it is 'first receptive of Intellect' (v.3). The 'middle' level can thus be the accomplice and vehicle of our fall into the body, but also decisively conducive to transcending the body and ascending towards the Intellect (Stern-Gillet 2014: 403–4).

Let me conclude this section by citing a much-celebrated passage in which Plotinus describes his personal experience of the unity with the Intellect. The passage is worth including since it brings together the main points discussed in the previous paragraphs, while also anticipating themes to be addressed in the next section:

> Often, after waking up to myself from the body, that is, externalising myself in relation to all other things, while entering into myself, I behold a beauty of wondrous quality, and believe then that I am most to be identified with my better part, that I enjoy the best life, and have become united with the divine and situated within it, actualizing myself at that level, and situating myself above all else in the intelligible world. Following on this repose within the divine, and descending from Intellect into acts of calculative

reasoning, I ask myself in bewilderment, how on earth did I ever come down here, and how ever did my soul come to be enclosed in a body, being such as it has revealed itself to be, even while in a body? (*Enn.* iv.8.1)

The experience of realisation that there is a 'better part' of the soul is described in terms of an awakening. For the most part, we are infatuated by the sensible world and forget that we also participate, without knowing about it, in the life of intellect. In this state of forgetfulness, we fail to 'actualise' what we truly are and live a life of those who are asleep. While it may not be possible to separate ourselves from the embodied condition altogether, we should 'above all' try to shift the centre of our life to the intelligible realm. And this is what it means, on Plotinus' account, to achieve happiness. To this account we shall now turn.

6.3 Happiness as the Abundance of Life

In the Plotinian universe, the measure of goodness is proximity to the One, or the Good. Whatever is closer to the One – whatever is more simple, unified and self-sufficient – is also better than what is further from it and, since the One is also the source of being, also has a higher degree of existence. All things strive for the Good, that is, desire the assimilation to the One (vi.7.24–25). Humans are no exception. Due to their association with body, and hence matter, their default condition is that of 'fall': 'And this is the fall of the soul; to come in this way into matter and to be weakened, because all of its faculties are not present in the activity ... and what is seized by a kind of theft it [the matter] makes evil, until such soul can lift itself up again' (i.8.14.45–48). The soul is weakened both because the body to which it is attached inhibits the optimal actualisation of its faculties, and because it generally gets engrossed in the bodily realm, 'busying itself with trivialities' (iv.8.4.16), 'severing itself from the whole' (iv.8.4.18) and increasing its distance from the One.

Nonetheless, it is possible for the soul, even in its embodied condition, to 'lift itself up', or 'ascend' back towards the One. The approximation to the One is understood as an 'assimilation' (*homoiôsis*), in which one strives to become *like* the One. This means, for human beings, following 'the best part of themselves' (ii.9.2.8) – their intellect – and in so doing partaking in the activity of divine Intellect. The possibility of this assimilation is premised on the view that we are by our constitution always anchored in the intelligible world, and whatever life we choose for ourselves, we shall always be connected to the One. So we only need to 'actualize', by a refocusing of our attention, the intellectual powers of our souls.

Plotinus envisages this process as consisting of several consecutive stages that coincide with different kinds or indeed grades of virtues. Virtues are the means of assimilation (i.2.1.49–51). At the initial stage, humans should acquire so-called 'civic virtues' (*politikai aretai*), four cardinal virtues that correspond to virtues from Plato's *Republic* (iv.428b ff). These virtues are 'measures in matter', which itself is 'unassimilated to everything' (i.2.2.21), and hence help us to avoid the absolute evil of matter. The main role of civic virtues is to impose, with the help of discursive reasoning, order and limit on our desires and appetites; so, for instance, the civic virtue of temperance is the 'agreement or concord of the spirited faculty with the faculty of calculative reasoning' (i.2.1.19–20). Once the embodied soul has been put in order, the next step is to dissociate from the body altogether, as far as possible. This dissociation is the job of the 'purificatory' or kathartic virtues. So, for instance, the kathartic counterpart of civic self-control is 'not to feel the same things as the body' (i.2.3.17). These virtues are acquired through certain kathartic practices, notably aesthetic pursuits (i.6), mathematics and dialectic (i.3). All these are conducive to turning the soul towards the intelligible and making it impervious, as far as possible, to the feelings and disturbances of the body (i.2.5–6).

The purified soul is ready to embrace the life of intellect, and, by so doing, become one with it insofar as is possible. Rather than merely having 'images or impressions' of Beings, 'we think them by being them' (vi.5.7.3–5), and in so doing we are 'together with all things' (ibid. 8). Since Intellect is the unity of activity of thinking and the object of thought, becoming one with Intellect means that we are in perfect unity with ourselves, being the object of our own intellection. So, focusing one's attention on 'the voices from the high' (vi.4.12.19–20) means that one also achieves the greatest possible intimacy with oneself (v.8.11.31–33). This 'feeling of presence in which the duality between subject and object is abolished' (Aubry 2014: 313) also brings a sense of self-sufficiency and satisfaction, since there is no desire for an external object, and one has no desire other than to remain immersed in this state.

In Plotinus' treatise *On Happiness* (i.4), this outlook on the human good is affirmed in the context of ancient debates about *eudaimonia*.[7] In the first two sections of the treatise (i.4.1–2), Plotinus critically discusses

---

[7] The following account of Plotinus' treatise on *eudaimonia* has been informed by Schniewind (2015), McGroarty (2006) and Gerson (2013), though I focus more persistently than these treatments on Plotinus' view of happiness as the maximisation of life itself and pass over some other noteworthy elements of his theory. For a comprehensive study of the notion of Life in Plotinus' thought, see Ciapalo (1987).

an approach to defining *eudaimonia* that he attributes to Aristotle and the Stoics. In Plotinus' eyes, this approach is inconsistent. On the one hand, Aristotle and the Stoics presuppose a specific understanding of 'life', on which all living things are, at some level, alive in the same sense. 'Life' is a genus, whereas 'human life' or 'life of plants' are different species of this genus. On the other hand, these philosophers deny that non-human forms of lives could ever achieve *eudaimonia*. For it is only by virtue of having a share in reason, i.e. by virtue of a peculiar quality of their life, which distinguishes human life from non-human lives, that humans can aspire to happiness. The problem is this: if all living beings share in the same definition of 'life', what good reasons are there to deny that they all can 'live well', that is, happily? This denial is not plausible, since plants, for instance, typically exercise their natural function if they have enough light and nutrients. The exclusion of plants from living well is particularly precarious for naturalists such as the Peripatetics. Since the lives of plants also 'unfold in the direction of a goal' (i.4.1.19), such as the bearing of fruit, they evidently can also be said to live well (or badly) (cf. iii.8.1).

Of these two conflicting views, as Plotinus identifies them, it is the for- mer – the underlying conception of life and its value – that needs to be abandoned in the first place. Lives of humans, animals and plants should be differentiated not in terms of having different qualitative attributes, but in terms of having a different degree of metaphysical priority: 'not in the sense of a logical distinction within a genus, but in the sense in which we speak of one thing being prior (*proteron*) and another being posterior (*hus- teron*)' (i.4.3.17–19). Effectively, Plotinus uses Aristotle's notion of meta- physical priority to challenge Aristotle's own understanding of 'life'. Life must be predicated 'homonymously': 'it is said in one way of a plant and in another of a non-rational animal, according to the clarity and dimness of the live they have' (i.4.3.20–22). Of course, to make Plotinus' position consistent, 'clarity' and 'dimness' cannot stand for yet another set of quali- ties that qualify 'life', but for different degrees of life itself. These degrees correspond to different levels on the metaphysical ladder that leads from the One to matter (or the other way round): thus, the life of intellect is metaphysically prior to the vegetative life; it is 'life' in a more proper, original sense of that word.

This metaphysical understanding of life has implications for related views about 'living well' and life's value. It is a mistake to derive the goodness of life from its specific quality (*poiotês*), namely rationality, rather than from life itself (i.4.3.10–15). The notion of 'life' is infused with value from the start, and does not become good by virtue of a superadded quality such as rationality. Correspondingly, living well consists not in having a life of a peculiar quality but simply in living: one should not presume, like Aristotle and Stoics did, that 'being happy is not just living' (i.4.3.11–12). That is why even plants, though deprived of perception and reason, can live well in their own way. But if all living beings can live well in their own peculiar way, is it still possible to say that the human life is, in some sense, better or more desirable than the life of a plant? Clearly, someone like Plotinus would like to say that it is: if proximity to the One is the measure of goodness, and humans are more proximate thanks to their intellects, human life should be better than the life of plants. And indeed this is what Plotinus thinks. Even though 'life' is predicated equivocally, different kinds of life are axiologically commensurable since the difference among them in all cases turns out to be a difference of degree; they all refer to a single Life – the life of Intellect – from which they all derive. The lives of entities that are higher up in the metaphysical hierarchy are better than the lives of those that are lower, and since good-ness is coextensive with being, this also means that those who have better lives can also be said to be more alive. All living things can be said to 'live well': but the living well of, say, plants will be a 'reflection' (*eidôlon*) of the living well of philosophers, that is, it will be derivative and metaphysically posterior (i.4.3.23–24).

This metaphysical-cum-axiological hierarchy explains why human lives that involve the activity of the intellect are lives in a fuller and better sense: they are closer to the Intellect as the source of the principle of life – indeed they can become identical with it (i.4.4.15). This is why Plotinus defines *eudaimonia* proper, i.e. the life of intellect, as 'living fully', or the 'super-abundance of life' (*agan zên*) itself. Those who live best are also those who live most; they are those who assimilate to Intellect as the source of life:

> And if the good belongs to whatever has a superabundance of life – this is whatever is in no way lacking in life – only to whatever lives superabun-dantly would *eudaimonia* belong (*tôi agan zônti to eudaimonein huparchoi*); for to this the best [will belong], if that which is really the best in life is in real beings and is the perfect life. (i.4.3.25–28; transl. McGroarty)

The 'real life' is also 'the perfect life', and this is the life of intellect. All humans, insofar as they are humans, have the perfect life in 'potency', but those who are happy have 'actualized' it and in fact have 'transformed' themselves so that they are identical with the intellect (i.4.4.10–15).

The lives of happy humans are contrasted with other sorts of lives, those that are mere imperfect images of the real life, and 'are no more lives than their opposite' (i.4.3.36–37). These shadowy lives are lived in 'darkness' and are 'small and faint and cheap' (vi.7.15.3–4). And yet, despite his disdain for these inferior lives, Plotinus does think that even they have a grain of goodness: though distant, they are nonetheless derivations of the Good, and are genuinely better than matter, the principle of evil and death. So the 'hierarchical thinking has to be kept in tension with the anti-hierarchical immediacy of the Good's presence to everything' (Corrigan 2014: 387). But there is a sharp gap within the otherwise continuous hierarchy between those who live real lives, happy sages, on the one hand, and all other living things, including humans, who only live a 'reflection' of life, on the other.

The idea of happiness as superabundance of life recalls those passages from Aristotle that equate living better with living more. In both cases, self-perfection (living better) also implies self-realisation (living more): by perfecting those capacities that define who I am, I come to exist more fully. For Aristotle, these capacities – such as rationality – are those that define me as a member of the human species; likewise, for Plotinus, the capacity for both discursive reasoning and pure intellection is character- istic of humans (i.4.4.7–12). The differences between these philosophers come to light when one asks whether Aristotle would accept the implicit Plotinian view that good humans are more alive than well-functioning plants, or that humans in general can be said to be more alive than plants or other less complex organisms. Neither seems to be a view that Aristotle, or at least the Aristotle of the *Nicomachean Ethics*, would be inclined to endorse.[8] Humans cannot generally be said to be more alive than plants or jellyfish, since both living humans and living jellyfish *equally* fulfil the defi- nition of life – that is, they engage in the activity of the nutritive soul. That is why the notion of 'being alive' (*zēn*) is excluded from the definition of the human function in NE i.7: being alive *per se* does not contribute to the goodness of life; it is the quality of life that matters. What Aristotle does say in the *Nicomachean Ethics* ix.9, as we have seen, is that corrupted lives are not lives proper, and for that reason vicious humans cannot achieve the fullness of life of the virtuous. But plants or jellyfish are generally no more corrupted than humans; in fact, they tend to be rather more successful in completing the natural capacities that they have. And so in this sense they cannot be regarded as 'living less' than humans do. So it seems that,

[8] Things may appear differently from the perspective of Aristotle's *Protrepticus*. When we read that only those who are 'intelligent' are 'truly alive' (*Protr.* 59.4–11), this does imply that degrees of life are coextensive with degrees of rationality. So when Plotinus chooses Aristotle as a target of his criticism in *Enn.* i.4, he seems to direct this criticism at the eudaimonist theory from the *Nicomachean Ethics* rather than from the *Protrepticus*, which seems to be more compatible with Plotinus' own position.

for Aristotle, the notion of degrees of life can be used to refer to different degrees of actualisation within a particular species, but not to compare degree of lives across different species. For Plotinus, in contrast, differences in substance can, if they imply differences in the proximity to the One, in themselves entail differences in the degrees of life. Humans can be said, in general terms, to be better and more alive than jellyfish, because they are, thanks to their intellect, closer to the One and to the Intellect as the source of life.[9]

Since degrees of life are coextensive with degrees of goodness, we can further ask how would the value of bad humans, on the Plotinus' view, compare with the value of well-functioning jellyfish. In Section 2.8, I have suggested that Plato and Aristotle would parse the value of a life along two axiological axes: the value of its complexity and the value of its perfection. The degree of complexity determines the magnitude of the overall value, the degree of perfection determines its direction. Human lives are complex, and therefore high-risk high-gain; that is why vicious human lives end up being worse than normal jellyfish lives: vice gives the axiological magnitude of their lives a bad direction. Plotinus does not have a discussion that would directly bear on this issue, but it follows from the premises of his metaphysical system that the differences in perfection (good versus bad) and the differences in complexity (jellyfish versus humans) can in principle be cashed out on a single axiological axis, that of goodness that depends on one's proximity to the One. The magnitude of value is not independent of its direction. Vice does not generate a robust badness that parasitically capitalizes on the value of human complexity; rather, it diminishes life's complexity (or rationality), which again explains why bad humans live less fully. Vice is not an axiological inversion of good potentials into the negative, but only a lack, a privation of goodness, that amounts to a fall on the metaphysical-cum-axiological ladder. By becoming vicious, humans fall in the direction of well-functioning jellyfish.

Having defined happiness as the abundance of life, Plotinus dedicates the remaining part of the treatise to some implications of his account in the context of ancient debates. The most important among these implications is the claim concerning the happy person's self-sufficiency and imperviousness to external misfortunes. These attributes follow from the principal achievement of the Plotinian sage, namely the identification with the intellect as the true self. All other aspects of the sage's existence,

---

[9] This does not mean that Plotinus would generally dismiss the value of non-living things. For a discussion of anti-anthropocentric elements in Plotinus' thought, see Corrigan (2014).

including the body and the composite soul, are 'just something he happens to be wearing, which no one would actually suppose to be a part of him, since he does not want to wear these things' (i.4.4.6–19).

The identification with intellect goes hand in hand with the separation from the embodied existence, since 'it is not possible to live happily in the composite of body and soul' (i.4.15.9–10) – and this is where Plotinus departs from Aristotle, the Stoics and even Plato. This dissociation from the composite soul does not necessarily mean that soul exits the body. In fact, the sage continues to be subject to much of the suffering and disturbance that non-sages typically experience, but he regards this experience as belonging not to his 'inner soul' but to 'the outer shadow of human being' (iii.2.15.49). The hallmark of Plotinian happiness is a radical shift of perspective on one's individual existence, and a resolute, wilful detachment from the embodied soul and whatever it suffers: 'Even if the dying of the relatives and close ones causes pain, it does not pain him, but only that in him which is apart from intellect, that whose pains he will not accept' (i.4.4.35–37). He regards these sufferings as belonging to a role, a character that he is playing, but never forgets that his true self is detached from the worldly fates of this character (iii.2.15.45–55). This detachment is the reason why misfortunes cannot penetrate into his innermost self and disturb his happiness: 'So his happiness will not be diminished by adverse fortune, for this sort of life remains as it is' (i.4.4.30–31; cf. also i.4.8.11–12).

In deploying the imagery of roles, Plotinus follows the example of the Stoics, who also used it to bring out that many of those things that people strive for or experience in their lives are actually indifferent things that do not ultimately matter for happiness. There are indeed suggestive parallels between Plotinus' axiological views and the Stoic distinction between the good and the indifferent things.[10] So when Plotinus insists that the sage 'must give to this embodied life what it needs, insofar as he can, he himself being other than it' (i.4.15.17–18), that reminds us of the Stoic category of preferred indifferents, such as bodily health (cf. i.4.6.27–30). The sage should not neglect his body, but neither should he regard it as something that matters for his happiness. Asking why the sage would care at all about things such as health, Plotinus answers: 'In fact, we will say that it is not because of their contribution to being happy, but because of their contribution to existence' (i.4.7.3–4). This is consistent with Plotinus' view that

---

[10] Brittain (2003: 245) and Emilsson (2017: 316) have noted the parallel.

happiness does not increase with time (i.5): staying alive longer will not make you happier, but perhaps embodied existence, or staying alive, is a value that motivates the sage to take care of his body, independently of his happiness. This, too, echoes the Stoic view of life as a preferred indifferent. Moreover, as we shall see in the next section, Plotinus, like the Stoics, seems to regard bodily health – in contrast to happiness itself – as an important consideration in the deliberation about staying alive.

However, Plotinus is not an axiological dualist in the Stoic sense. Unlike the Stoics, he does not think that it is in the pursuit of preferred indifferents that our rationality should find its proper expression; thinking so amounts to disregarding the true status and calling of our intellect, which is at home in the immaterial realm of true being. The necessities of life are to be acquired by discursive reasoning (i.4.6.16–17); they are therefore not objects of intellection, the activity where the highest human good is to be found. Most importantly, Plotinus does not regard things such as health or wealth as non-instrumentally valuable; rather, they are mere 'necessities of life' (i.9.1.13), possessions that are indispensable for the continuation of embodied existence. All these differences ultimately derive from the fact that the Stoics and Plotinus have a different understanding of the self for whom these things should be good. While the Stoics emphasise that human beings are, first and foremost, defined by their rational capacities, they also regard them as 'rational animals' (e.g. DL vii.51); as such, humans have legitimate reasons to strive for many of the body-related things that other animals do.

So the 'necessities of life' are instrumental for the continuation of embodied existence. But why does Plotinus think that the sage should care about his continuation at all if the disembodied state seems much more favourable? The answer is, I think, that the embodied state, too, is instrumental to the flourishing of the soul, even though the soul is an immaterial entity. But that also means that the continuation of embodied life is not unconditionally valuable or choiceworthy. I explore these views in the next two sections, starting with the value of being born *qua* composite of body and soul, and then turning to the conditions in which it is worth staying in this embodied state.

6.4   Life Worth Beginning

In the context of Plotinus' thought, the question whether it is worth being born at all can be formulated as a question about whether it is worthwhile for the human soul to 'descend' into a body, in comparison to remaining in the disembodied state. As noted in the introductory section, Plotinus' views about the worth of embodied existence appear to be ambivalent. This ambivalence goes back to Plato, but Plotinus makes the question a central problem of his philosophy. While he is no less emphatic than Plato in the *Phaedo* about the soul's life in the embodied state as a difficult exile, he also offers two lines of arguments in favour of the incarnate existence that are without a recognisable parallel in Plato.

The first set of arguments can be found in an important treatise *On the Descent of Souls into Bodies* (iv.8), where Plotinus tries to reconcile competing views about the value of embodiment.[11] This treatise has been regarded as expressing a 'world-affirming attitude' towards the physical world, and hence also to the soul's embodiment (Gerson et al. 2019: 510). Before we turn to these life-affirming arguments, it should be said clearly that Plotinus' default perspective on the soul's embodiment is, here as elsewhere, that it is a necessary evil. It is necessary because it is in the essential nature of soul. Given the twofold nature of the soul, says Plotinus, it is 'better' for it to be in the intelligible realm, but also necessary for it to partake of the sensible (iv.8.7.1–3). Drawing closely on the *Timaeus*, Plotinus explains that just as the soul of the universe was 'sent down by the god' to make the universe intelligent (iv.8.1.46–49), so it is the necessary expression of the essential nature of the human soul that it descends into bodies in order to take care of them, administer them and master them (iv.8.2.7–9; iv.8.3.26–31). The soul chooses a particular life, but this 'choice' (*prohairesis*) is 'more like a natural leap, as it might be towards a natural desire for marriage' (iv.3.14.19–20). The soul enters the appropriate body it 'must' enter, and cannot but choose a life that fits its individual 'disposition', which again is determined by the conduct of its previous life (iii.2.13.11–15). This insistence on the necessity of embodiment puts our question into perspective: when we ask whether it would not be better for the soul to remain disembodied, this does not mean that this is an option that was actually open to the soul.

Besides being necessary, the embodiment is evil in the sense that it entangles the soul with matter. For if souls are to fulfil their function of administering the bodies, they 'are constrained to descend deep inside them' (iv.8.2.9). At the very least, this constraint is that of being impeded or disturbed, to a bigger or smaller extent, in the exercise of the soul's rational and intellectual capacities. Worse yet, the body is bound to 'infect'

---

[11] For an excellent discussion of this theme in general, and Plotinus' arguments in *Enn.* iv.8. in particular, see Song (2013).

the soul with pleasures, appetites and pains (iv.8.2.42–45), though this evil can in principle be minimised or eliminated by the acquisition of virtues. That embodiment is an evil is also implied by the view that it is a punishment for the soul's former actions (iv.8.5.9–10; cf. iv.3.24.15–16).[12]

This negative perspective on the soul's descent into body is counterbalanced by some arguments in favour of the embodiment. Consider the following passage:

> In this way, then, though soul is a divine being and derives from the places above, it comes to be encased in a body, and though being a god, albeit of low rank, it comes thus into this world by an autonomous inclination and at the bidding of its own power, with the purpose of bringing order to what is inferior to it. And if it extricates itself promptly, it suffers no harm, acquiring a knowledge of evil (*ouden beblaptai gnôsin kakou prosbalousa*) and learning the nature of vice,[13] while bringing its own powers into the light and exhibiting deeds and productions (*erga kai poiêseis*) which, if it had remained inactive in the incorporeal world (*en tôi asômatôi êremounta*), would have been useless, as never coming to actuality (*eis to en ergein aei ouk ionta*); and the soul itself would never have known what capacities it had, since they would never have been revealed or developed (*ouk ekphanenta oude proodon labonta*). This is so, if indeed in all cases actualization reveals the potentiality (*energeia tên dunamin edeixe*) that would otherwise have been entirely hidden and in a way blotted out and non-existent (*hoion aphanistheisan kai ouk ousan*), since it never would truly exist. As it is, however, everyone is brought to wonder at what is inside it by reason of the variegation of what is outside, reflecting on what sort of a thing it is from the observation of its sophisticated acts. (iv.8.5.23–37)

Although the descent of the soul into the body is necessary, it is a positive expression of the soul's 'autonomous inclination'. In particular, it is an expression of its benevolent nature, which not only cares about the realisation of its own intelligible nature, but also attends to the 'need of something else' (*eis allou tou chreian*) (iv.8.5.11–12). So is it the inevitable fate of the soul to be harmed, as it were, by its own benevolence? Not quite; in the above passage, the incarnation is presented in positive terms as the prerequisite for the actualisation and development of some of the soul's capacities, which would remain idle in a disembodied state. This

---

[12] This claim also puts Plotinus in a position to regard embodiment as at once necessary and voluntary (iv.8.5).

[13] Compare a slightly different translation by Fleet: 'If it escapes quickly it will have suffered no damage *by* [emphasis mine] acquiring a knowledge of evil' (Fleet 2012: 159). On this reading, the soul suffers no harm *in spite* of acquiring a knowledge of evil, because this knowledge presupposes a risky interaction with matter. More on this 'risk' later in this section.

actualisation also has an epistemological benefit, insofar as it 'reveals' the full potential of the soul. But then this argument seems to stand in sharp tension with Plotinus' repeatedly expressed view that the body does not promote but rather impedes the soul: 'soul actualizes more what belongs to it without body' (*mallon energei ta autês aneu sômatos*) (i.7.3.7–8). An obvious strategy to reconcile these claims is to point out that in each case Plotinus has different capacities of the soul in mind: some are enabled by the body and some are impeded by it.

The psychic capacities that are enabled must be those that bear on the soul's function as the administrator of the body, and belong to the composite soul. This includes, in particular, the discursive reasoning that puts affections and appetites into order, and more broadly all capacities that are employed in the practical realm of 'deeds and productions'. The capacities of the soul that are impeded by the body, and whose activation does not depend on the embodied state, are the pure noetic capacities of the separate soul. If this is right, and Plotinus does think that the activation of the capacities of the composite soul makes embodied existence worthwhile, his reasoning could be spelled out along the following lines. In the incarnate state, the soul can activate both intellect, though with impediments, and body-related capacities; in the disembodied state, it can activate only intellect, albeit without impediments. Thus, the embodied condition comes out better, all things considered, at least from the perspective of the whole soul.

This argument in favour of the embodied life has two important limitations. First, the surprising benefits of embodiment can be reaped only 'if the soul extricates itself promptly' and 'suffers no harm'. This seems to exclude all those who fail to avoid the harm by acquiring at least the civic virtues. If the soul is in a disordered state and subjected to the body, all its wonderful capacities for mastering the body lie largely inactive. Secondly, the perspective of the whole soul is not necessarily identical with the perspective of the self. The embodiment may well be worthwhile for my soul, but is it for that reason good *for me*? If indeed my true self is the separate soul, or undescended intellect, then this does not follow. But the sages do identify themselves with their intellect. Thus, jointly considered, these limitations seem to undermine the argument in favour of the embodiment: incarnate existence can be worthwhile neither for the bad nor for the good.

There are also those who are neither sages nor vicious, that is, those who have avoided falling into vice but have yet to fully dissociate themselves from the body to embrace the intellect. It is for them, actually, that the incarnation could be worthwhile. For their their souls are exercising their body-related capacities and, in addition, the experience of the embodied condition can promote their *katharsis*. Notably, Plotinus suggests that the experience of the sensible world is epistemically valuable insofar as it enables the soul to grasp more clearly the contrast between the sensible and the intelligible worlds, and thus also augment the knowledge of intelligible reality: 'For the experience of evil results in a clearer knowledge (*epistêmê*) of the Good in those whose power is too weak to attain knowledge of evil prior to experiencing it' (iv.8.7.15). So Plotinus here apparently affirms, rather audaciously, that the soul cannot properly come to know itself if it remains in a disembodied state (cf. Brisson and Pradeau 2002: 488). Plotinus typically uses the word *epistêmê* for the 'non-intuitive cognition of necessary, eternal truths' (Gerson et al. 2019: 922), and hence this cognitive increase serves the discursive reasoning of the composite soul, rather than the intuitive intellection of the separate soul. Still, this knowledge has the potential to positively contribute to the spiritual ascent.

But what about the sages? Are we to conclude that the embodied existence is only necessary, but not really worthwhile for them? To offer an answer to this question, I shall now turn to the second set of arguments in favour of the embodied existence, which comes chiefly from Plotinus' treatise *On Providence* (iii.2–3). In this treatise, Plotinus discusses the worth of human lives not so much from the perspective of individual souls but rather from the perspective of the contribution of these lives to the universe. In other words, the focus is on the contributive value of lives rather than on whether life is worth living for the person who lives it. But I shall suggest that the contributive value also has implications for the personal value.

Like the Stoics, Plotinus envisages the world as providentially ordered, so that each thing cannot fail to make a contribution to the harmony and unity of the whole. The ruling principle is like a general who 'keeps an eye on actions and experiences and what must be there, food and drink and indeed all the weapons and mechanical aids; and all that flows from the interweaving of these activities has been foreseen so that their consequences have their place in good organization' (iii.3.2). But in fact the power of the ruling principle is even greater than the power of generals, since it can 'also control the enemy camp as well' (ibid.). This means that it can integrate and make a constructive use even of evil such as, 'for example … from the leading away of captives other cities [may come to be] better than those that have been plundered by wicked men' (iii.2.18.17–18). Plotinus goes as far as to maintain that 'if we deprive the ruling principle of wicked deeds we will be depriving it of good ones, too' (iii.2.18.20–21), affirming a strict interdependence between good and evil.

He uses artistic imagery to bring out this point: the world is like a play that needs both good and evil characters, or like a musical composition that needs both high and low tones (iii.2.17). Bad humans are as necessary in the providentially organised world as a public executioner is indispensable in a well-ordered city: the city needs this kind of person, 'though he is a rogue' (iii.2.17.85–88).

From this perspective, then, even bad human lives are meaningful, since they make a positive contribution to the whole. In this respect Plotinus' position is close to that of the Stoics, but on a closer inspection it turns out that his view about the value of bad lives is not quite like the Stoic one. For he regards evil deeds as being caused by the necessity of nature, not by the providence of the ruling principle (iii.3.5.25–6; 33–34).[14] The necessity causes these evil deeds through the choices of actions of bad souls, who, however, in making these choices, do not act truly of themselves, but under the blind diktat of the matter that has come to dominate their disordered souls. So in the second part of *On Providence* (iii.3), Plotinus does not so much regard evil deeds as necessary counterparts of their opposites, but rather as regrettable and unintended flaws. The providence does not cause them, nor does it presuppose them; rather, it resourcefully manages to find a good use for them or rectify them:

> Virtue everywhere is in control since what has gone wrong is changed and encounters correction, just as in a single body when health has been bestowed through providence's care of the living being, when there is a cut or wound of any kind the ruling principle which organizes it once more fixes, brings together, heals and rights the painful part. (iii.3.5.27–32)

The ruling principle is powerful enough to prevent these flaws from tainting the beauty of the universe, like a general that can contain even the army of the enemy, but that does not mean that the world would be worse off without them. This makes the axiological status of bad lives, from the cosmic point of view, somewhat ambivalent. They are indeed indispensable and, eventually, make a positive contribution, but they are made indispensable only by an intervention of the providential ruling principle.

We can now revisit the question whether embodied lives are worth living for the sages: would they not be better off entirely dissociated from the bodily realm? This question acquires special urgency when we turn, as in the next section, to the worth of continued existence. Should sages not hasten to extricate themselves from their bodies? Plotinus' philosophical

---

[14] Emilsson (2017: 254) talks about the 'unintended consequences' of providence.

theory of providence implies a negative answer to this question. All human lives, and good lives in a less problematic way than bad lives, are meaningful. Could this meaningfulness also make my life worth living *for me*? The answer is that it could: the sages identify themselves with the Intellect, and in so doing approximate the One, but that means that their individual perspective approximates that of the universe. What is good for the One they also regard as what is good for themselves. On this basis, I think, Plotinus could plausibly maintain that embodied life is worth living for the sages even though, but also precisely because, they identify themselves with intellect as their true self. Their lives are worthwhile for them because they are meaningful from the perspective of the One.

6.5   Life Worth Continuing

The discussions about the worth of being born provide a sound basis for an understanding of Plotinus' views about the worth of staying alive. The Plotinian material that bears most explicitly on this question comprises scattered discussions about the appropriateness of suicide, or the voluntary departure of the soul from the body. These discussions have attracted considerable scholarly attention, with diverging views about Plotinus' position. Some commentators have argued that Plotinus was categorically against suicide, since the good soul will 'always choose to stay' (Rist 1967: 175; cf. also Wallis 1972); others have thought that his position is quite close to that of the Stoics,[15] or that it shifted in the course of his philosophical career from rejection to acceptance (McGroarty 2006: 205–7; Kalogiratou 2009).

The reserved attitude towards suicide is informed by the providentialist outlook. In the treatise *On Exiting from the Body* (i.9), Plotinus counsels against the voluntary departure from life by appealing to one's 'allotted time'. The soul should leave the body only in what we could call natural death, namely when 'the soul is no longer bound to it, with the body unable to bind it any longer, and its harmony no longer present' (i.9.1.5–7). This anti-suicide outlook is further elaborated in a fragment *Plotinus on Voluntary Death* preserved by Elias:

> [T]he philosopher should imitate god and the sun, not being careless of the body just because they care for the soul, but taking providential care of it until such time as it becomes unfit, distancing itself from the association with the soul. For it is absurd to exit before one's time, which is when the one who joined the body and soul together loosens the bond. (Gerson et al. 2019: 126)

[15]   Graeser (1972), Dillon (1996), Stern-Gillet (2013).

The idea here is that everything in the world has its job to do, and just as it is the job of the sun to shine, so it is a job of human beings to take good care of the body and remain associated with it as long as possible. While the philosopher knows that his embodied existence is other to him, he continues to be attached to it, playing the role assigned to him, until the time comes when it is 'necessary' to depart.

And such time may indeed come. This includes cases when he can no longer 'endure' staying in his body (i.4.16.23–24), or when he starts to 'lose his mind' (i.9.1.12), or, generally when the 'burden is too heavy' (i.4.7.43). These cases could perhaps be understood as situations in life when the soul can no longer properly activate the capacities that have to do with administering and mastering the body. When the body overwhelms the soul with unmanageable, chronic pain, or when the cognitive and motivational capacities of the soul rapidly decline, the soul is hardly in a position to exercise its function as the caregiver of the body. If the activation of these capacities is one of the reasons why the descent of the soul into the body is worthwhile, it would make good sense to regard, conversely, the failing of these activations as a reason to return to the disembodied state.

The combination of these two perspectives on suicide, providentialist and functionalist, does not necessarily amount to an inconsistency or a doctrinal shift. For the condition when the soul cannot exercise its functions and the 'burden is too heavy' can quite plausibly be regarded as a sign that one's time has come and one is supposed to depart.[16] In fact, in cases when the soul is no longer capable of administering the body, the bond between body and soul has *already* started to be loosened, so suicide does not violate but rather assists the providential order of things.

So far, we have been discussing suicide from the perspective of the sage. But what about non-sages? Let us first consider those among the non-sages who are not irreparably vicious. Plotinus says about them that they should stay alive because 'soul should not exit while there is an opportunity for progress' (i.9.1.18–19). This coheres with the view, mentioned in Section 6.4, that the experience of embodied existence can be conducive to progress. Those making such progress have a good reason to stay in their bodies not only in spite of their embodied condition, but also, at least in part, because of it.

When it comes to bad humans, the outlook is much bleaker. Like Plato or Aristotle, Plotinus too establishes a connection between performing

---

[16] In this sense, Plotinus endorses the notion of the 'divine sign' adopted by Plato and the Stoics (see Section 3.6)

one's 'function' (*ergon*) and the worthwhileness of life. What makes life worth choosing *for* all living things is the exercise of their specific function: 'for example, musically disposed animals, who are otherwise in a good state, certainly sing naturally, and have a life that is in this respect choice-worthy for them' (i.4.1.9–11). Note that this reference to function may be the reason why Plotinus says, as cited the second epigraph to this chapter, that the existence of animals is preferable for them to their non-existence: the reason may well be that they typically exercise the function of their animal soul. Since bad humans fail to perform their function, namely to exercise the rational and intellectual capacities of their soul, their life is not 'doing its job', like an eye that cannot see clearly (i.7.3.3). By implication, then, their life is not worth choosing for them, so much so that death may be preferable. This is corroborated by the claim that for bad humans, or those who fail to preserve the purity of their soul, life is not a good but an evil (i.7.3.12–13). This pessimistic perspective is further reinforced by a remark from *On Providence* where Plotinus flatly says about bad humans that 'death would be better for them than continuing to be alive (*hoi thanatoi autois beltious ê to houtô zôntas einai*) in the way that the laws of the universe do not want them to live' (iii.2.8.47–49). The universe would not be worse off without these humans, and they themselves would be better off dead.[17]

These claims, pessimistic as they are, need to be put into the broader context of Plotinus' metaphysical commitments. It follows from these commitments that bad actualisation cannot be, all things considered, worse than no actualisation at all. For evil is the privation of goodness, which is a privation of being, and hence extremely bad lives are, strictly considered, not lives at all. 'Even if there are punishments in Hades', Plotinus says, they will not make a bad life better because this life is 'not simply life' (i.7.3.15). In his treatise on evil, Plotinus describes the extremely vicious condition of the soul as virtual death, no matter that the soul still remains in body: 'It dies, then, as much as a soul can die, and death for it while still immersed in the body is to be sunk into matter and to be filled with it and, when it leaves the body, to lie there until it should turn away and lift up its gaze from the mud' (i.8.13.18–26). So wholly vicious persons are hardly alive at all. But that means that the question whether their lives are worth living is moot, or at least largely

---

[17] Note that this does not amount to a claim that suicide is generally allowed or recommended for the vicious, but only that their lives are not worth living. But Plotinus nowhere says anything that would categorically block this conclusion, and in fact there is a strong reason in its favour: by curtailing their lives, the vicious would prevent their souls from suffering, in the course of their miserable lives, even greater harm.

insignificant, as insignificant as these 'dim' lives themselves. Since this life is only a distant, faint image of the true life of the Intellect, it does not really matter that much whether it is or is not worth living. The more vicious a person is, the less substance this question actually has.

6.6 Plotinus, Plato, the Stoics and Aristotle on the Value of (Mere) Life

We started this chapter by noting Plotinus' ambivalence about the worth of embodied existence. The subsequent discussion has revealed that this ambivalence derives from the twofold nature of the soul: on the one hand, the body impedes the soul and possibly infects it with evil; on the other, in descending into bodies, the soul lives out, as it were, its essential nature as the administrator of the body and can fully activate its capacities. Souls cannot but descend into bodies, and in so doing contribute to the providential order of the universe. In addition, if and insofar as they can avoid harm and corruption, the embodied existence seems, all things considered, genuinely worthwhile for them. As for the embodied lives of vicious souls, their contributive value is compromised, nor are these lives of benefit for these souls. But when Plotinus says these lives are not worth living, the tension between this claim and the life-affirming strand in his thought is somewhat mitigated by the qualification that bad lives hardly qualify as lives at all.

We have seen little explicit evidence in favour of a distinction between the target notion of happiness and the threshold notion of life worth living. Clearly, given the monistic axiology, this distinction can be based only on different degrees of approximating to the Good, and so indeed it is. Plotinus regards as unhappy but still worth living the lives of those who have not achieved full identification with the life of intellect but have at least acquired civic virtues and/or have a chance of progressing towards wisdom.

Perhaps the most distinctive aspect of Plotinus' axiology of life is his view that happiness is a 'superabundance of life', or that the more life is worth living for you, the more alive you really are. According to this view, it is not a superadded quality that makes your life good, because life is good in itself. Hence you live better simply by living to a greater degree. I conclude this chapter by several comments about this view from the perspective of a comparison with other philosophers in the tradition.

Surprisingly, perhaps, the account that appears to be most different from Plotinus' view is that of Plato. At least for the Plato of *Euthydemus* or *Clitophon*, life – the fact of having a soul – has purely instrumental value: all non-instrumental value depends on how you use your soul, or how you live. Since Plotinus regards *all* life to be an emanation of the One, it has non-instrumental value. Even bad lives, insofar as they can be regarded as lives, have a degree of non-instrumental goodness, no matter how insignificant or miserable they are. This is, ultimately, the consequence of the immanentist dimensions in Plotinus' cosmology: whereas the One, or the Good, radically transcends the realm of nature, it is nonetheless present, albeit derivatively, in all kinds of lives. To avoid confusion, it should be noted that the view that life has non-instrumental value does not conflict with the instrumental value of embodied existence. It is life as non-instrumental value to which the embodied existence is instrumental. One can be alive only by virtue of having soul, which itself receives life from the Intellect. But the characteristic *modus vivendi* of the human soul lies in the state of embodiment.

The Stoics, in contrast to Plato, grant that mere living has non-instrumental value. This is, indeed, what one would expect from the combination of their ethical naturalism with the monistic and providentialist cosmology. All things are nothing but elements of the godly breath, and through their existence they contribute to the good of the universe. However, the monistic cosmology comes with a radically dualistic axiology that is unparalleled in Plotinus. So the value of life, non-instrumental though it is, is separated from what is good in the strict sense – that is, the rational *modus operandi* of the universe which finds its particular expression in human virtue. So the Stoics cannot say, as Plotinus indeed can, that we live better by living more, just as they cannot say that we live better by being healthier or wealthier.

When we ask, in the Peripatetic context, whether living more amounts to living better, and the other way round, it is useful to distinguish between two senses of 'living more', or between two senses of actualisation in general. In one sense, 'living more' has to do with perfecting the characteristically human capacities: in becoming a better human, one becomes more fully a human, and therefore more fully exists (*qua* human) (see Section 2.3). In the Peripatetic account of moral development from Cicero's *On Ends* (discussed in Sections 5.2 and 5.4), this kind of actualisation amounts to satisfying the natural desire for perfection. In another sense, 'living more' amounts simply to achieving a higher degree of activity; in this sense, those who are awake, or those whose activities are free from external impediments, are more alive than those who are asleep or those who are impeded in their activities. In the account of moral development, this kind of actualisation amounts to satisfying the natural desire for activity.

Whereas it is clear how the former sense of 'living more' can amount to 'living better', it is less clear how this can be in the latter case. Being more active, regardless of a degree of perfection, *could* mean to have a better life, but this would presuppose significant shifts in the Peripatetic account of the good life (as discussed in Section 5.6).

When Plotinus likens the ascent to the life of intellect to an awakening from sleep (e.g. iii.6.6.71–75; iv.8.1), this is a clear indication that he does not want to distinguish sharply between these two senses of actualisation. Developing the virtues needed to embrace the life of intellect does not only amount to an increase in perfection; it also entails a fuller, more active life, similarly to awakening from sleep. Insofar as those who are asleep live only in a diminished sense, this is in line with Plotinus's view that bad human lives hardly count as lives at all, and stands in contrast to Plato's view from the *Clitophon* or to Aristotle's position from the *Nicomachean Ethics*.[18] That you use your soul badly does not mean, for Plato, that you use it less; vice does not make you less active. The reason for Plotinus' claim that bad humans can hardly be said to be alive is that the very notion of being alive is understood normatively: goodness is built into the very definition of what life is. We have encountered this move in Aristotle (think of the view that 'life' in itself is something definite, and hence good), but Plotinus is more radical in redefining life *not* as a physical or biological, but as a metaphysical – which in his case also means a normative – notion. So there is, in the end, hardly any substantive difference between the life of eternal sleep and the lives of active but vicious humans. This heavily revisionist understanding of life also explains why Plotinus can regard humans as generally being more alive than plants or jellyfish. As implausible as this may seem from a biological perspective, this is the conclusion one reaches if all life is understood as a top-down derivation from the life of Intellect: humans have intellect, and are thus closer to the source than other living things.

---

[18] But shows affinity with some claims from Aristotle's *Protrepticus*, see Sections 2.3 and 6.3.

Conclusions

At the beginning of this book, I situated the ancient philosophical views about the life worth living in the broader context of early Greek literature, and also discussed them with regard to modern philosophical accounts of the related themes. It is now time to summarise the main lessons of these interpretations. To do so, let me contrast the views of ancient philosophers both with the outlook of the Greek poets and with the modern philosophical views. In the following discussion, I focus on the big picture, and hence these conclusions do not necessarily apply in all cases, but for the most part.

The question about the life worth living can be understood in two different senses: whether it is worth being born at all; and whether it is worth staying alive. We have seen that it is only starting with the Hellenistic period that these two questions were treated on separate terms, whereas in Plato and Aristotle the discussions about life worth living seem to imply both senses without a clear discrimination. The Hellenistic philosophers were chiefly interested in the problem of the worth of continued existence, which reflects the importance of suicide as a major ethical theme of this period. The problem of the worth of being born received comparatively less attention, though we find an interesting discussion in the Stoic sources and the theme was later addressed in Plotinus' reflections on the value of embodied existence.

C.1 Philosophers and the Poets

Ancient poets such as Theognis or Euripides regard human existence as a pitiable lot. Some philosophers, notably Epicurus, challenge this pessimistic outlook head-on. But can we say that philosophers are indeed bringing the good news about the human condition, as Williams or Nussbaum suggested? What are the chances that we shall have a life that we have good reasons to be glad for having? How accessible is such a life, considering the variety of natural and social predicaments that different humans find themselves in? If happiness is the goal – if this is the most worthwhile life for humans – then the bar is quite high. All major philosophical schools, including the Epicureans, concur that virtue, a psychological excellence or health, is necessary to be happy. To acquire virtue, one needs, at the very least, a good upbringing and education, as well as a nature that is amenable to cultivation. In addition, some philosophers, such as Aristotle, hold that virtue can be adequately enacted only in certain social roles (philosopher, politician) and not in others (craftsman, slave). But even when one is privileged and fortunate enough to have all of these, being virtuous may still not be enough. Consider, for instance, Aristotle's and Epicurus' views about the necessity of friendship for the good life.

Hence, happiness is not widely accessible. But what about a life that, if not happy, is at least worth living? On the one hand, no ancient philosopher thinks that a life is worth living by default: mere living does not have value that is sufficient to make a life worth living. On the other hand, various kinds of imperfect lives could be worth living even though they are not happy. An important reason for such a concession is the distinction between a life worth living, as the more accessible threshold notion, and a happy life, as the distant ideal. Plato, Aristotle and their followers do grant such a distinction. In their view, a life at least barely worth living is intermediate between a happy and a wretched life, so that it possesses some but not all goods necessary for the happy life. Every happy life is also worth living, but not every life worth living is also happy.

The intermediate space for a life worth living is based on axiological theories that allow for a plurality of several different kinds of goods: when you have some of them, or to some degree, your life is at least worth living; when you have them all, it is happy. Most importantly, in comparison with happiness, the requirement for virtue is eased. You do not need to have virtue to the extent that you need it for the happy life; what suffices is a degree of virtue, or even freedom from vice. Vice as the state of corruption must be distinguished from various other states that constitute less serious forms of imperfection. Here belong, for instance, Plato's good carpenters, who have some virtues but not others, or Aristotle's self-controlled persons, who are half-virtuous. Along with relaxing the requirement for virtue, there is a concession that one can achieve a life worth living in a range of social roles that is broader than the roles required for happiness. The lives of philosophers are best, but even workers have a reasonable claim to have lives worth living, if certain conditions are met. Thinking of later Peripatetics, there are also hints towards the concession that unperfected lives, perhaps even vicious lives, can be worth living if only they are free from impediments.

Thus the distinction between a happy life and a life worth living gives some grounds for optimism. But this optimism has its limits. One is that a degree of virtue, or freedom from vice, may not be an unconditional worthmaker. Some conditional worthbreakers, such as grave external misfortunes or serious bodily ailments, may override conditional worthmakers. More importantly, perhaps, there are two unconditional worthbreakers that have a common denominator, namely that they spoil the exercise of human function: the state of injustice or vice; and the state of cognitive impoverishment, typically a life reduced to the passive consumption of bodily pleasures, one that makes a human life human only in name and not in substance. If your life is irreversibly tainted by either of these two worthbreakers, no amount of other good contents can possibly get you above the threshold. One might think that most humans can stay clear of these unconditional worthbreakers; after all, you do not need to be a philosopher to avoid injustice (for Plato), and you do not need to be virtuous to avoid vice (for Aristotle). Still, it is difficult to overestimate the extent to which the chance of sailing through life unscathed by these worthbreakers depends on living under a good political constitution. Plato's carpenter can have a life worth living only on the condition that he lives in a well-governed city ruled by the philosophers; take that condition away, and his case is hopeless.

But not all philosophical schools of antiquity committed to the distinction between the target notion of happiness and the threshold notion of a life worth living. Two Hellenistic schools, Stoics and Epicureans, are the notable exceptions. The Stoics maintained that a happy life and a life worth living amount to two different and non-overlapping notions: there are both unhappy lives worth living and happy lives not worth living. So there is a distinction between a happy life and a life worth living, but the latter is *not* conceived as a threshold on the same continuum of value on which happiness is the target; a life most worth living is not necessarily a happy life. There are two different, incommensurable scales of evaluation: one for life's worthwhileness, which admits of more or less; and another one for life's happiness, which allows only happiness or unhappiness, with nothing in between. From the Stoic perspective, to measure the worth of being alive by virtue and vice, as Plato and Aristotle did, amounts to a categorical mistake that devaluates virtue and overrates life. Life is not a good, only virtue is; therefore, the deliberation about staying alive must be referred not to virtue or vice but to other indifferent things besides life or, more precisely, to the balance of preferred indifferent things and their opposites. Leaving aside how philosophically compelling this twofold perspective on well-being is, this account of a life worth living can be regarded as quite optimistic. The Stoics notoriously had a very demanding account of virtue and themselves admitted that humans who achieved such a rational perfection, and hence escaped vice, were extremely rare. For Plato and Aristotle, this would amount to a concession that virtually no human lives are worth living. This does not follow for the Stoics. Even if you are a fool, and therefore unhappy, you may have perfectly good reasons to carry on living if you have a preponderance of things in accordance with nature, combined with the confidence of maintaining these in the future.

Thus, three major philosophical traditions of the Greek and Roman antiquity – Platonic, Peripatetic and the Stoic – commit to the view that it is possible to have a life worth living without having achieved the best possible life, and even without having the prospect of achieving it in the future. There are different philosophical motivations for this concession, but one of them stands out, namely the role of naturalism. At its most general, the thought is that nature is a source of norms, so that to live in accordance with a nature, whether of one's own, of the city or of the kosmos, is a good. This view is behind the optimistic contention of philosophers that humans can aspire to *eudaimonia*, even though they can never be gods; they can aspire to a good life, because that life is a perfection of human nature, nothing less (not the nature of jellyfish), but also nothing more (not the nature of the gods). The naturalistic perspective also helps to justify the distinction between the best human life and a life worth living. This is especially the case in the Peripatetic and Stoic tradition. It is Aristotle's view that if one is not virtuous, one's nature can still be uncorrupted, and therefore even non-virtuous life can be worth living. For the Stoics, even a non-virtuous life that is well-supplied by things in accordance with nature would be worth living. But the elements of the naturalistic approach are also detectable in Plato. In the *Republic*, the appeal to natural types is instrumental in justifying the principle of specialisation, which ultimately makes it possible to include the lives even of non-philosophers in the category of lives worth living. Some people are by their nature such that they flourish in roles that do not enable them to reach the perfection of the best element of the soul, but still allow them to achieve and maintain a condition of psychological health.

A particularly strong expression of the naturalistic perspective is the recognition by some ancient philosophers of non-instrumental value at the lowest level of the axiology of life, that is, at the level of mere human living. No ancient philosopher regarded mere human living as an unconditional worthmaker. But both Peripatetics and the Stoics considered it as non-instrumentally valuable, precisely because it is a work of nature, and hence an end and a good. If you have a human constitution, Aristotle maintained, then doing what you are supposed to do as a human – perceive and think – is already something fine to start with. But naturalism was not the only perspective in antiquity that warranted the affirmation of the non-instrumental value of life *per se*. In the Neoplatonist thought of Plotinus, all forms of life are regarded as non-instrumentally valuable, insofar as all of them are emanations of the transcendent One.

As for the relationship between the non-instrumental value of life *per se* and the value of good life, we have encountered three models of this relationship. First, there is the view from Plotinus and Aristotle's *Protrepticus* on which life *per se* is defined in revisionist, normative terms: you can be said to be alive precisely to the extent that you live well. Secondly, on the opposite spectrum, there is the Stoic view that the value of life *per se* and the value of good life belong to two incommensurable axiological realms, that of indifferent things and that of goodness. Thirdly, there is the view I attributed to Aristotle's other ethical works, and to later Peripatetic tradition, that human life has a virtue-independent value but one which does not belong to an axiological realm incommensurable with that of virtue. This third view allows, in theory at least, for a competition between value in the sense of life's perfection and value in the sense of life's abundance, for being more alive in the sense of being more active does not necessarily converge with being alive in the sense of being more perfect. This potential tension explains, I suggested, a wavering in the Peripatetic sources in the assessment of the worthwhileness of vicious but successful lives.

The remaining major philosophical school are the Epicureans, who are the exception in their reluctance to grant the possibility of unhappy lives that are worth living. This is a result of their monistic axiology that regards freedom from disturbance, which does not allow for degrees, as the dominant good. If you achieve freedom from disturbance, your life is both happy and worth living; if not, it is neither. There is an important qualification to this general picture: your life may be worth living, though unhappy, if you are making progress in philosophy or have a chance to make such progress in the future. So it is only the prospect of achieving happiness that makes a continued existence worthwhile. Thus, whether we regard the Epicurean outlook on the life worth living as optimistic or pessimistic depends crucially on the accessibility of philosophical study. And what the Epicureans have to say on this score is ambivalent: on the one hand, philosophy is envisaged as an intellectually fairly low-threshold activity that you can practise with the help of like-minded friends; on the other, there are Epicurean remarks to the effect that not everyone is naturally suited to making philosophical progress.

Let me conclude this section by some general observations about the ancient accounts of life's worthwhileness with regard to their meaningfulness. Some philosophers, most notably Plato in the *Republic*, understand these two values in strictly interdependent terms. What makes your life worth living is the exercise of the function of your soul; this entails the exercise of your social role in the city, which makes your life meaningful. In general, accounting for goodness in terms of function bodes for the convergence of worthwhileness and meaningfulness: on the one hand, good functioning (or even mere functioning) entails a degree of health and fulfilment; on the other, it entails that you accomplish a mission, that you live in a way that you are meant to live, whether by your city, by nature or by the providential god.

At the same time, some philosophers allow for a gap, or even a degree of antagonism, between worthwhileness and meaningfulness. Aristotle's slaves or craftsmen may have meaningful lives, from the political perspective, but whether that makes their lives worth living is uncertain. The Stoics and Plotinus hold that we cannot escape, even if we wanted, the fate of having meaningful lives because we cannot fail to make our contribution to the harmony of the universe. But this contribution does not necessarily translate to the worthwhileness of our lives; in fact, if it is our fate to suffer from lifelong illness and poverty (for the Stoics), or from vice (Plotinus), then the contribution of our life to the universe precludes our lives being worthwhile for us.

There is a broad convergence, however, on the point that a life cannot be worth living without also being meaningful in some way. This holds even for the Epicureans, who did not endorse teleological axiology. For if a life worth living is impossible without friendship, and if friendship consists in committed mutual care, then your life, if happy, is necessarily also meaningful by providing a source of security for your friend. So as for the relationship between worthwhileness and meaningfulness, a fitting conclusion would be that ancient philosophers generally tend to regard meaningfulness as a necessary condition of a life worth living, and that some of them (Plato) regard it even as a sufficient condition.

C.2   Ancients and Moderns

Some ancient claims about the life worth living, such as the claim that the vicious or unexamined life is not worth living, have been deemed extreme or puzzling in the eyes of many modern philosophers. We have now seen that these views follow from the functionalistic perspective on the value of human life, and are therefore well within the ancient philosophical mainstream. Hence some modern worries about these claims could well apply to ancient philosophy more broadly considered. The charge is that the ancient approach to defining a life worth living is unnecessarily pessimistic and elitist. The ancients deny, on philosophically dubious grounds, a worthwhile life to many humans who are quite content with their lives, for all their imperfections. This tendency testifies to an elitism that goes hand in hand with an overemphasis on the performance of a function or role and, at the same time, with a questionable disregard of the value of subjective well-being. In this final section, I sketch some strategies for how the ancient philosophers could be vindicated against these objections.

Let us first consider the charge of pessimism. One part of the rebuttal derives from the distinction between happy life and life worth living. If the general outlook of philosophers is that a human life is worth living if it is not too bad, in different senses of that word, then it is neither too pessimistic nor too optimistic. This holds also for contrast with the modern approaches. One could perhaps argue, on behalf of the ancients, that it is modern, not ancient approaches, that tend to embrace extreme positions. Consider the doctrine of the sanctity of life, which attributes to human life unconditional value, in contrast to anti-natalism, which attributes to it unconditional disvalue. Neither of these positions has parallels in ancient philosophy. On the one hand, the ancients believed that no life is worth living by default or unconditionally; its worthwhileness must be earned by remaining free from fatal imperfections. On the other hand, they did not go as far as to deny that human life can ever be genuinely worthwhile; in fact, some of them even go as far as to argue that all human lives have non-instrumental value. On the whole, then, we could say that the ancient outlook on life worth living is rather moderate or discriminating; the worthwhileness depends on the contents. This is confirmed by the fact that in ancient philosophy we find categorical opposition neither to human procreation nor to the practice of suicide.

The alleged ancient pessimism can be further qualified by appreciating important non-elitist or even anti-elitist elements of some ancient theories. Consider Plato's carpenter, who can do just fine if he heeds his job, or a Stoic fool who enjoys good health, has enough to eat and has a satisfactory social life. There is a widely shared idea in ancient philosophy that it is sufficient for having a life worth living if you are able to function reasonably well in your social context. This functioning typically presupposes some level of bodily health, some level of rationality and cognitive richness, as well as some decency of character, but not necessarily impressive political or intellectual achievements. Even Epicureans, who do insist that one cannot ever have a life worth living without philosophical studies, programmatically tried to make a life informed by the Epicurean philosophy a widely accessible option.

Now, it is true that no ancient philosopher would ever be willing to grant a life worth living to someone like Wolf's 'Blob', whose life is reduced to the socially isolated consumption of passive pleasures. The possibility that such a life could be worth living is less alien to the modern philosophical imagination than it is to the ancient. Recall, for instance, the modern view that a life is worth living for a person if only that person wishes to carry on living; if only Blob wants to stay alive, his life must be worth living for him. But the decisive ancient denial of this possibility is not so much an expression of an elitist sentiment but rather of the ancient insistence that a life worth living is necessarily also meaningful, that is, it is connected to the larger social and cosmic context in a way that meaningfully contributes to it. A life worth living must be meaningful; but meaningfulness does not guarantee worthwhileness. Is this view any more pessimistic that the modern possibility – or worry, rather – that the worthwhileness of a life does not guarantee its meaningfulness?

These differences notwithstanding, Susan Wolf argued against Blob's chances of having a life worth living, and a number of other modern philosophers would concur with the ancient view that a life worth living must also be a meaningful life. We can think of Nozick's criticism of the experience machine, which makes precisely the point that a worthwhile life must be connected to the real world. After all, I have mentioned a strand in the contemporary philosophy of well-being that draws directly on ancient eudaimonism. One argument espoused by these philosophers is that virtue reliably generates a subjective well-being that can be characterised in terms of a psychological health; in the long term, it feels good to be virtuous and it feels bad to be vicious. We have seen that some ancient sources offer vivid accounts of the troublesome consequences of vice for subjective well-being. Consider Plato's tyrant, whose life is a hell on earth: he suffers not only a lot of pain but also frustrated desires. This would be his response to Haybron's Genghis Khan case: you cannot be vicious and prosperous, not on a closer look. From the perspective of subjectivist accounts of well-being, a tyrant is doing poorly; but in Plato's view, this is a necessary consequence of the injustice in his soul. It would be a mistake, therefore, to associate the ancient emphasis on objective perfection with the wholesale deprecation of subjective feelings and experiences. It is true that no ancient philosopher would agree with the view that it is sufficient to have a life worth living that you desire your life to continue. But they did think that the presence of some important objective values in your life promotes, or even is indispensable for, feeling well in your life and having the actual desire to carry on living.

These last remarks indicate that there is less discontinuity between ancient views and modern views, or at least some of them, than some potentially disturbing ancient claims would make one think. But it is one thing to grant that virtue plays an important role for well-being, and another to make serious recommendations to hopelessly vicious or mentally retarded humans, or to crippled carpenters, that they would better die. Indeed, if politicians or doctors were to make such recommendations, they would meet with outrage. Why, precisely, are similar ancient views bound to remain so alienating to the modern mind? The reason is, perhaps, not so much that the ancient commitments would be fundamentally unrelatable to the modern mind but rather than they tend to compete with, or to be overridden by, sensitivities that emerged, and prevailed, in the later history of thought. These include, in particular, the view that every human life has a value that derives from it being a God's creation, or from its dignity or moral status, as well as the tendency to regard the feelings and desires of individuals as sources of normativity. Insofar as these sensitivities did not play a major role in ancient views about life's worthwhileness and value, we can perhaps say that the ancient outlook was simpler or, if you like, less conflicted.

Bibliography

Ackrill, J. L. 1974. 'Aristotle on Eudaimonia'. In *Essays on Aristotle's Ethics*, ed. by A. O. Rorty. Berkeley: University of California Press, 15–34.

Ademollo, F. 2020. 'Cosmic and Individual Soul in Early Stoicism'. In *Body and Soul in Hellenistic Philosophy*, ed. by B. Inwood and J. Warren. Cambridge: Cambridge University Press, 113–144.

Agar, N. 2001. *Life's Intrinsic Value: Science, Ethics, and Nature*. New York: Columbia University Press.

Altman, W. 2011. 'Reading Order and Authenticity: The Place of *Theages* and *Cleitophon* in Platonic Pedagogy'. *Plato Journal* 11: 1–50.

Annas, J. 1981. *An Introduction to Plato's Republic*. Oxford: Oxford University Press.

Annas, J. 1985. 'Self-Knowledge in Early Plato'. In *Platonic Investigations*, ed. by D. J. O'Meara. Washington, DC: Catholic University of America Press, 111–137.

Annas, J. 1992. *Hellenistic Philosophy of Mind*. Berkeley: University of California Press.

Annas, J. 1993. *The Morality of Happiness*. New York: Oxford University Press.

Annas, J. 1996. 'Aristotle and Kant on Morality and Practical Reasoning'. In *Aristotle, Kant and the Stoics*, ed. by S. Engstrom and J. Whiting. Cambridge: Cambridge University Press, 237–258.

Annas, J. 1999. *Platonic Ethics: Old and New*. Ithaca, NY: Cornell University Press.

Annas, J. and Woolf, R. eds. 2001. *Cicero: On Moral Ends*. Cambridge: Cambridge University Press.

Arenson, K. 2019. *Health and Hedonism in Plato and Epicurus*. London and New York: Bloomsbury Press.

Atkins, E. M. and Griffin, M. T. eds. 1991. *Cicero: On Duties*. Cambridge: Cambridge University Press.

Aubenque, P. 1963. *La prudence chez Aristote*. Paris: Presses Universitaires de France.

Aubry, G. 2014. 'Metaphysics of Soul and Self in Plotinus'. In *The Routledge Handbook of Neoplatonism*, ed. by P. Remes and S. Slaveva-Griffin. London: Routledge, 310–323.

Baier, K. 1988. 'Threats of Futility: Is Life Worth Living?' *Free Inquiry* 8: 47–52.

Baier, K. 1997. *Problems of life and death*. Amherst: Prometheus Books.

Baranzke, H. 2012. '"Sanctity-of-Life" – A Bioethical Principle for a Right to Life?' *Ethical Theory and Moral Practice* 15: 295–308.

Barney, R. 2003. 'A Puzzle in Stoic Ethics'. *Oxford Studies in Ancient Philosophy* 24: 303–340.

Barney, R. 2008. 'Aristotle's Argument for Human Function'. *Oxford Studies in Ancient Philosophy* 34: 293–322.

Barney, R. 2020. 'Becoming Bad: Aristotle on Vice and Moral Habituation'. *Oxford Studies in Ancient Philosophy* 57: 273–308.

Barney, R., Brennan, T. and Brittain, C. eds. 2012. *Plato and the Divided Self.* Cambridge: Cambridge University Press.

Barry, R. L. 2002. *The Sanctity of Human Life and Its Protection.* Lanham, MD: University Press of America.

Bayertz, K. ed. 1996. *Sanctity of Life and Human Dignity.* Dordrecht: Springer.

Benatar, D. 2006. *Better Never to Have Been: The Harm of Coming into Existence.* Oxford: Clarendon Press.

Bénatouïl, T. 2013. 'The Stoic System: Ethics and Nature'. In *The Routledge Companion to Ancient Philosophy*, ed. by F. Sheffield and J. Warren. London: Routledge, 424–437.

Betegh, G. 2020. 'Plato on Illness in the Phaedo, the Republic, and the Timaeus'. In *Plato's Timaeus. Proceedings of the Tenth Symposium Platonicum Pragense*, ed. by C. Jorgenson, F. Karfík and Š. Špinka. Leiden: Brill, 228–258.

Bett, R. 2010. 'Socratic Ignorance'. In *The Cambridge Companion to Socrates*, ed. by D. Morrison. Cambridge: Cambridge University Press, 215–236.

Bobonich, C. 2002. *Plato's Utopia Recast: His Later Ethics and Politics.* Oxford: Clarendon Press.

Bonhöffer, A. F. 1996. *The Ethics of the Stoic Epictetus*, transl. by W. Stephens. New York: Peter Lang.

Bowe, G. S. 2007. 'In Defense of Clitophon'. *Classical Philology* 102.3: 245–264.

Boys Stones, G. R. 2001. *Post-Hellenistic Philosophy: A Study of Its Development from the Stoics to Origen.* Oxford: Oxford University Press.

Bradford, G. 2016. 'Perfectionism'. In *Routledge Handbook of Philosophy of Well-Being*, ed. by Guy Fletcher. London and New York: Routledge, 124–134.

Bradley, B. 1998. 'Extrinsic Value'. *Philosophical Studies* 91: 109–126.

Bradley, B. 2002. 'Is Intrinsic Value Conditional?' *Philosophical Studies* 107: 23–44.

Bradley, B. 2013. 'Intrinsic Value'. In *International Encyclopedia of Ethics*, ed. by H. Lafollette. Oxford: Blackwell.

Brennan, T. 2000. 'Reservation in Stoic Ethics'. *Archiv für Geschichte der Philosophie* 82.2: 149–177.

Brennan, T. 2005. *The Stoic Life: Emotions, Duties, and Fate.* Oxford: Clarendon Press.

Brisson, L. 2006. 'The Doctrine of Degrees of Virtue in the Neoplatonists: An Analysis of Porphyry's Sentence 32, Its Antecedents, and Its Heritage'. In *Reading Plato in Antiquity*, ed. by H. Tarrant and D. Baltzly. London: Duckworth, 89–106.

Brisson, L. and Pradeau J.-F. eds. 2002. *Plotin: Traités 1–6.* Paris: Flammarion.

Brittain, C. 2003. 'Attention Deficit in Plotinus and Augustine: Psychological Problems in Christian and Platonist Theories of the Grades of Virtue'. *Proceedings of the Boston Area Colloquium of Ancient Philosophy* 18.1: 223–275.

Brouwer, R. 2014. *The Stoic Sage: The Early Stoics on Wisdom, Sagehood and Socrates*. Cambridge: Cambridge University Press.

Brickhouse, T. C. and Smith, N. D. 1989. 'A Matter of Life and Death in Socratic Philosophy'. *Ancient Philosophy* 9: 155–165.

Broadie, S. 1991. *Ethics with Aristotle*. New York: Oxford University Press.

Broadie, S. and Rowe, C. eds. 2002. *Aristotle: Nicomachean Ethics: Translation, Introduction and Commentary*. Oxford: Oxford University Press.

Broome, J. 1985. 'The Economic Value of Life'. *Economica* 52: 281–294.

Broome, J. 2008. 'What Is Your Life Worth?' *Daedalus* 137: 49–56.

Brunschwig, J. 1986. 'The Cradle Argument in Epicureanism and Stoicism'. In *The Norms of Nature: Studies in Hellenistic Ethics*, ed. by M. Schofield and G. Striker. Cambridge: Cambridge University Press, 113–144.

Burnet, J. 1916. 'The Socratic Doctrine of the Soul'. *Proceedings of the British Academy* 7: 235–259.

Cagnoli Fiecconi, E. 2019. 'Aristotle's Peculiarly Human Psychology'. In *Aristotle's Anthropology*, ed. by K. Geert and N. Kreft. Cambridge: Cambridge University Press, 60–76.

Camus, A. 1951. *L'Homme révolté*. Paris: Gallimard.

Christensen, A. 2017. 'Better Off Dead: Suicide in Plato's Philosophy'. PhD dissertation, Washington University in St. Louis.

Christensen, A. 2020. 'As the God Leads'. *Ancient Philosophy* 40.2: 267–284.

Chroust, A. H. 1966. 'Eudemus or on the Soul: A Lost Dialogue of Aristotle on the Immortality of the Soul'. *Mnemosyne* 19: 17–30.

Ciapalo, R. T. 1987. 'Life (Zōḗ) in Plotinus' Explanation of Reality'. PhD dissertation, Loyola University Chicago.

Claus, D. 1981. *Toward the Soul: An Inquiry into the Meaning of ψυχή before Plato*. New Haven: Yale University Press.

Connell, S. 2015. *Aristotle on Female Animals. A Study of the* Generation of Animals. Cambridge: Cambridge University Press.

Cooper J. 1989. 'Greek Philosophers on Euthanasia and Suicide'. In *Suicide and Euthanasia: Philosophy and Medicine*, ed. by B. A. Brody. Dordrecht: Springer, 9–38.

Cooper, J. ed. 1997. *Plato: Complete Works*. Indianapolis: Hackett.

Cooper, J. 1999. 'Pleasure and Desire in Epicurus'. In *Reason and Emotion: Essays on Ancient Moral Psychology and Ethical Theory*, ed. by J. Cooper. Princeton: Princeton University Press, 485–514.

Cooper, J. M. 2012. *Pursuits of Wisdom: Six Ways of Life in Ancient Philosophy from Socrates to Plotinus*. Princeton: Princeton University Press.

Corrigan, K. 2014. 'Humans, Other Animals, Plants and the Question of the Good: The Platonic and Neoplatonic Traditions'. In *The Routledge Handbook of Neoplatonism*, ed. by P. Remes and S. Slaveva-Griffin. London: Routledge, 372–392.

Crisp, R. 2006. *Reasons and the Good*. Oxford and New York: Oxford University Press.

Crisp, R. 2018. 'Prudential and Moral Reasons'. In *The Oxford Handbook of Reasons and Normativity*, ed. by D. Star. Oxford: Oxford University Press, 800–820.

Csikszentmihalyi, M. and Csikszentmihalyi, I. S. eds. 2006. *A Life Worth Living: Contributions to Positive Psychology*. Oxford: Oxford University Press.

Devereux, D. 2017. 'Virtue and Happiness in Plato'. In *The Cambridge Companion to Ancient Ethics*, ed. by C. Bobonich. Cambridge: Cambridge University Press, 53–71.

Dillon, J. 1996. 'An Ethic for the Late Antique Sage'. In *The Cambridge Companion to Plotinus*, ed. by L. Gerson. Cambridge: Cambridge University Press, 315–335.

Dimas, P. 2015. 'Epicurus on Pleasure, Desire, and Friendship'. In *The Quest for the Good Life: Ancient Philosophers on Happiness*, ed. by Ø. Rabbås, E. K. Emilsson, H. Fossheim and M. Tuominen. Oxford: Oxford University Press, 164–182.

Echeñique, J. 2021. 'A Peripatetic Argument for the Intrinsic Goodness of Human Life: Alexander of Aphrodisias' *Ethical Problems* I'. *Apeiron* 54.3: 367–384.

Emilsson, K. E. 2017. *Plotinus*. London: Routledge.

Engelhardt, H. T. 1996. 'Sanctity of Life and Menschenwürde: Can these Concepts Help Direct the Use of Resources in Critical Care?' In *Sanctity of Life and Human Dignity*, ed. by K. Bayertz. Dordrecht: Kluwer, 201–219.

Englert, W. 1994. 'Stoics and Epicureans on the Nature of Suicide'. *Proceedings of the Boston Area Colloquium of Ancient Philosophy* 10.1: 67–98.

Fagles, R. transl. 1996. *Homer: The Odyssey*. London: Penguin.

Fainlight, R. and Littman, R. transl. 2009. *Sophocles: The Theban Plays: Oedipus the King, Oedipus at Colonus, Antigone*. Baltimore: Johns Hopkins University Press.

Feldman, F. 1994. *Confrontations with the Reaper: A Philosophical Study of the Nature and Value of Death*. New York: Oxford University Press.

Feldman, F. 2006. *Pleasure and the Good Life: Concerning the Nature, Varieties and Plausibility of Hedonism*. First paperback ed. Oxford: Clarendon Press.

Fleet, B. 2012. *Plotinus Ennead IV.8: Translation, with an Introduction, and Commentary*. Las Vegas: Parmenides Publishing.

Fletcher, G. 2016. *The Philosophy of Well-Being: An Introduction*. London; New York: Routledge.

Foot, P. 1977. 'Euthanasia'. *Philosophy and Public Affairs* 6.2: 85–112.

Fortenbaugh, W. ed. 2018a. *Arius Didymus on Peripatetic Ethics, Household Management, and Politics: Text, Translation, and Discussion*. London; New York: Routledge.

Fortenbaugh, W. 2018b. 'Didymus on Types of Life'. In *Arius Didymus on Peripatetic Ethics, Household Management, and Politics: Text, Translation, and Discussion*, ed. by W. Fortenbaugh. London; New York: Routledge, 227–254.

Frede, M. 1999. 'On the Stoic Conception of the Good'. In *Topics in Stoic Philosophy*, ed. by K. Ierodiakonou. Oxford: Oxford University Press, 71–94.

Fumagalli, R. 2018. 'Eliminating "Life Worth Living"'. *Philosophical Studies* 175.3: 769–792.

Gauthier, R. A. and Jolif, J. Y. 1958–1959. *L'Éthique à Nicomaque. Introduction, traduction et commentaire*. Louvain: Nauwelaerts.

Gerson, L. 1994. *Plotinus*. London; New York: Routledge.

Gerson, L. ed. 1996. *The Cambridge Companion to Plotinus*. Cambridge: Cambridge University Press.

Gerson, L. 1997. 'Socrates' Absolutist Prohibition of Wrongdoing'. *Apeiron* 30.4: 1–11.

Gerson, L. 2013. 'Platonic Ethics'. In *The Oxford Handbook of the History of Ethics*, ed. by R. Crisp. Oxford: Oxford University Press, 129–146.

Gerson, L. et al. transl. 2019. *Plotinus: The Enneads*. Cambridge: Cambridge University Press.

Graeser, A. 1972. *Plotinus and the Stoics: A Preliminary Study*. Leiden: Brill.

Gill, C. 2006. *The Structured Self in Hellenistic and Roman Thought*. Oxford: Oxford University Press.

Gill, C. 2013. 'Cynicism and Stoicism'. In *The Oxford Handbook of the History of Ethics*, ed. by R. Crisp. Oxford: Oxford University Press, 93–111.

Gill, C. forthcoming. *Learning to Live Naturally. Stoic Ethics and Its Modern Significance*. Oxford: Oxford University Press.

Gomez-Lobo, A. 1989. 'The Ergon Inference'. *Phronesis* 34.2: 170–184.

Gosling, J. C. B. and Taylor, C. C. W. 1982. *The Greeks on Pleasure*. Oxford: Oxford University Press.

Graver, M. 2015. 'Honor and the Honorable: Cato's Discourse in De Finibus 3'. In *Cicero's De Finibus: Philosophical Approaches*, ed. by J. Annas and G. Betegh. Cambridge: Cambridge University Press, 118–146.

Graver, M. and Long, A. A. transl. 2015. *Letters on Ethics: To Lucilius*. Chicago: Chicago University Press.

Griffin, M. 1986. 'Philosophy, Cato, and Roman Suicide: I'. *Greece & Rome* 33.1: 64–77.

Grube, G. M. A. 1931. 'The Cleitophon of Plato'. *Classical Philology* 26.3: 302–308.

Hahm, D. 2007. 'Critolaus and Late Hellenistic Peripatetic Philosophy'. In *Pyrrhonists, Patricians, Platonizers: Tenth Symposium Hellenisticum*, ed. by A. M. Ioppolo and D. Sedley. Naples, 49–101.

Harris, J. 1985. *The Value of Life*. London: Routledge.

Hatzimichali, M. 2018. 'Bodily and External Goods in Relation to Happiness'. In *Arius Didymus on Peripatetic Ethics, Household Management, and Politics: Text, Translation, and Discussion*, ed. by W. Fortenbaugh. London; New York: Routledge, 205–226.

Haybron, D. M. 2010. *The Pursuit of Unhappiness: The Elusive Psychology of Well-Being*. Oxford and New York: Oxford University Press.

Henry, W. B. ed. 2009. *Philodemus: On Death*. Atlanta: Society of Biblical Literature.

Holmes, B. 2010. *The Symptom and the Subject: The Emergence of the Physical Body in Ancient Greece*. Princeton: Princeton University Press.

Hurka, T. 2009. *Perfectionism*. New York: Oxford University Press.

Hursthouse, R. 1999. *On Virtue Ethics*. New York: Oxford University Press.

Hutchinson, D. S. and Johnson, M. R. 2017. *Aristotle:* Protrepticus, *or* Exhortation to Philosophy. *Citations, Fragments, Paraphrases, and Other Evidence.* Online version at protrepticus.info.

Indelli, G. and Tsouna-McKirahan, V. eds. 1995. *Philodemus: On Choices and Avoidances.* Naples: Bibliopolis.

Inwood, B. 1985. *Ethics and Human Action in Early Stoicism.* Oxford: Clarendon Press.

Inwood, B. 2005. *Reading Seneca: Stoic Philosophy at Rome.* Oxford: Oxford University Press.

Inwood, B. 2014a. *Ethics After Aristotle.* Cambridge, MA: Harvard University Press.

Inwood, B. 2014b. 'Ancient Goods: The *Tria Genera Bonorum* in Ethical Theory'. In *Strategies of Argument: Essays in Ancient Ethics, Epistemology and Logic*, ed. by M.-K. Lee. Oxford: Oxford University Press, 255–280.

Inwood, B. 2017. *Stoicism: A Very Short Introduction.* Oxford: Oxford University Press.

Inwood, B. and Gerson, L. 1994. *The Epicurus Reader: Selected Writings and Testimonia.* Indianapolis: Hackett.

Inwood, B. and Gerson, L. 2008. *The Stoics Reader.* Indianapolis: Hackett.

Ionescu, C. 2019. *On the Good Life: Thinking through the Intermediaries in Plato's Philebus.* Albany: SUNY Press.

Irwin, T. 1977. *Plato's Moral Theory: The Early and Middle Dialogues.* Oxford: Clarendon Press.

Irwin, T. 1991. 'Aristippus against Happiness'. *The Monist* 74: 55–82.

Irwin, T. 1995. *Plato's Ethics.* New York; Oxford: Oxford University Press.

Irwin, T. 1999. *Aristotle: Nicomachean Ethics.* Indianapolis: Hackett.

Irwin, T. 2012. 'Antiochus, Aristotle and the Stoics on Degrees of Happiness'. In *The Philosophy of Antiochus*, ed. by D. Sedley. Cambridge: Cambridge University Press, 151–172.

James, W. 1895. 'Is Life Worth Living?' *International Journal of Ethics* 6: 1–24.

Joachim, H. 1951. *Aristotle: Nicomachean Ethics.* Oxford: Clarendon Press.

Johansen, T. 2004. *Plato's Natural Philosophy.* Cambridge: Cambridge University Press.

Johnson, M. 2005. *Aristotle on Teleology.* Oxford: Oxford University Press.

Kagan, S. 1998. 'Rethinking Intrinsic Value'. *The Journal of Ethics* 2: 277–297.

Kalogiratou, A. 2009. 'Plotinus' View on Soul, Suicide and Reincarnation'. ΣΧΟΛΗ 3: 387–400.

Kamm, F. M. 2003. 'Rescuing Ivan Ilych: How We Live and How We Die'. *Ethics* 113: 202–233.

Kamtekar, R. 1998. 'Imperfect Virtue'. *Ancient Philosophy* 18: 315–339.

Kamtekar, R. 2001. 'Social Justice and Happiness in the Republic: Plato's Two Principles'. *History of Political Thought* 22: 189–220.

Kass, L. 2008. 'Defending Human Dignity'. In *Human Dignity and Bioethics*, ed. by E. Pellegrino, A. Schulman and T. Merrill. Washington, DC: President's Council on Bioethics, 297–332.

Keil, G. and Kreft, N. eds. 2019. *Aristotle's Anthropology*. Cambridge: Cambridge University Press.

Keown, J. 2002. *Euthanasia, Ethics, and Public Policy: An Argument against Legalisation*. Cambridge; New York: Cambridge University Press.

Keyt, D. 2006. 'Plato on Justice'. In *A Companion to Plato*, ed. by H. Benson. Malden: Blackwell, 341–355.

Kietzmann, C. 2019. 'Aristotle on the Definition of What It Is to Be Human'. In *Aristotle's Anthropology*, ed. by G. Keil and N. Kreft. Cambridge: Cambridge University Press, 25–43.

Klein, J. 2015. 'Making Sense of the Stoic Indifferents'. *Oxford Studies in Ancient Philosophy* 49: 227–281.

Konstan, D. 2009. 'Epicurus'. In *The Stanford Encyclopedia of Philosophy*.

Korsgaard, C. 1983. 'Two Distinctions in Goodness'. *The Philosophical Review* 92.2: 169–195.

Korsgaard, C. 2008. *The Constitution of Agency: Essays on Practical Reason and Moral Psychology*. Oxford and New York: Oxford University Press.

Kraut, R. 1973. 'Reason and Justice in the Republic'. In *Exegesis and Argument: Studies in Greek Philosophy. Presented to Gregory Vlastos*, ed. by E. Lee, A. Mourelatos and R. Rorty. *Phronesis* Supplementary Volume, 207–224.

Kraut, R. 1984. *Socrates and the State*. Princeton: Princeton University Press.

Kraut, R. 1989. *Aristotle on the Human Good*. Princeton: Princeton University Press.

Kraut, R. 2007. 'The Examined Life'. In *A Companion to Socrates*, ed. by S. Ahbel-Rappe and R. Kamtekar. Malden: Blackwell, 228–242.

Kraut, R. 2009. *What Is Good and Why: The Ethics of Well-Being*. Cambridge, MA: Harvard University Press.

Kraut, R. 2010a. 'What Is Intrinsic Goodness?' *Classical Philology* 105.4: 450–462.

Kraut, R. 2010b. 'Ordinary Virtue from the Phaedo to the Laws'. In *Plato's Laws: A Critical Guide*, ed. by C. Bobonich. Cambridge: Cambridge University Press, 51–70.

Kremer, M. ed. 2004. *Plato's Cleitophon: On Socrates and the Modern Mind*. Lanham: Lexington Books.

Kuhse, H. 1987. *The Sanctity of Life Doctrine in Medicine: A Critique*. Oxford: Clarendon Press.

Kymlicka, W. 1990. *Contemporary Political Philosophy*. Oxford: Oxford University Press.

Lampe, K. 2015. *The Birth of Hedonism: The Cyrenaic Philosophers and Pleasure as a Way of Life*. Princeton: Princeton University Press.

Landau, I. 2017. *Finding Meaning in an Imperfect World*. Oxford: Oxford University Press.

Latham, R. E. and Godwin, J. eds. 1994. *Lucretius: On the Nature of the Universe*. Penguin Books.

Lear, Richardson G. 2004. *Happy Lives and the Highest Good: An Essay on Aristotle's Nicomachean Ethics*. Princeton: Princeton University Press.

Lear, Richardson G. 2006. 'Aristotle on Moral Virtue and the Fine'. In *The Blackwell Guide to Nicomachean Ethics*, ed. by R. Kraut. Blackwell, 116–136.

Lear, Richardson G. 2015. 'Aristotle on Happiness and Long Life'. In *The Quest for the Good Life: Ancient Philosophers on Happiness*, ed. by Ø. Rabbås, E. K. Emilsson, H. Fossheim and M. Tuominen. Oxford: Oxford University Press, 127–145.

LeBar, M. 2013. *The Value of Living Well*. Oxford: Oxford University Press.

Lee, A. 2022. 'The Neutrality of Life'. *Australasian Journal of Philosophy*, on-line first version. https://doi.org/10.1080/00048402.2022.2033284

Lennox, J. 1999. 'Aristotle on the Biological Roots of Human Virtue'. In *Biology and the Foundations of Ethics*, ed. by J. Maienschein and M. Ruse. Cambridge: Cambridge University Press, 10–31.

Lennox, J. 2001. *Aristotle: On the Parts of Animals I–IV. Translation with an Introduction and Commentary*. Oxford: Clarendon Press.

Lennox, J. 2010. 'Bios and Explanatory Unity in Aristotle's Biology'. In *Definition in Greek Philosophy*, ed. by D. Charles. Oxford: Oxford University Press, 329–55.

Lesses, G. 1989. 'Virtue and the Goods of Fortune in Stoic Moral Theory'. *Oxford Studies in Ancient Philosophy* 7: 95–127.

Leunissen, M. 2010. *Explanation and Teleology in Aristotle's Science of Nature*. Cambridge: Cambridge University Press.

Leunissen, M. 2017. *From Natural Character to Moral Virtue in Aristotle*. Oxford: Oxford University Press.

Levin, S. 2014. *Plato's Rivalry with Medicine: A Struggle and Its Dissolution*. Oxford: Oxford University Press.

Lewis, C. I. 1955. *The Ground and Nature of the Right*. New York: Columbia University Press.

Long, A. A. and Sedley, D. N. 1987. *The Hellenistic Philosophers*. Cambridge: Cambridge University Press.

Long, A. A. 2015. *Greek Models of Mind and Self*. Cambridge, MA: Harvard University Press.

Long, A. G. 2019. *Death and Immortality in Ancient Philosophy: Key Themes in Ancient Philosophy*. New York: Cambridge University Press.

Lorenz, H. 2003. 'Ancient Theories of the Soul'. Entry in the *Stanford Encyclopedia of Philosophy*. https://plato.stanford.edu/entries/ancient-soul/

Machek, D. 2021. 'Is the Life of a Mediocre Philosopher Better Than the Life of an Excellent Cobbler? Aristotle on the Value of Activity in *Nicomachean Ethics* x. 4-8'. *The Journal of Value Inquiry*. Online-first version. https://doi.org/10.1007/s10790-021-09805-1

Machek, D. 2022. 'Aristotle on the Goodness of Unhappy Lives'. *Journal of the History of Philosophy* 60.3: 359–383.

Matheson, D. 2020. 'The Worthwhileness of Meaningful Lives'. *Philosophia* 48.1: 313–324.

McMahan, J. 2002. *The Ethics of Killing: Problems at the Margins of Life*. Oxford Ethics Series. New York: Oxford University Press.

Matson, W. 1998. 'Hegesias the Death-Persuader; or, the Gloominess of Hedonism'. *Philosophy* 73: 553–558.

McCabe, M. M. 2015. *Platonic Conversations*. Oxford: Oxford University Press.

McGroarty, K. 2006. *Plotinus on Eudaimonia: A Commentary on Ennead I 4*. Oxford: Oxford University Press.

Mensch, P. and Miller, J. eds. 2018. *Diogenes Laertius. Lives of the Eminent Philosophers*. Oxford; New York: Oxford University Press.

Metz, T. 2012. 'The Meaningful and the Worthwhile: Clarifying the Relationships'. *The Philosophical Forum* 43: 435–448.

Metz, T. 2014. 'Life Worth Living'. In *Encyclopedia of Quality of Life and Well-Being Research*, ed. by A. C. Michalos. Dordrecht: Springer, 3602–3605.

Meyer, S. S. 2008. *Ancient Ethics: A Critical Introduction*. London: Routledge.

Michael of Ephesus. 2001. *On Aristotle Nicomachean Ethics 9*. In *Aspasius, Michael of Ephesus, Anonymous: On Aristotle Nicomachean Ethics 8–9*, transl. D. Konstan. London, New York: Bloomsbury, 131–232.

Mitsis, P. 1988. *Epicurus' Ethical Theory: The Pleasures of Invulnerability*. Ithaca, NY: Cornell University Press.

Moraux, P. 1973. *Der Aristotelismus bei den Griechen. Von Andronikos bis Alexander von Aphrodisias*. Berlin: De Gruyter.

Morrison, D. 1987. 'The Evidence for Degrees of Being in Aristotle'. *The Classical Quarterly* 37: 382–401.

Nagel, T. 1970. 'Death'. *Noûs* 4.1: 73–80.

Nagel, T. 1971. 'The Absurd'. *The Journal of Philosophy* 68.20: 716–727.

Narbonne, J.-M. 2014. 'Matter and Evil in the Neoplatonic Tradition'. In *The Routledge Handbook of Neoplatonism*, ed. by P. Remes and S. Slaveva-Griffin. London: Routledge, 231–244.

Natali, C. 2009. '*Nicomachean Ethics* VII, 1148b15–1150a8: Beastliness, Irascibility, Akrasia'. In *Aristotle's Nicomachean Ethics. Book VII*, ed. by C. Natali. Oxford: Oxford University Press, 103–129.

Nehamas, A. and Woodruff, P. 1989. *Symposium: Translated with Introduction & Notes*. Indianapolis: Hackett.

Nikolsky, B. 2001. 'Epicurus on Pleasure'. *Phronesis* 46.4: 440–465.

Nozick, R. 1974. *Anarchy, State, and Utopia*. New York: Basic Books.

Nozick, R. 1989. *The Examined Life: Philosophical Meditations*. New York: Simon & Schuster.

Nussbaum, M. 1972. 'ΨΥΧΗ in Heraclitus I'. *Phronesis* 17.1: 1–16.

Nussbaum, M. 1986. *The Fragility of Goodness*. Chicago: Chicago University Press.

Nussbaum, M. 1995. 'Aristotle on Human Nature and the Foundations of Ethics'. In *World, Mind and Ethics: Essays on the Ethical Philosophy of Bernard Williams*, ed. by J. Altham and R. Harrison. Cambridge: Cambridge University Press, 86–131.

O'Keefe, T. 2001. 'Is Epicurean Friendship Altruistic?' *Apeiron* 34: 269–305.

O'Meara, D. 1993. *Plotinus: An Introduction to the Enneads*. Oxford: Clarendon Press.

O'Meara, D. 2003. *Platonopolis: Platonic Political Philosophy in Late Antiquity*. Oxford: Clarendon Press.

O'Meara, D. 2005. 'The Metaphysics of Evil in Plotinus: Problems and Solutions'. In *Essays in Honour of D. O'Brien*, ed. by J. M. Dillon and M. Dixsaut. Aldershot: Ashgate, 179–185.

O'Reilly, K. 2019. 'The Jellyfish's Pleasures in Philebus 20b-21d'. *Phronesis* 64.3: 277–291.

Orwin, C. 2004. 'On the *Cleitophon*'. In *Plato's* Cleitophon: *On Socrates and the Modern Mind*, ed. by M. Kremer. Lanham: Lexington Books, 59–70.

Osborne, C. 2007. *Dumb Beasts and Dead Philosophers: Humanity and the Humane in Ancient Philosophy and Literature*. Oxford: Oxford University Press.

Owen, G. E. L. 1960. 'Logic and metaphysics in some earlier works of Aristotle'. In *Aristotle and Plato in the mid-fourth century*, ed. by I. Düring and G. E. L. Owen. Göteborg: Almquist & Wiksell, 163–90.

Pakaluk, M. 2008. *Aristotle: Nicomachean Ethics: Books VIII and XI*. Oxford: Clarendon Press.

Papadimitriou, J. D. et al. 2007. 'Euthanasia and Suicide in Antiquity: Viewpoint of the Dramatists and Philosophers'. *Journal of the Royal Society of Medicine* 100.1: 25–28.

Parfit, D. 1984. *Reasons and Persons*. Oxford: Clarendon Press.

Purinton, J. 1993. 'Epicurus on the Telos'. *Phronesis* 38.3: 281–320.

Rabbås, Ø. 2015. 'Eudaimonia, Human Nature, and Normativity. Reflections on Aristotle's Project in *Nicomachean Ethics* Book I'. In *The Quest for the Good Life: Ancient Philosophers on Happiness*, ed. by Ø. Rabbås, E. K. Emilsson, H. Fossheim and M. Tuominen. Oxford: Oxford University Press, 88–112.

Rabbås, Ø., Emilsson, E. K., Fossheim, H. and Tuominen, M. eds. 2015. *The Quest for the Good Life: Ancient Philosophers on Happiness*. Oxford: Oxford University Press.

Rachels, J. 1986. *The End of Life*. New York: Oxford University Press.

Rackham, H. transl. 1932. *Aristotle: Politics*. Loeb Classical Library 264. Cambridge, MA: Harvard University Press.

Rawls, J. 1999. *A Theory of Justice*. Cambridge, MA: Belknap Press of Harvard University Press.

Raz, J. 2001. *Value, Respect, and Attachment: John Robert Seeley Lectures*. Cambridge; New York: Cambridge University Press.

Remes, P. 2008. *Neoplatonism*. Stocksfield: Acumen.

Remes, P. and Slaveva-Griffin, S. eds. 2014. *The Routledge Handbook of Neoplatonism*. London: Routledge.

Remes, P. and Sihvola, J. eds. 2008. *Ancient Philosophy of the Self*. Dordrecht: Springer.

Reeve, C. 1998. *Aristotle: Politics*. Indianapolis: Hackett.

Reydams-Schils, G. 2005. *The Roman Stoics*. Chicago: Chicago University Press.

Rider, B. 2020. 'Epicureans on Pleasure, Desire and Happiness'. In *The Routledge Handbook of Hellenistic Philosophy*, ed. by K. Arenson. London: Routledge, 295–306.

Rist, J. 1967. *Plotinus: The Road to Reality*. Cambridge: Cambridge University Press.

Rist, J. 1969. *Stoic Philosophy*. Cambridge: Cambridge University Press.

Rist, J. 1983. *Human Value: A Study in Ancient Philosophical Ethics*. Leiden: Brill.

Roochnik, D. 2004. 'The Riddle of the *Cleitophon*'. In *Plato' Cleitophon: On Socrates and the Modern Mind*, ed. by M. Kremer. Lanham: Lexington Books, 43–58.

Rosenbaum, S. 1990. 'Epicurus on Pleasure and the Complete Life'. *The Monist* 73: 21–41.

Russell, D. 2012. *Happiness for Humans*. New York: Oxford University Press.

Santas, G. 2010. *Understanding Plato's Republic*. Malden: Wiley-Blackwell.

Schniewind, A. 2003. *L'éthique du sage chez Plotin. Le paradigm du spoudaios*. Paris: Vrin.

Schniewind, A. 2015. 'Plotinus' Way of Defining "Eudaimonia" in Ennead I 4 [46] 1–3'. In *The Quest for the Good Life: Ancient Philosophers on Happiness*, ed. by Ø. Rabbås, E. K. Emilsson, H. Fossheim and M. Tuominen. Oxford: Oxford University Press, 212–221.

Schofield, M. 1991. *The Stoic Idea of the City*. Cambridge: Cambridge University Press.

Sedley, D. 1991. 'Is Aristotle's Teleology Anthropocentric?' *Phronesis* 36.2: 179–196.

Sedley, D. 2017. 'Epicurean versus Cyrenaic Happiness'. In *Selfhood and the Soul: Essays on Ancient Thought and Literature in Honour of Christopher Gill*, ed. by R. Seaford, J. Wilkins and M. Wright. Oxford: Oxford University Press, 89–106.

Segev, M. 2022. 'Death, Immortality, and the Value of Human Existence in Aristotle's Eudemus Fragment 6 Ross.' *Classical Philology* 117.3: 438–461.

Seidler, M. J. 1983. 'Kant and the Stoics on Suicide'. *Journal of the History of Ideas* 44.3: 429–453.

Sellars, J. 2006. *Stoicism*. Berkeley: University of California Press.

Sharples, R. 2007. 'Peripatetics on Happiness'. In *Greek and Roman Philosophy 100BC–200AD, Volume 2*, ed. by R. Sharples and R. Sorabji. London: Institute of Classical Studies, University of London, 627–637.

Sharples, R. 2010. *Peripatetic Philosophy 200 BC to AD 200: An Introduction and Collection of Sources in Translation*. Cambridge Source Books in Post-Hellenistic Philosophy. Cambridge: Cambridge University Press.

Sheffield, F. 2018. 'Plato on Virtue and the Good Life'. In *The Routledge Companion to Ancient Philosophy*, ed. by J. Warren and F. Sheffield. London: Routledge, 471–501.

Simpson, P. 2017. transl. *The Great Ethics of Aristotle*. London: Routledge.

Singer, P. 1995. *Rethinking Life and Death: The Collapse of Our Traditional Ethics*. New York: St. Martin's Press.

Singer, P. 1993. *Practical Ethics* (2nd ed.). Cambridge: Cambridge University Press.

Slings, S. 1999. *Plato: Clitophon*. Cambridge: Cambridge University Press.

Smith, N. 'Return to the Cave'. In *Plato's Republic. A Critical Guide*, ed. by M. McPherran. Cambridge: Cambridge University Press, 83–102.

Smuts, A. 2014. 'To Be or Never to Have Been: Anti-Natalism and a Life Worth Living'. *Ethical Theory and Moral Practice* 17.4: 711–729.

Snell, B. 1946. *Die Entdeckung des Geistes. Studien zur Entstehung des europäischen Denkens bei den Griechen*. Hamburg: Claassen & Goverts.

Song, E. 2013. 'Ashamed of Being in the Body? Plotinus versus Porphyry'. In *Plato Revived: Essays on Ancient Platonism in Honour of Dominic J. O'Meara*, ed. by F. Karfík and E. Song. Berlin; Boston: De Gruyter, 96–116.

Sorabji, R. 1993. *Animal Minds and Human Morals: The Origins of the Western Debate*. Ithaca: Cornell University Press.

Sorabji, R. 2006. *Self: Ancient and Modern Insights about Individuality, Life and Death*. Chicago: University of Chicago Press.

Stern-Gillet, S. 2013. 'When Virtue Bids Us Abandon Life. (Ennead VI 8 [39] 6, 14–26).' In *Plato Revived: Essays on Ancient Platonism in Honour of Dominic J. O'Meara*, ed. by F. Karfík and E. Song. Berlin; Boston: De Gruyter, 182–198.

Stern-Gillet, S. 2014. 'Plotinus on Metaphysics and Morality'. In *The Routledge Handbook of Neoplatonism*, ed. by P. Remes and S. Slaveva-Griffin. London: Routledge, 396–420.

Striker, G. 1996. 'Antipater, or the Art of Living'. In *Essays on Hellenistic Epistemology and Ethics* ed. by G. Striker. Cambridge: Cambridge University Press, 185–204.

Strycker, E. de. 1968. 'Prédicats univoques et prédicats analogiques dans le Protreptique d'Aristote'. *Revue Philosophique de Louvain* 66: 597–618.

Sumner, L. W. 1996. *Welfare, Happiness, and Ethics*. Oxford and New York: Clarendon Press and Oxford University Press.

Szaif, J. 2012. *Gut des Menschen. Untersuchungen zur Problematik und Entwicklung der Glücksethik bei Aristoteles und in der Tradition des Peripatos*. Berlin; Boston: De Gruyter.

Szaif, J. 2018. 'Two Conceptions of "Primary Acts of Virtue" in Doxography C'. In *Arius Didymus on Peripatetic Ethics, Household Management, and Politics: Text, Translation, and Discussion*, ed. by W. Fortenbaugh. London; New York: Routledge, 161–203.

Taylor, C. 1989. *Sources of the Self: The Making of the Modern Identity*. Cambridge, MA: Harvard University Press.

Taylor, P. 1986. *Respect for Nature: A Theory of Environmental Ethics*. Princeton: Princeton University Press.

Tiberius, V. 2014. 'Well-Being, Philosophical Theories Of'. In *Encyclopedia of Quality of Life and Well-Being Research*, ed. by A. Michalos. Dordrecht: Springer, 7110–7113.

Torres, J. 2020. 'Plato's Medicalisation of Ethics'. *Apeiron: A Journal for Ancient Philosophy and Science* 54.3: 287–316.

Torres, J. 2021. 'Plato's Anthropocentrism Reconsidered'. *Environmental Ethics* 43.2: 119–141.

Trisel, B. 2007. 'Judging Life and Its Value'. *Sorites* 18: 60–75.

Tsouna, V. 2002. 'Is There an Exception to Greek Eudaimonism?' In *Le style de la pensée. Mélanges J. Brunschwig*, ed. by M. Canto and P. Pellegrin. Paris: Les Belles Lettres, 464–489.

Tsouna, V. 2007. *The Ethics of Philodemus*. Oxford: Oxford University Press.

Tsouna, V. 2020. 'Hedonism'. In *Oxford Handbook of Epicurus and Epicureanism*, ed. by P. Mitsis. Oxford: Oxford University Press, 141–188.

Tsouni, G. 2017. 'Didymus' Outline of Peripatetic Ethics, Household Management and Politics: An Edition with Translation'. In *Arius Didymus on Peripatetic Ethics, Household Management, and Politics: Text, Translation, and Discussion*, ed. by W. Fortenbaugh. London; New York: Routledge, 1–67.

Tsouni, G. 2019. *Antiochus and Peripatetic Ethics*. Cambridge Classical Studies. Cambridge: Cambridge University Press.

Velleman, D. 1991. 'Well-being and time'. *Pacific Philosophical Quarterly* 72: 48–77.

Visnjic, J. 2021. *The Invention of Duty: Stoicism as Deontology*. Philosophia Antiqua 157. Leiden: Brill.

Vlastos, G. 1978. 'Justice and Happiness in the Republic'. In *Plato: A Collection of Critical Essays* vol. 2, ed. by G. Vlastos, Notre Dame: Notre Dame University Press, 66–95.

Vlastos, G. 1985. 'Happiness and Virtue in Socrates' Moral Theory'. *Topoi* 4: 3–22.

Vlastos, G. 1991. *Socrates: Ironist and Moral Philosopher*. Cambridge: Cambridge University Press.

Vogt, K. 2014 'Taking the Same Things Seriously and Not Seriously: A Stoic Proposal on Value and the Good'. In *Epictetus: His Continuing Influence and Contemporary Relevance*, ed. by D. R. Gordon and D. B. Suits. RIT Press, 55–76.

Wallis, R. T. 1972. *Neoplatonism*. London: Duckworth.

Warren, J. 2001. 'Socratic Suicide'. *The Journal of Hellenic Studies* 121: 91–106.

Warren, J. 2002. *Epicurus and Democritean Ethics: An Archaeology of Ataraxia*. Cambridge: Cambridge University Press.

Warren, J. 2004. *Facing Death: Epicurus and His Critics*. Oxford and New York: Clarendon Press.

Warren, J. 2014. *The Pleasures of Reason in Plato, Aristotle, and the Hellenistic Hedonists*. Cambridge: Cambridge University Press.

Warren, J. 2018. 'The Cyrenaics'. In *The Routledge Companion to Ancient Philosophy*, ed. by J. Warren and F. Sheffield. London: Routledge, 974–1006.

Werner, D. 2018. 'Suicide in the Phaedo'. *Rhizomata* 6.2: 157–188.

White, S. 2002. 'Happiness in the Hellenistic Lyceum'. *Apeiron*, suppl. 35: 69–93.

Wilkinson, D. 2011. 'A Life Worth Giving? The Threshold for Permissible Withdrawal of Life Support from Disabled Newborn Infants'. *The American Journal of Bioethics* 11.2: 20–32.

Williams, B. 1973. 'The Makropulos Case: Reflections on the Tedium of Immortality'. In *Problems of the Self*, ed. by B. Williams. Cambridge: Cambridge University Press, 82–100.

Williams, B. 1985. *Ethics and the Limits of Philosophy*. London: Routledge.

Williams, B. 1993. *Shame and Necessity*. Berkeley: University of California Press.

Wolf, S. 2015. *The Variety of Values: Essays on Morality, Meaning, and Love*. New York: Oxford University Press.

Wolfsdorf, D. 2013. *Pleasure in Ancient Greek Philosophy*. Cambridge: Cambridge University Press.

Woods, M. 1982. *Aristotle's Nicomachean Ethics: Books I, II and VIII*. Oxford: Clarendon Press.

Woolf, R. 2009. 'Pleasure and Desire'. In *The Cambridge Companion to Epicureanism*, ed. by J. Warren. Cambridge: Cambridge University Press, 158–178.

Zavaliy. A. 2019. 'Cowardice and Injustice. The Problem of Suicide in Aristotle's Ethics'. *History of Philosophy Quarterly* 36.4: 319–336.

Zillioli, U. 2012. *The Cyrenaics*. London: Routledge.

Index Locorum

247

Subject Index

For EU product safety concerns, contact us at Calle de José Abascal, 56–1°,
28003 Madrid, Spain or eugpsr@cambridge.org.

www.ingramcontent.com/pod-product-compliance
Ingram Content Group UK Ltd.
Pitfield, Milton Keynes, MK11 3LW, UK
UKHW020355140625
459647UK00020B/2483